BOB DYLAN

BOB DYLAN

Jewish Roots, American Soil

Harry Freedman

BLOOMSBURY CONTINUUM
LONDON • OXFORD • NEW YORK • NEW DELHI • SYDNEY

BLOOMSBURY CONTINUUM
Bloomsbury Publishing Plc
50 Bedford Square, London, WC1B 3DP, UK
Bloomsbury Publishing Ireland Limited,
29 Earlsfort Terrace, Dublin 2, D02 AY28, Ireland

BLOOMSBURY, BLOOMSBURY CONTINUUM and the Diana logo are trademarks of
Bloomsbury Publishing Plc

First published in Great Britain 2025

Plate section image credits: Page 1: © Michael Ochs Archives/Getty Images;
Page 2: © Michael Ochs Archives/Getty Images; Poster © Blank Archives/Getty
Images; Page 3: Poster © Black Archives/Getty Images; Image © Brian Shuel/
Redferns; Page 4: © Michael Ochs Archives/Getty Images; © CBS Photo Archive/
Getty Images; Page 5: images x 2 © Bettmann/Getty Images; Page 6: images x 2
© Rowland Scherman/Getty Images; Page 7: © Blank Archives/Archive Photos/Getty
Images; Page 8: © Michael Ochs Archives/Getty Images; © Bettmann/Getty Images

For legal purposes the Acknowledgements on pp. 227–8 constitute an extension
of this copyright page

A catalogue record for this book is available from the British Library

Library of Congress Cataloguing-in-Publication data has been applied for

ISBN: HB: 978-1-3994-1630-6; TPB: 978-1-13994-1629-0; eBook: 978-1-3994-1628-3;
ePDF: 978-1-3994-1627-6

2 4 6 8 10 9 7 5 3 1

Typeset by Deanta Global Publishing Services, Chennai, India
Printed and bound in Great Britain by Clays Ltd, Elcograf S.p.A

To find out more about our authors and books visit www.bloomsbury.com
and sign up for our newsletters

For product safety related questions contact productsafety@bloomsbury.com

Dedicated to the memory of Stuart Cohen (1949–1998).

CONTENTS

INTRODUCTION

When Bob Dylan was awarded the prestigious Nobel Prize in Literature in 2016, there blew up something of a storm. The media and cognoscenti queried the Nobel Committee's judgement, prominent literary voices expressed outrage at the choice. Bob Dylan, these voices said, was a singer, not a writer, there were many more credible candidates who deserved the prize, the Ideals of Literature had been betrayed, and so on. Bob Dylan didn't exactly help to calm the rage. For weeks he refused even to acknowledge he'd won the award. He didn't turn up to receive his gold medal at the official ceremony in Stockholm, where the prize-winners from all the other categories were gathered. Only finally, several months later, did he agree to accept the prize. Because Dylan was scheduled to play two concerts in Stockholm as part of a European tour, the Nobel Committee arranged a small private event, just twelve of them and him. Sneaking in, according to *The New Yorker*, wearing a hoodie, leather jacket and gloves, he collected his medal, drank some champagne, and went off to play his gig. He didn't tell the audience what he'd done that afternoon.[1]

Dylan fans were neither surprised nor outraged at the award. They were in no doubt he deserved the prize. Yes, he was a musician, but his music was the garment, superbly tailored to be sure, in which he clothed his words. His lyrics were the product of genius, his poetic powers far outweighing those of any of the naysayers. His was the outstanding, creative voice of mid- to late-twentieth-century American culture. As for the controversy over the award of the prize, well, when had Dylan not been controversial? It may not have been his plan, but controversy and dissension stalked his career. At least until the late 1960s, when his critics finally accepted that he would always remain true to himself and that their complaints were just phantoms in the wind.

Bob Dylan went from unknown to superstardom during some of the most turbulent times in modern American history. The McCarthy years, when anyone suspected of communist leanings was ostracised, however weak the evidence, took a terrible toll among musicians, writers and creatives, some of whom moved in the same circles as Dylan. The struggle for civil rights tore American society apart and the assassination of President Kennedy traumatised it, destroying hopes, ideals and dreams. If that wasn't enough, the Vietnam War radicalised the post-war generation, baby-boomers as they were known. Dylan was not a boomer, he was born four years before the end of the war, but he was the artist they regarded, though he rejected the categorisation, as their spokesman and voice. In a period of tremendous social and technological change, Bob Dylan fuelled himself with the energy of the age, transforming in seemingly no time at all from an aspiring Greenwich Village folk singer into a cultural icon deserving of a Nobel Prize.

Those few years are the subject of this book. Relentlessly driven, unafraid of change, and seeing far into its consequences, Dylan harnessed the spirit of the age to explore new ways of delivering his messages and ideas. Provocative or accusatory, inspirational, mystifying or entertaining, Dylan never lacked the element of surprise. Speaking out in the service of justice and truth, daring to stand up to his detractors, a man never prepared to be cowed. Even when it meant upsetting some of his fans and alienating segments of his audience.

Like any outstanding creative, Bob Dylan's work is the product of multiple influences. Widely read, there seems to be no end to the poets and authors he echoes. Musically too, he draws upon the entire spectrum of contemporary genres, from folk and blues through to jazz, country, rock and pop. However, three great cultural influences, two American, one ethnic, truly moulded him as an artist: Woody Guthrie, the man he wanted to emulate as a folk singer at the start of his career. The Beat poets, notably Allen Ginsberg and Jack Kerouac, whose use of language, seemingly boundless perspective and elevated awareness opened new horizons, expanding his world view — in time, he would add Rimbaud and Verlaine to his pantheon of poets. And third, his Jewish ancestry, which rarely affected him consciously but furnished him with traits and values, shaping him into the person he had no choice other than to be. All three of these primary influences are encapsulated in the title of this book, *Bob Dylan: Jewish Roots, American Soil*.

STARTIN' OUT

A SMALL TOWN

It is hard growing up as a Jew in a small town. It is hard, even if your family doesn't stand out as being particularly Jewish, even if they look much the same as everybody else, apart perhaps from being a bit smaller, a bit darker, and with curlier hair. It is hard even if, on the surface, your parents' lives are much the same as everybody else's, except for the fact that they are never seen in church. Nor does it help if you happen to be born with a German surname in America in 1941, above all in the Midwest, a child during World War II. Even though, by the time you were old enough to understand the slurs, everyone knew what the Germans had done to the Jews. One way or another, you and your family were bound to be seen as outsiders.

The Zimmermans, in the mining town of Hibbing, Minnesota, were such a family. A mother, father and two sons, four of just 280 Jews in a town of around 16,000 souls.

Your parents might play down their differences when they live in a town like Hibbing. They'd think of themselves as no different to everybody else, and they'd encourage you to do the same. They might point out from time to time that there are a few other Jews in the town and they'd remind you that you have family in nearby Duluth, where you were born and lived until you were six, where there are nearly 3,000 Jews. They'd tell you that America is a free and open society, where it doesn't matter which religion you were born into, where nobody discriminates against Jews. Even if that wasn't particularly true. Although it was easier to be Jewish than to be black.

But even as they tell you that, you might begin to wonder. You may hear them talking, when you are four or five, about the news coming out of Europe. About what had happened to the Jews. You would not understand much about it at that age, and your parents would have done their best to keep it from you. Nevertheless, you'd start to form an impression that there is something different about being a Jew; that you are not exactly the same as everybody else. And that impression would grow stronger, and your sense of difference would deepen, as you grew older and went to school. Where quite possibly, on occasion, you might be drawn into a fight with another child who had sneered at you, calling you something like 'Jew-boy' or 'dirty Jew', something they'd heard at home.

That can, and does, happen anywhere. But growing up in a small town, where you might be the only Jew in your class, where there was nobody else feeling as different as you did, you would be more aware of it.

It does something to children, this sense of difference. It can damage them profoundly, make them fearful, embarrassed to tell anyone they are a Jew. Or, it can have the opposite effect; it can raise their hackles, toughen them, make them want to show the world who they really are. It can infuse them with single-minded ambition, invigorate them with the urge to excel.

Some children may feel both emotions; both embarrassed about their Jewishness and determined to show the world what they are truly capable of. Such people may try to conceal their Jewishness while doing their utmost to make a name for themselves, garnering recognition, admiration and respect, proving themselves to be exceptional at what they do, ensuring that their Jewishness is no impediment to success. Then, if they do achieve their aims, if they gain the recognition they were desperate for, and have accumulated the fame, money or whatever else impelled them, then might they relax, accept the reality of their difference, express pride in who they are, and exude confidence in their Jewishness.

That's the paradigm. It doesn't often work out like that, many Jews are embarrassed, few achieve success. Some respond to embarrassment by changing identity, maybe exploring a different spiritual path or faith for a while. Perhaps even becoming a Christian. But, as long as the paradigm holds, as long as they are destined for success, the day will most likely come when they acknowledge their Jewishness again. It is all part of the journey, the transformation that a determined Jew from a small town might go through in their unwavering ambition to succeed.

If you read *Chronicles*, the first and only published volume of Bob Dylan's autobiography, you will learn that he came from a small town. You might deduce that his surname was Zimmerman. However, you would not know that he was Jewish. The word Jew only occurs once in the autobiography, and even that is only in a reference to the Pope. His first girlfriend, Echo Helstrom, who he met in the eleventh grade, once asked him if he was Jewish. She told Anthony Scaduto, Dylan's earliest biographer, that he gave her a funny look.[1] Their friend John Buckland, who overheard the exchange, told Echo never to ask him that again. And Scaduto reports conversations with other former acquaintances of Dylan too, all of whom are adamant that he was not prepared to own up to his origins.

Dylan's early desire to conceal his origins may have come as a surprise to Scaduto and his readers. It shouldn't really; thousands of sensitive, teenage Jewish boys have felt the same. Particularly in those days when identity was not something one shouted about, when the pressure to conform and fit in was still strong, before the social upheavals of the 1960s, upheavals in which self-conscious, reluctantly identifying Jews played a disproportionate part. The desire to conceal his origins would have been particularly apposite in Hibbing, a town where, according to a teacher in Dylan's old school, speaking some years later, 'the Finns hated the Bohemians and the

Bohemians hated the Finns. Nearly everyone hated the Jews.' It sounds like a quote from Tom Lehrer's song, 'National Brotherhood Week', but pretty accurate, nevertheless: 'Oh, the Protestants hate the Catholics, / And the Catholics hate the Protestants, / And the Hindus hate the Moslems, / And everybody hates the Jews.'[2]

Thirteen years older than Dylan, a Jew from Manhattan where the need to conceal one's Jewishness was never much of a priority, Tom Lehrer never seems to have had a problem sounding or appearing Jewish. He even gave up his successful musical career to go and teach Mathematics – academic subjects don't come more Jewish than that. But Dylan was not Lehrer and Hibbing was not Manhattan. In small towns, prejudices reign supreme. As a Jew, Dylan's father Abe Zimmerman wasn't even able to join the local golf club.[3]

There may have been only a scattering of Jews in Hibbing but Dylan's parents played their part in the Jewish community. Abe served on committees of the B'nai B'rith charitable fraternity, his wife Beatty performed a leading role in the local branch of the women's fellowship, Hadassah. Dylan's parents invited 500 people to his barmitzvah party – or, to be more precise, the barmitzvah of Robert Zimmerman, because that is who he was at the age of 13 – of whom 400 came. Not a bad turnout for a small town with only 280 Jews. Unlike some Jewish boys, those at the most disconnected end of the religious spectrum, Bobby Zimmerman's barmitzvah was not an outlier in an otherwise secular life.

Barmitzvahs are a big deal in families, particularly for the parents and grandparents. Their boy has come of age; it is a moment to cherish. Technically he is now subject to the rights and duties imposed by Jewish law, but that is not what most parents are celebrating. Their pride comes from watching their son sing a portion of the Torah, the Five Books of Moses, in synagogue. Standing up in a room full of adults, strangers as well as family, reading something in Hebrew that he barely understands, that he has learnt by rote because in many cases he is not familiar with the language, and singing it in a voice that's on the point of breaking, a voice with a mind of its own, wavering between falsetto, cracking and bass.

He's probably more nervous than he has ever been before, because, unlike the adults, he is too young to realise that no matter how good or bad his performance is, nobody will care. It's the occasion that counts, that's all. Everyone will *kvell*, particularly the old people. Though some of the girls will think it unfair that boys receive all the attention, whereas they get none. Batmitzvahs, the comparable ceremony for girls, still hadn't become a thing in 1954, when Bobby Zimmerman was called to read from the Torah. It would be another decade or two before the girls' ceremony really took off.

Following the trauma of the synagogue service, there will be a party. The boy might give a speech, and he'll get lots of presents – mainly briefcases, wallets and fountain pens, the barmitzvah gifts of choice in the 1950s. He'll like the presents, particularly from those guests who give him money rather than fountain pens, and he will enjoy the party more if he's allowed to invite his friends. But he is 13 years old. He has had to work hard to learn his Torah portion, his hormones are exploding, the stress of the occasion has seriously aggravated his acne, and he is worried that those two girls over there, the one he thinks he likes and her friend, are laughing at him. Barmitzvahs are great for the adults. How much do they really do to strengthen the Jewish identity of a typical 13-year-old boy?

Abe and Beatty Zimmerman, Bobby's parents, were both children of immigrants from the old country. The two families lived at opposite extremes of the *heim*, the Pale of Settlement to which Eastern European Jews were mainly confined, stretching from one sea to another, from the Baltic to the Black. His mother's family came from Lithuania or Latvia in the north of the region, his father's from Odessa on the south coast of Ukraine. Like all immigrants fleeing the poverty and pogroms of the late nineteenth century, Bobby's grandparents arrived in America with nothing. Abe's father, Zigman Zissel Zimmerman, born in 1873 or 1875, arrived in Duluth in 1905, in the wake of a pogrom that had killed 400 Jews in Odessa.

He had gone straight to Duluth after arriving in America, because other people from Odessa had gone there, hoping to take advantage of the town's growing economy, centred around the port and the newly arrived railroad. That was the pattern of Jewish settlement in the West: you went where your *landsleiten*, your fellow countrymen, had gone. Like most of his fellows, Zigman began by working in Duluth as a pedlar. In 1910, when he had scraped enough money together, he brought his wife Anna over with their four children, the oldest of whom was 8. Their fifth child, Abe, was born in Duluth in 1911.

Beatty's parents, Ben and Florence Stone, originally surnamed Solemovitz and Edelstein respectively, came to Hibbing as young children with their parents. Ben's father was a pedlar in Hibbing who, speaking no English himself, encouraged his son to fight his way up to a degree of prosperity, opening a general store in the small town of Stevenson and marrying Florence in 1911. Born in the *shtetl* of Vilkomir, in Lithuania, in 1892, she arrived in Hibbing with her parents Boruch and Faige at the age of 10. Dylan's antecedents, immigrants all, made it their overriding priority to provide their children with a reasonable helping of financial security and an education.

Bob Dylan is an enigma; we can never fully understand what is in his head. When he recorded 'I Pity the Poor Immigrant' in 1967, we can't know if he was singing of immigrants in general or whether he had anyone specific in mind. The fact that he was born into a generation of American Jews graced with Yiddish-speaking grandparents may not even have occurred to him. But the immigrant who Dylan pities is besotted by material prosperity, cheating, lying, and falling in love with wealth. Is this sarcasm, Bob Dylan sneering at antisemitic stereotypes? At those who unjustly denigrate impoverished Jewish immigrants for the very fact of their immigration, for their desire to flee the pogroms and dream of a better life?

And what of the biblical images in the song? You shall eat and be satisfied, says Deuteronomy, but Dylan's immigrant is never full.

He is weighed down by skies of iron, his strength consumed in emptiness, the dooms pronounced in Leviticus. Dylan was 26 when he recorded 'I Pity the Poor Immigrant'. The Judaism we cast off in our teenage years has a habit of coming back.

Seemingly disinterested in his Jewishness, as a teenager Bobby couldn't get away from it. Four years in a row he spent a few weeks each summer at a Jewish camp run by his mother's Hadassah organisation. It was a pretty conventional thing to do, a tame experience, sports and games, innocent romances, discussions about Israel, the state founded just a few years earlier, Hebrew songs around a campfire at night. They would have sung 'Hava Negilah', the Israeli folk song that everybody knew. Dylan parodied it in 1962 to poke fun at folk purists obsessed with the origins of their tunes, describing it as a foreign song that he had come across in Utah. The only resemblance between his 'Talkin' Hava Negilah Blues' and the Israeli folk song is in the name.

Jewish parents tend to be ambitious for their children. It's an aspiration forged in the immigrant experience, in the imperative for physical and material security. Bobby's parents were ambitious for him, they tried to explain that there was no future in being a poet. Beatty, resorting to Jewish mother stereotype, told him he would be dead before he started earning any money as a poet or musician. They tried to encourage him to join his father in the family business, in the appliance store that he ran with his brothers. Either that or study hard to earn a degree and become a doctor or a lawyer. But Bobby's head was somewhere else. A generation earlier he may have listened to them. Now, in the mid-1950s he lay in bed at night listening to his radio beneath the covers, discovering music that had never been dreamed of in Hibbing: Hank Williams his first idol, Johnny Ray whose voice he fell in love with, Little Richard, Bill Haley, Buddy Holly, Roy Orbison and Elvis. Not just listening to the music, like most of his peers, but dissecting, analysing, internalising it all. Folk music was what he was looking for; he considered the folk singers of America to be his cultural forebears, but he listened to everything. For Bobby Zimmerman, music, the right music, was a constellation of sounds and emotions to be explored, each song worth listening to for its array of different influences, genres and styles; an intricate pathway to the recesses of his soul. If he liked a song, he loved it. If he didn't like it, it was empty and banal. He called the range of music coming out of his radio the 'Jekyll and Hyde themes of the times'.[4]

His intense, analytical approach to the music that stirred him would serve him well. For Dylan it wasn't a question of following trends, of listening to what everyone else was listening to. Rather he peered into everything he heard, where and how the changes came, how different styles fused, the mix of influences, the harmonies and rhythms. His deconstruction of each and every song he considered important helped him to understand why one song, one musician, would endure while another was destined for oblivion. When the time came for him to move on from the folk music that launched his career, to evolve from protest singer to megastar, there was nothing random about the musical choices he made. The time would come when some of his fans would accuse him of selling out, of betraying them. But there was no betrayal; he had told them early on that the times were a-changing, they just hadn't understood the full extent of what he meant. We forget today that Dylan didn't simply *sing* about the changing of the times; he was one of the few who first *noticed* that the times were a-changing. That song, 'The Times They Are A-Changin'', wasn't commentary, it was perspicacity, some might even say prophecy. From the day that Bobby Zimmerman first turned on the radio in his parents' home in Hibbing, he'd had a pretty good idea that big things were happening, that the old values were changing, that something new was on the way. He couldn't yet see how it would pan out, but it felt exciting, fresh, revolutionary. He'd known from his early teens that he wanted to be part of it, that his understanding of music would shape his future life. What he needed to do to make it happen wasn't fully clear, but he was certain that it didn't involve him following in his parents' footsteps, subscribing to their beliefs or doing the things they had done, like settling down and getting a steady job.

FAREWELL HIBBING

Ditching your parents' values, paying little attention to your Jewish identity, such things are easy to do. They involve arguments at home, but once you walk out of the door, when you are with your friends, your life is your own. What seems to have been much harder for young Bobby Zimmerman was getting away from Hibbing itself. An old mining town on the Iron Range, the mines had seen their best days. By the mid-1950s, Hibbing had sunk into a depression. Years later, Dylan sang about the town's decline in 'North Country Blues', the semi-fictional story of a miner and his family, destroyed by the closure of the mines.

Whatever there was for teenage kids to do in Hibbing wasn't much, and Bobby wasn't the only youngster desperate to get out. And get out he did. Several times in fact, but only ever in his imagination, in fantasies and tales. It took him much longer to do so in reality.

When he did finally leave, when he first experienced the world beyond Hibbing, and that world began to take an interest in him, he told nobody that he was a middle-class Jew from Hibbing where his father ran an appliance store. He fantasised an origin for himself as a freewheeling itinerant. He told his first interviewers that he had worked in the circus when he was 13, that he had lived in Gallup, New Mexico, and that he had no religion, having tried a bunch of different ones.

A couple of years later he recounted an alternative backstory. Owning up this time to a childhood in Hibbing, he said he'd run away from home at the age of 10 with his guitar and harmonica, only to be picked up by the police 900 miles to the south and taken back. He had then run off five more times before finally leaving home at the age of 18. The story was nothing but make-believe, yet was seized on over and again during the next few years by interviewers and journalists, trying to present their subject as even more iconic than he actually was.

Leaving home at the age of 18 was the only truth in his fantasy. He had wandered a little beforehand, working for a few weeks in the summer of 1959 at a café in the nearby town of Fargo and exploring the folk scene in Denver, Colorado, 1,000 miles from his home. He had played in a band at school and while in Fargo had been roped in to play piano for the future heart-throb Bobby Vee, in the most unlikely of circumstances, the specifics of which vary, depending on who is telling the story. The gist of it is that Buddy Holly had been due to play a gig in Fargo but had been tragically killed in a plane crash. Vee, in those days still known as Bobby Velline, was in a band with his brothers and, although only 15 years old, had landed the opportunity to fill in for Holly at the concert he had been due to play. Now, Vee's band were looking for a rock pianist to accompany them, and somebody told them about Bobby Zimmerman who was stacking dishes at the Red Apple café. Bobby failed the audition but even being called upon boosted his self-belief; it was the first time he had come close to a professional gig. Despite his parents trying their hardest to persuade him otherwise, he could now realistically dream of a musical career. Meanwhile, his father and mother had other plans for him.

In line with those plans, Bobby left home in September 1959, to take up a place on a liberal arts programme at the University of Minnesota in Minneapolis, a couple of hundred miles south of Hibbing. He was supposed to major in music but he didn't remain a student long enough for his major to make any impact on him, or for him to make a meaningful contribution to the university. He dropped out after just a few months. He'd found a more productive way to spend his time.

Bobby's sojourn in Minneapolis was perhaps the most formative period of his life. Partly because he arrived as Bobby Zimmerman and left as Bob Dylan. But mainly because of the changes he went through in that short period, inducting him into the social and emotional world in which he belonged, actuating the potential he always knew he had and hoisting him to the crest of the cultural tsunami about to be unleashed by his generation.

America had never known a decade like the 1950s. A time of growing prosperity yet one overshadowed by overwhelming social division, political paranoia and unyielding conservatism. The end of World War II, advances in medicine and technology along with an unprecedented economic boom should have ushered in an era of tranquillity. Instead, in the minds of many, a monster loomed over the nation, albeit one more imagined than tangible. A spectre from the East, an unimaginable evil named communism that threatened to overwhelm the American Way of Life, its values, and the sanctity of all that was held dear. An all-consuming paranoia, obsessing the politicians. An inquisition of dissenters and free-thinkers, damaging reputations, destroying livelihoods and ruining lives. Moderate voices, fearful they themselves might become victims, by and large remained silent. Meanwhile, cohorts of teenagers, confident and invincible as only youth can be, watched dumbfounded, unable to comprehend, identifying more with the persecuted than their inquisitors. Their parents' world was not one they wished to be a part of.

It had begun in 1950, when Senator Joseph McCarthy instigated an investigation into suspected communists and fifth columnists. As paranoid as only a conspiracy theorist can be, he warned that Stalin, the Soviet leader, whose crimes we now know were second only to Hitler's, had a legion of sympathisers and agents in the United States aspiring to destroy the nation's way of life. Preparing to contaminate American democracy with the poison of communism. McCarthy's was a warning that terrified the uninformed. It was common knowledge that the Soviet Union had already successfully tested an atomic bomb – in 1949 at a test site in Kazakhstan. Not content with subverting democracy, it was evident that the Soviets planned to blow the United States to smithereens.

America's leaders crowed that the nation was responding to the Soviet threat. While Joe McCarthy's witch-hunt was, in their eyes, doing a fine job of protecting free speech and democracy, the armed forces were engaged in a decisive war against the communists in Korea. No matter that it was a catastrophic war that would blindly lead to the creation of a belligerent, nuclear-armed dictatorship in the north of that unhappy land, making things truly dangerous for future generations. That would be in the future. Rare is the paranoid politician endowed with generous powers of foresight.

The perceived communist threat was everywhere. In 1953 Ethel and Julius Rosenberg were executed, having been convicted (unjustly in her case) of espionage on behalf of the Soviets. In nearby Cuba, a communist insurgency led by Fidel Castro and Che Guevara was gearing up to overthrow the American-backed government of Fulgencio Batista. Fear was rampant. Unless you were under 25 years old.

It is little wonder that America's youth turned their backs on the national paranoia. With more money and time on their hands than ever before, they had little reason or incentive to worry. While ordinary Americans were struggling to make sense of the manifold threats, fears and dangers, others, particularly among the young, paid them no mind at all. College and high-school students lavished far more attention on the new phenomenon of rock 'n' roll than on communist conspiracies or the risk of nuclear war, despite being instructed in how to hide beneath their school desks, should they suffer a nuclear attack. All they wanted were the good times. When Bill Haley and his Comets released 'Rock Around the Clock' in 1955, topping the *Billboard* charts for two months, rock 'n' roll moved from the fringes to the mainstream. Elvis, The Everly Brothers, Buddy Holly and handfuls of scarcely remembered names followed in quick succession, each with their own distinctive sound. In 1956 Elvis followed his first-ever number-one hit, 'Heartbreak Hotel', with three more chart-toppers and repeated the feat the following year. Elevated by their new music, American youth mostly turned their backs on the preoccupations and prejudices of their parents' generation.

This was the age of the pop-music single, new releases coming out each week, seven-inch vinyl discs, just one song on each side, stacked up on spindles poking out of their gramophone turntables. As each disc finished playing, the arm with its needle and cartridge would retract and the next record would drop down, ready to spin at 45 rotations per minute. Unlike the long-playing, 12-inch albums that went around at 33 rpm.

Record stores became social hangouts; the best had listening booths where you could hear the latest release, or any other record of your choice, before deciding whether to buy. The singles craze forced even the staid *Billboard* newspaper to rebrand its weekly 'Music Popularity Charts', containing separate listings for discs sold in stores, played in jukeboxes and on the radio. *Billboard* consolidated them into a 'Hot 100', a sharper name to reflect the new image of popular music, now universally called 'pop'. Kids bought singles in droves, dropping dimes into jukeboxes to play the latest hits, dancing in the cafés and dance halls, creating for the first time a distinctive teen culture, a world from which their parents were excluded and which sharp-minded entrepreneurs quickly saw as a new commercial opportunity. Record companies paid disc jockeys to spin their latest offerings on the radio, advertisers piled in, the top stars minted it. Teenagers with their money were the new gold mines. Like Bobby Zimmerman, teenagers were all listening to their radios. Unlike other teenagers, Bobby listened with a discerning ear, only paying attention to those records with distinctive musical qualities; taking an interest exclusively in those performers whose music expressed their creativity, for whom recording a single was not just a way of cashing in.

The teens were looking for fun, at this stage in their lives they weren't looking to change the world. But change the world they would. There was no colour bar to their love of music. The Cleveland disc jockey Alan Freed brought African American rhythm and blues to white audiences through artists like B. B. King, Fats Domino and The Drifters. Little Richard credited Elvis with opening the door to black musicians. Black kids were dancing to the same music as whites; the 1956 Rock 'n' Roll Number Five concert in Camden, New Jersey, drew a mixed-race crowd numbering 4,500. Ralph Bass, the president of Chess Records, spoke of how black dance halls would only let white kids in on certain nights, putting 'a rope across the middle of the floor. The blacks on one side, whites on the other, digging how the blacks were dancing and copying them. Then, hell, the rope would come down, and they'd all be dancing together.'⁵ When it came to colour, young Americans were generally blind. And when racial tensions exploded in the late 1950s, not for the first time but in a way that now shocked America as never before, it was young people, through their activism and their energy, who took the initiative in bringing about change.

1955 had been a dreadful year for race relations. In August, Emmett Till, a 14-year-old black boy, was murdered by two white men: beaten, shot and thrown in a Mississippi river, for allegedly whistling at a white woman. His murderers were arrested, acquitted at trial by an all-white jury, and the following year sold their story, complete with confession, to a newspaper. Dylan chronicled the murder in his rarely heard 'The Death of Emmett Till', written in 1962 but not released until 2010, on the *Witmark Demos* album.

Emmett Till's murder and the acquittal of his assassins sparked an inferno of protest that reached its climax four months later, in December, when Rosa Parks, a black woman in Montgomery, Alabama, refused to give up her seat to a white man on a bus. Her arrest led to a year-long boycott of buses in Montgomery, the passing of anti-segregation laws, the flowering of the civil rights movement and a spate of white-supremacist violence that only ended when seven bombers from the absurdly named Ku Klux Klan were arrested.

Like any social phenomenon, rock 'n roll did not thrill everyone. Many considered it shallow and paid it no attention at all. Some, generally a little older and with greater life experience, had no interest in teenage escapism, in finding ways to distract themselves from the confusion of contemporary life. They actively promoted their rejection of contemporary values, expressing themselves through political activism, art or the written word. Jack Kerouac, Allen Ginsberg, Lawrence Ferlinghetti, William Burroughs and a small number of like-minded poets and writers collectivised themselves as Beats, a status Ginsberg described as 'a poetic conception, an attitude toward the world'. The Beats considered themselves to be innovators in the literary world but in doing so they underestimated their impact. Their cultural influence was far greater than merely their literary output, despite the undoubted quality of much of what they wrote. Their principled rejection of the expectations and mores of their middle-class neighbours would help shape the hippie and anti-establishment movements of the 1960s and 1970s, which acknowledged a debt to the Beats, yet extolled Bob Dylan as a greater inspiration. Dylan, who grew close to Ginsberg, was a generation younger than many of the Beats. Had he been born 20 years earlier, he might have been numbered among them.

The Beats bestowed a hallucinogenic, quasi-mystical character upon the era; their poetry was metaphysical, consciousness-expanding, surreal; the closest the mid-twentieth century came to having its own William Blake or Rumi. But born too late and still in Minneapolis, Dylan was not ready for the Beats. Music was still his obsession.

DISSENT

The folk music that Dylan was hoping to find among the blues and the new rock 'n' roll issuing from his radio had been through something of a revival during the 1940s. The traditional songs and melodies of marginalised and working people were playing on specialist radio shows and sung by wandering troubadours, reawakening America to

the nation's rich, informal musical heritage. The roots of the revival
lay both in African American music, spirituals, gospels, calypso and
the songs of the white rural classes, but the musicians were more
likely to be urban eggheads who reformatted the tunes into a
somewhat synthetic, contemporary offering that their peers could
more easily relate to. That's how the ubiquitous anthem of protest
'We Shall Overcome' was born, from an amalgam of two songs: the
words from Charles Tindley's 1901 hymn 'I'll Overcome Some Day'
and the melody from the traditional gospel song 'I'll Be Alright'.

Folk songs can evoke powerful emotions. Often reflecting the
burden that their composers were labouring under, their tragedies,
dreams of liberation or prayers for salvation, folk music lends
itself to protest, to calls for freedom and the need to take action.
Little wonder that folk music owed its revival to the gestating civil
rights and freedom movements. With their egalitarian, socialist
undertones these were the very activities that Senator Joe McCarthy
and his allies would soon strive to suppress. Keenly aware of their
disruptive powers, folk musicians and singers sometimes adapted
traditional lyrics to give them greater contemporary relevance,
turning themselves into the priests and prophets of the political left.

In 1940, shortly before the United States entered World War II,
four young folk musicians in their twenties banded together to form
The Almanac Singers. All four were politically engaged, active in
the growing social struggle for civil and workers' rights in America.
They played at rallies, union meetings, benefits and parties, any
place where they could use their music for political effect. They
urged their audiences to sing along with them in protests about
exploitative corporations and appalling working conditions. They
extolled strikers and disparaged scabs, castigated hatred and racial
persecution, called for social justice, condemned war and the
oppression of the masses.

Whether all four were members of the Communist Party has never
been conclusively determined, but they moved in the same circles
and, in the eyes of the authorities, even if they were not members,

they were guilty by association. In 1942 the FBI branded them as seditious because of their anti-war activity, the press condemned them as communist agitators and music commentators gave them hostile reviews. Perhaps fortuitously for their own safety, World War II intervened and they disbanded after two years. Years later the House Un-American Activities Committee, Congress's myopic investigation into communism, denounced two of them, Pete Seeger and Lee Hays, as communists and declared them blacklisted. They didn't denounce the other two, Woody Guthrie or Millard Lampell, but they stuck them on the blacklist anyway. Radio and TV stations refused to employ them, record labels shunned them, no major venue would welcome them onto the stage. And that was just the impact on their careers and their pockets. To be blacklisted in 1950s America was to be ostracised socially, though of course the sort of people who were prepared to shun them were not those they had any interest in spending time with anyway.

The people who they were keen on associating with tended to be on the left of the political spectrum. They were often members of cultural or ethnic minorities: other musicians, artists, writers, blacks and Jews. A disproportionate number were Jews, reflecting the political leanings of the immigrant generation and their children, leanings that they had brought with them from the old country. Many Jews were involved in the folk-music scene in one way or another: it appealed to their traditional instincts, political outlook, creativity, and awareness of their outsider status. The vast majority of Jewish folk musicians paid little attention to their ethnicity, though they may have been aware that they belonged to a Jewish radical stream with roots in pre-revolutionary Russia. The radical stream's influence trickled down into The Almanac Singers through Pete Seeger. Seeger was not a Jew; he was born into a Christian family who could trace their roots in America back through generations. But it was Seeger who did more than most to propagate Jewish and Hebrew folk music in America, through songs like 'Hineh Ma Tov' and 'Tzena, Tzena, Tzena'.

Pete Seeger had inherited his political outlook from his parents, who saw their mission as disseminating socialism and bringing 'good' music to the American people.[6] His mother Constance was a violinist and his father Charles a pianist and distinguished professor of musicology. Seeger's parents divorced when he was seven and his new stepmother, a former student of his father's, was the modernist composer Ruth Crawford Seeger, a specialist in folk music.

Seeger's affinity with Jewish and Hebrew music most likely came to him through his father Charles. He in turn had been influenced politically by the composer Aaron Copland, a direct heir to the Jewish radical tradition. Charles Seeger and Copland had both been members of the Composers' Collective, founded in 1932 as an offshoot of the Communist Party's International Music Bureau.

The Composers' Collective was a forum that aspired to harness music to address the social and economic problems besetting the country. As Charles Seeger would say years later, 'We felt urgency in those days . . . The economic and social system is going to hell over here. Music might be able to do something about it. Let's see if we can try. We *must* try.'[7] He became an evangelist for the idea that folk music was how the working classes of America expressed themselves politically. Copland shared similar views. In 1945 he joined the Board of Sponsors of People's Songs Inc., an organisation that Pete Seeger had created to use folk music in the service of left-wing causes. It was Charles and Pete Seeger who formally allied folk music and left-wing politics. Copland completed the triangle by adding the Jewish dimension. Bob Dylan, in his early years, would absorb their influences.

During the war Pete Seeger served in the Army as a mechanic, while also performing for the troops. In 1948 he teamed up again with Lee Hays, his former Almanac Singers colleague, and two others to form a new band. They called themselves The Weavers. The anti-communist paranoia, the Red Scare as it was called, which had briefly raised its head in the wake of the Russian Revolution of 1917, was just then reappearing. It felt all the more ominous now, in the post-war years, with the Soviet Union extending its hegemony across Eastern Europe and Winston Churchill declaring that an 'iron curtain has descended across the Continent'.[8] By 1950, America was in the grip of the twin anti-communist tyrannies of Senator McCarthy and the House Un-American Activities Committee. The Weavers were advised that if they wanted to be commercially successful, they should steer clear of politics. Needing money more than they needed persecution they turned themselves into a commercial combo, or at least as commercial as a folk band could be in those days. Their first record was 'The Hammer Song', better known today as 'If I Had a Hammer'. The song eventually became hugely successful, a staple both of protest movements and church services, but The Weavers' version flopped; it didn't become a hit until it was recorded in 1962 by Peter, Paul and Mary. Nevertheless, *Billboard* thought The Weavers had potential, writing that 'the act is rough, unpolished, needs costuming and better routining. But allowing for the individual shortcomings, the group has a drive and a spirit that indicates more than casual commercial value.'[9]

The Weavers did better with their version of Lead Belly's 'Goodnight, Irene'; it reached number 1 in 1950 and sold a million copies. They released it along with Seeger's version of the Yiddish folk song 'Tzena, Tzena, Tzena'.

In adopting their commercial image, The Weavers were trying their hardest not to be political. But they couldn't shake off their past. The Decca record label had stood by them while 'Goodnight, Irene' was selling its one million copies, even though Seeger's name was being bandied about by Senator McCarthy's witch-finders. But by 1953, when his left-wing leanings had resurfaced in the media, when radio stations blacklisted him and the FBI took an interest, Decca dropped Seeger from their catalogue, and The Weavers' career came to a sudden end. Their decision to turn commercial had helped usher in a folk-music revival; when The Weavers disappeared so did the revival. Folk music went underground.

As it turned out, that was no bad thing. For it was then, away from the spotlight of the *Billboard* charts, record labels, radio stations and major concert venues, that folk music was able to reconnect with its political roots. Folk singers were now to be found in radical coffee houses and small clubs, the haunts of people who would soon be labelled beatniks or dropouts, who had something of a left-wing, anti-establishment outlook, or were social misfits, or very often both. Haunts where a makeshift stage in the front window of a café or at the back of the room might be occupied by a local jazz combo, an aspiring folk singer or a wannabe Beat poet trying out his latest lines. Known as basket houses, because the only money a performer earned was from passing a basket around the audience, these were the sort of places to which the young Bobby Zimmerman gravitated, shortly after enrolling at the University of Minnesota – after he'd discovered that college life was not all that it was cracked up to be.

AN OUTSIDER

When he first arrived in Minneapolis, Bobby lived in the university's Jewish fraternity house, Sigma Alpha Mu. It was the conventional thing for a student to do, to live in a frat house and, if you were a Jew, to live in a Jewish fraternity. But Bobby Zimmerman was not the conventional type and the other boys in Sigma Alpha Mu were not the sort of people he was interested in hanging around with. Sober young men, in sensible clothes, with square tastes in music and mainstream political views, people who didn't see that there was much wrong with the country and thought that Senator McCarthy was doing a reasonable sort of job, young men who were going to college before marrying and settling down, who rang their parents regularly – these had never been Bobby Zimmerman's kind of people. Even though, to look at, he wasn't much different from them. He was clean-cut, rather dumpy, wore college boy clothes and combed his hair a lot. You could easily mistake him for any other 18-year-old Jewish kid. Unless, that is, you were another 18-year-old Jewish kid, trying to talk to him. You'd then know straightaway, from the absence of a reply, or at best a grunt, that this was somebody who had no interest in speaking to you. He didn't want to be a part of you. And although you might feel a little miffed, from that moment on you too had no intention of being a part of him.

The Jewish college scene is inclusive, welcoming and sociable, if you feel a part of it, if you find it easy to connect with your peers. And if you can't connect, or you don't find it easy, if their interests are not your interests, if their world is not yours, then you are always going to be an outsider.

Bobby Zimmerman didn't care that he was an outsider. But he did care that the kids in the Jewish fraternity house didn't want much to do with him, that they didn't respect him for refusing to have the same middle-class ambitions as them, for clearly not having any intention of taking up a respectable Jewish career, as a doctor, lawyer or accountant. He had an elevated sense of his self-worth; he knew he was different, and special, and it meant nothing to him if they considered him surly and vain. But he did want them to appreciate that he had good reason to be surly and vain. He didn't care about impressing them but nor did he want them to put him down or disrespect him. There were other people in Minnesota who he did care about impressing but they weren't students at the university; they were the cool cats who hung around in the coffee houses downtown. Granted, a fair few of them did happen to be Jewish, but that meant nothing, it was just a coincidence. Unlike the frat kids, Bobby didn't want to be around people just because they were Jews.

Bobby didn't live at the frat house for long and he stayed at the university for not much longer. A few years later he wrote that he had failed his science course for refusing to watch experiments on a live rabbit, had been thrown out of English for using four-letter words when writing about the teacher, and was expelled from the communications course for never turning up. Of course,

none of that may have been true, in the same article he said that
he had been jailed as a suspect in an armed robbery and was
once held on a murder charge.[10] If anything might cause us to
regard Bob Dylan as a Jewish mystical dreamer, it is his erosion
of the boundaries between observable and potential realities. It
is a quality born out of a cultural optimism, shaped by a history
of exclusion and deprivation, a mechanism for responding to
adversity, or, conversely, fuelling ambition, encapsulated in the
Talmudic saying 'this too is for the best'. If everything, no matter
how bad, is for the best, or at least tolerable, then anything
is possible. Actual and potential blur into one another; how
otherwise could a slave nation's dream of freedom become real,
a man wrestle with an angel and prevail, a destitute milkman, a
Fiddler on the Roof, ask how it might damage the Great Eternal
Plan if he were to be a wealthy man?

The University of Minnesota did not play a large part in Bob
Dylan's life story but his time in Minneapolis certainly did.
Still looking clean-cut and fresh of chubby face, he headed for
Dinkytown, the city's cool neighbourhood on the edge of the
university. Dinkytown was no Greenwich Village but its coffee
houses were hangouts for Minneapolis's small crowd of dropouts,
artists, beatniks and aspiring sages. They were Bobby's kind
of people; once he found them he seemed more accepting of
observable reality, more willing to transcend his fantasy origins. In
Dinkytown, the backstories didn't disappear altogether, but he did
recite them less frequently.

One of the Dinkytown coffee houses was the Ten O'Clock
Scholar. As the name suggests it was mainly a student haunt. A
dozen or more vacant-looking customers were mooching around
the place, most of them without even a drink in front of them,
when Bobby Zimmerman walked in, one day in October 1959. A
flamenco guitarist was playing on a low platform in the window.
Bobby stood, watching, listening, then walked over to the owner.

'Mind if I play?' he asked.

'What's your name?' replied the owner, David Lee, mildly amused at this frat brat, with his neatly combed hair, chinos and sports jacket.

Bobby Zimmerman thought quickly. He hated his German, Jewish name, hated the idea that anyone might think he was German, or Jewish. If only he had been born with a name that sounded erudite; that sounded original, idiosyncratic and intelligent.

'Bob Dylan,' he said.

And so Bob Dylan was born.

Those who heard him sing at the Ten O'Clock Scholar were far from impressed. His guitar playing wasn't too great, his voice was an adenoidal monotone. But Bob Dylan wasn't performing for his audience. He was singing and playing for himself, learning how to be a folk singer. Dylan may not have got on well with the courses he studied at university but that was no reflection on his intelligence, nor on his thirst for education. The Ten O'Clock Scholar became his surrogate university, the college he kept going back to, the one he didn't drop out of. Instead, it was the Scholar's new owners, after David Lee had sold the joint, who got rid of him.

The problem was that Bob Dylan was a prima donna. As he was entitled to be, he was Bob Dylan, and even though his audience didn't know where he was headed, he had a pretty good idea. Self-belief issued from every pore. He may not have been able to describe in detail how his future would turn out but he knew that as long as he kept on working at it, playing and learning, he would succeed. Driven and single-minded, in a way that only an aspirational, far-sighted Jewish outsider from a small town can be, he would not let up in his quest for success. A time would come when people would pay good money to see him perform, and having paid good money, they wouldn't spend his performance chatting to their friends. Since they wouldn't dream of doing that in the future, there was no reason, in the mind of the new, freshly minted persona called Bob Dylan, why they should do it now.

So when customers of the Ten O'Clock Scholar spoke to each other while he sang and played, wandered in and out, or displayed any other of the myriad ways of not paying his performance any attention, he'd let them know. He'd yell at them, stomp off the stage, go and sulk in the basement. Bob Dylan could be insufferable. His audience knew it, the coffee house's owner knew it, most particularly his Jewish frat house acquaintances knew it. His attitude towards his audiences was the same as his attitude to his fraternity: he was better than they gave him credit for and he wanted them to acknowledge it. He was still a poor guitarist and his nasal voice sounded dreadful but he knew he was going places and he didn't have the humility to indulge his audience, nor the patience to develop his career slowly. He'd now been playing at the Ten O'Clock Scholar for about three months and was still only earning two dollars a night, less than his friend Spider John Koerner who was also playing there. When Bob Dylan asked for a pay rise, the new owners of the Ten O'Clock Scholar stopped inviting him to play.

Listen to Dylan's music today and you will hear all sorts of literary influences: Whitman, Rimbaud, the Bible, William Blake, Bertolt Brecht, William Burroughs; the list goes on and on. But in his Minneapolis days, according to his former friends, Dylan read nothing and took no serious interest in anything other than his music, in learning his craft. He left the Scholar and started playing at the Bastille coffee house, earning five dollars a night, more than twice the fee he'd been earning before. He made himself distinctive, and not just for his nasal monotone. He strapped a contraption that looked as if had been made from a wire coat hanger around his neck, attached a harmonica to it, and blew it between verses while strumming his guitar. It was a technique that came to define him, though it hadn't been his idea. Reportedly invented by the guitarist Les Paul, a harmonica rack had been used by Woody Guthrie, also Jesse Fuller and Ramblin' Jack Elliott. Woody had probably fashioned the rack himself, but by the time Bob began to play the harmonica, racks were being sold by specialist musical suppliers.

Bob's girlfriend in Minneapolis, Bonnie Beecher, bought him one. Nobody else in Minneapolis was playing harmonica and guitar at the same time, yet the combination of his rack and harmonica was a singularity that none of his audience seemed to notice. He got no credit or recognition for it.

Dylan allegedly did not read while in Minneapolis and nor did he pay any attention to politics. The 1960s were bustling in, carried along by a flurry of anticipation. Depending on one's political outlook, the augurs were either exciting or worrying. John Kennedy, the man who liberals heralded as the standard-bearer of a new era, was gathering support in his Democratic campaign for the White House. His supporters were certain that his presidency, if he succeeded in winning it, would propel America into an age of almost messianic promise. In Havana meanwhile, Fidel Castro's Cuban revolutionaries had succeeded in ejecting Batista's government, replacing it with a Soviet-allied, communist state from which all American interests were ejected. Just 100 miles off the coast of Florida, events in Cuba were causing nervousness in Washington, fascinating the Beats and galvanising the New Left. Fidel Castro had visited Washington in 1959 where he had met and impressed Vice President Richard Nixon. Now however, Nixon was shaping up as the Republican candidate to stand against Kennedy in the November 1960 presidential election. To add muscle to his campaign Nixon was loudly pressing for a full invasion of Cuba, to remove Castro from power. And if Cuba wasn't enough, in May 1960 Gary Powers, the pilot of an American U2 spy plane, was shot down over Russia. The Cold War felt more perilous than ever and the nuclear threat, which had been building all through the 1950s, was suddenly more immediate.

Things were no more settled in the South where the civil rights movement was coming of age. In February 1960 four young black students decided it was time to do something about the colour bar, the segregation of blacks and whites, invariably to the whites' advantage. They marched into the local town of Greensboro, North

Carolina, walked into the Woolworths store, sat at the lunch counter and demanded to be served. The lunch counter had a policy of only serving whites. As they sat down they were terrified, even more when a policeman arrived, walking around them tapping his night stick into his hand. But they kept their cool. They weren't served and sat there until five o'clock when the counter closed. The civil rights movement, the hottest political movement in early 1960s America, was reborn that day. The daring of the Greensboro Four first hit the local newspaper, then the national headlines. Sitting at a segregated lunch counter was such a simple act of resistance it proved inspirational. Across the South, students arose in protest. By the end of February there were sit-ins on more than 50 university campuses across the country. At Easter that year Dr Martin Luther King delivered a speech to over 200 student activists gathered at a meeting in North Carolina. The 19-year-old Joan Baez wasn't there that day, but she'd heard him speak a while earlier. 'Everyone in the room was mesmerised. He talked about injustice and suffering, and about fighting with the weapons of love, saying that when someone does evil to us we can hate the evil deed but not the doer of the deed, who is to be pitied . . . When he finished his speech I was on my feet cheering and crying.'[11] Events would become more dangerous and violent over the coming years, but after February 1960 there was no looking back.

1960 was turning into a year of huge political upheaval. Nevertheless, in Dinkytown's Bastille coffee house, it all seemed somehow to wash over the young Bob Dylan. The man who would shortly be considered the voice of the protest generation played his guitar, blew his harmonica, and learnt how to be a folk singer.

But not for long. When the change hit Dylan, it was sudden and all-consuming. He had been hanging around with 'Diamond' Dave Whitaker, a laid-back, politically astute savant on the Dinkytown coffee-house scene. A member of pro-Castro, left-wing groups in Minneapolis, Whitaker had recently arrived in the city after an extended bout of travelling, passing through London and Paris, and living on a kibbutz in Israel. Of all Dylan's Minneapolis friends, Whitaker was the most experienced; Dinkytown's sage and intellectual. Unlike the student fraternity he had been out there and seen the world, was widely read, had moved in Beat circles and knew Ginsberg, Kerouac and Ferlinghetti. He acted as a kind of mentor to the young, still naive Bob Dylan, grounding him and encouraging him to broaden his horizons. Whitaker's living room acted as a hangout for the Dinkytown crowd; it was there that Dylan smoked his first joint, an occasion Whitaker was still talking about over 50 years later.[12]

Dylan was in Whitaker's apartment one afternoon, playing a Woody Guthrie album, listening intensely to the music as he always did but not paying much attention to the message. Whitaker asked him if he had read *Bound for Glory*, Guthrie's autobiography. Dylan shrugged, said he'd never heard of it, so Whitaker proceeded to tell him all about Guthrie's life. By the time he'd finished Dylan was entranced, insisting that he needed to read the book right there and then. According to Whitaker, he handed the book to Bob to read, but another account claims that they spent the next couple of days searching the city's libraries and bookstores, trying to find a copy. Bob eventually located one and sat in the Ten O'Clock Scholar all day, devouring it. *Bound for Glory* would become a turning point in his life.

BOUND FOR GLORY

Woody Guthrie was born in 1912 into a farming family in Oklahoma. When he was 8 years old, oil was discovered near his home town of Okemah. Overnight the city's economy and population exploded, transforming the family's fortunes. The good times lasted for eight years, until the oil dried up, the town's economy collapsed, and Okemah sank deep into the overwhelming devastation of the Great Depression. Like so many others in those difficult years, the Guthrie family was financially ruined. Woody took off, heading for Texas.

He reached Pampa, just in time to fall in love with Mary Jennings, have three children, and face financial ruin once again, as drought and the great Dust Bowl storms destroyed the livelihoods of the region's farmers and their farmhands. By now he was playing guitar and singing professionally. Forced to hit the road again, this time he travelled with a musical talent that might earn him a crust or two.

Woody Guthrie walked, jumped freight trains and hitchhiked his way to California. He played his guitar as he went, singing in saloons to earn a few coins or a bed for the night, facing the opprobrium of the townspeople he passed along the way, who were sick of the sight of Dust Bowl refugees. He ended up in California, where he got a job in Los Angeles singing old-time songs on the KFVD radio station. He campaigned between songs, arguing for unions and civil rights, attacking corruption and the power of big business. He wove ideas of social justice into his songs, singing about the tragedies of the dust storms, the hardships of travelling and the evils of poverty. He sang about outlaws who just would not knuckle down, like 'Billy the Kid', of the irredeemably bad killer 'Stackolee' and of 'Pretty Boy Floyd', a Robin Hood character who robbed banks to help the poor and keep them in their homes, contrasting him with the bankers and capitalists who threw them out onto the streets. He wrote 3,000 songs during his career, his best have been covered by everyone from Dylan and Joan Baez to Bruce Springsteen, The Grateful Dead, Odetta, Billy Bragg and The Byrds. He was diagnosed (like his mother) with the incurable, degenerative brain disorder Huntington's disease in 1954, and lived out his final years in Creedmoor State Hospital in Queens, New York, dying in 1967.

Always an eclectic figure, Woody Guthrie cemented his name in leftist legend and folk music history in 1940, when he arrived in New York. Moses Asch, an immigrant from Warsaw, son of the noted Yiddish author and playwright Sholem Asch, signed him up for his recording company. Under the name of Folkway Records, Asch's company would soon become the most important of all the early folk labels. Alongside Woody Guthrie its artists included Pete

Seeger, Lead Belly, Duke Ellington and Dizzy Gillespie. Woody was a founder member of The Almanac Singers, but when they were reincarnated as The Weavers, their recording of his most famous song 'This Land Is Your Land' undermined the message he was trying to get across.

Woody had written 'This Land Is Your Land' in response to Irving Berlin's 'God Bless America'. Initially Guthrie had sarcastically called it 'God Blessed America for Me', before changing its name. Woody's original verses condemned the inability of the poor to own property, drew attention to the hunger besetting American cities, and emphasised the fact that America belonged to everyone, not just to the privileged. But when The Weavers recorded it in 1959, they omitted the controversial verses. The House Un-American Activities Committee was falling into disrepute by this time, being criticised by senior figures for intruding into the personal lives of citizens, described by former President Truman as 'The most Un-American thing in the country today', its abolition being called for by Representative James Roosevelt, son of former President Franklin D. Roosevelt.[13] Nevertheless, the members of The Weavers – Fred Hellerman, Lee Hays, Pete Seeger and Ronnie Gilbert – all of whom had suffered through the years of the blacklist, were many times bitten and more than a little shy. They played it safe and left out the controversial lyrics.

It took Bob Dylan most of the day to read *Bound for Glory*. By the time he finished, he knew he had found his role model. Guthrie's music, his travelling lifestyle, his insistence on expressing the truth no matter how controversial, his politics and his reputation – this was the image Bob Dylan wanted for himself. His search for his identity was over, he had no doubt about who he wanted to be. And the first steps he would take in being that person could only be towards New York. To visit Woody Guthrie, as he lay dying in hospital.

2

MAKING AN IMPACT

NEW YORK

As it turned out, when he left Minneapolis Dylan didn't head straight for New York. He stopped in Chicago for a while, hanging out with the folk crowd, playing like the novice he was, still inventing stories about himself, though now the stories included Woody. He told them that he had just come from seeing him in hospital, though it was a journey he was yet to make.

At this early stage in his life he was still trying to be someone he wasn't, still trying to divest himself of his not particularly cool Jewish and middle-class origins. He needn't have done so, for many of the radical, left-wing crowd in Chicago, and in Madison, Wisconsin, too, where he headed next, were also Jews from middle-class families. It's a fair bet that they were just as uncomfortable as he about their uncool origins (they called it being 'square' in those days). Like Dylan, they probably didn't talk about their backgrounds either; you didn't become a beatnik, a folkie, a leftie or whatever people called you, unless you were trying to leave part of your native identity behind.

Dylan's problem was that, at only 19 years old, he had not yet learnt to apply his genius to his music or his writing. His imagination and creativity lay dormant within him, asserting itself only when he felt the need to conceal something uncomfortable, like his origins. Then it burst out of him, in a maelstrom of fantasy. He was on his way to becoming the poet and storyteller who would win millions of fans and garner innumerable accolades, heading towards the Nobel Prize in Literature, one of only two musicians to be so honoured (the other being the poet and songwriter Rabindranath Tagore in 1913). But right now, the only stories Dylan told were about himself, trying to persuade those whose lives he passed through that he was an itinerant wayfarer, a boxcar hobo, long estranged from his coarse and brutish family, seasoned beyond his years. Turning himself into an incarnation of Woody Guthrie, the hero who, those who saw through him knew, he aspired to be.

He was maturing though and he was writing. His first composition, one that he later described as a homage in lyric and melody, was 'Song to Woody'. Adapted from the tune to Woody's song '1913 Massacre', he would record it a couple of years later on his first album, simply titled *Bob Dylan*. An elegy to his hero that he composed shortly after first meeting him, the song recalls Woody's rambling days, and plants Dylan firmly in his idol's shoes, travelling the same road as Woody, seeing the people and things he saw. In the last verse he namechecks Cisco Houston, Lead Belly and Sonny Terry, Woody's fellow artists and companions, second only to Woody himself in Bob Dylan's pantheon.

When she first heard Dylan sing 'Song to Woody', at a performance in Greenwich Village's Folk City, Joan Baez asked if she could record it. His friend Tony Glover advised him to keep it for himself; a wise recommendation since it is one of the two standout songs on his first album (the other being 'Talkin' New York'), the compositions that most clearly signalled the young songwriter's potential, even though the poetry was still immature. The recording betrays nothing of the Minneapolis Dylan, the keen amateur so desperate to learn that he didn't care how bad his public performances were. His voice is still raw, but in 'A Song to Woody' we hear for the first time the distinctive intonation and faux-hillbilly lyrics that would characterise Dylan's output until he went electric, and sometimes even beyond.

Bob Dylan arrived in New York at the end of December 1960, or in January 1961, depending on which of the many accounts we follow. Whatever the date, it was freezing. In his blues account of his arrival, 'Talkin' New York', he sang of how he froze to the bone, not warming up until reading in the *New York Times* that it was the coldest winter for fifteen years.

Having grown up in the even colder north country, Dylan was probably better equipped to deal with the cold than most people in the city. He headed for Greenwich Village; in search of the folk scene, looking for singers he wanted to hear and clubs he wanted to play. He was young, precocious and naive, too vulnerable for the city's hardened streets, a winning combination that made women mother him and men take him under their wing. But Dylan didn't think of himself as vulnerable. He was remaking himself in Woody's image and even though he had never jumped a train or ridden a boxcar in his life, had never stood in line for a handout of food or faced down a line of club-wielding boss's thugs, he tried to carry himself as if he had.

He certainly had the chutzpah for it. He had been born at the tail end of the last generation of self-made Jews; adventurers who, more often than not, started on the path to success by taking risks. They had no choice, they had left the old country to improve their lot and that of their families; the last thing they were going to do when they reached the land of opportunity was to sit demurely and wait for life to pass them by as their forebears had been obliged to do. Few Jews feel the same compulsion today, there is no need, their lives and careers are underpinned by education and sometimes by family money. But if you are starting from nothing, or in Dylan's case pretending to start from nothing, then you have to take a few risks. Just as Bob Dylan did when, as a small-town novice in a raw, hard city, he walked down MacDougal Street in Greenwich Village, hoisted his guitar through a narrow doorway, and descended a flight of steep stairs to a black-walled, subterranean cavern that went by the name of Cafe Wha?. Inside, he asked the owner, Manny Roth, if he could play a few songs. And, since he had no place to stay, followed up by asking if anybody could offer him a place to crash. Manny Roth said 'Sure'. Dylan had happened to wander in on one of the venue's hootenanny nights, an evening when anyone could get up and play. Then, out of compassion for the lost-looking, young fellow Jew, Roth went to the microphone and asked whether anyone in the audience had a couch he could crash on.

Born in 1919 to parents who, like the Zimmermans, ran a retail store, Manny Roth had studied acting, dropping out to join the Army Air Corps during World War II where he earned a Distinguished Flying Cross as a navigator on bombing flights. In 1959 he converted an old stable on MacDougal Street into a coffee house, painting the walls black, putting candles in blue glasses on the table, and inviting performers to play for whatever they could earn from a basket passed around the audience. For years Cafe Wha? served as a start-out venue for hosts of aspiring stars, musicians, comedians and poets. Jimi Hendrix played there, David Crosby, Lenny Bruce, Woody Allen, Joan Rivers, Richie Havens, Allen Ginsberg, Bruce Springsteen, and so many more. Dylan had turned up at the right place. Listening to him perform on that first winter's day, Roth thought: 'This kid doesn't have a prayer. He can't sing, can't play and certainly doesn't have any stage presence.' Ecstatic to be allowed to play there, Dylan said it was a place to stay out of the cold.'

Playing inside Cafe Wha?, Bob Dylan was Woody Guthrie. Hearing him, to Manny Roth and the few patrons of the Cafe Wha?, he was a new kid in town, radiating innocence, with a certain charisma about him, who needed looking after. Those were simple days and the folk scene was collegiate, a fellowship of radicals, visionaries and intellectuals. Even so, it was no small thing for Bob to take up the offer of a bed from a stranger in the audience in an unknown city; you almost certainly wouldn't do so today.

The passage of time along with Dylan's shifting backstories have left much forgotten or unknown. One of the unknowns is where Bob Dylan first played his guitar in New York. His first biographer, Anthony Scaduto, was in no doubt that it was at Cafe Wha?, on the very occasion that he first walked into the club, the same day he arrived in New York. Dylan himself says that he didn't play his guitar, that all he did was to accompany the club's MC, Freddy Neil, on harmonica. The journalist Robert Shelton, who catapulted Dylan onto the national stage, agrees. Then he hedged his bets on where Dylan first played his guitar by naming several places, before writing that 'some collectors maintain' that his first recorded stage words were at the Cafe Wha?.' But that's the enigma of Bob Dylan. Until he entered the public eye, until nearly everything he did and said was observed and noted, there is always more than one way of telling the story. The old aphorism, 'two Jews, three opinions', becomes, in Dylan's case, 'one Jew, three stories'.

Where everybody agrees is that during the first months of 1961 Greenwich Village was where Bob Dylan matriculated as an artist and a performer. He was everywhere, wearing his trademark dark corduroy cap, the one he wears on the cover of his first album, in and out of all the clubs, backing performers with his harmonica or guitar, playing his own sets when he could get them, making a name for himself. Cultivating his personal magnetism and getting to know others who were launching their own careers in the Village. Comedians like Joan Rivers, Woody Allen and Lenny Bruce. Tiny Tim, Ramblin' Jack Elliott, Peter, Paul and Mary, Dave Van Ronk and Joan Baez among the singers.

A few months after his arrival in New York he composed the aforementioned semi-autobiographical 'Talkin' New York', a sardonic song about his arrival and early days in the city. It was something of a homage to Woody Guthrie, sung in the 'talking blues' style that features in much of his output; more narrative than song; words spoken against a simple three-chord guitar background. He based the lyrics on a couple of Guthrie songs too, referencing his role model's complaint in 'Pretty Boy Floyd' about being ripped

off by people with fountain pens. It is the earliest insight into Bob
Dylan's feelings about New York and its folk music, seasoned with
humour and a *kvetch*.

Two formative, life-changing experiences befell Bob Dylan
in those first New York months. He met Woody Guthrie. And he
discovered the Beat poets.

WOODY

Dylan visited Guthrie in hospital shortly after he arrived in New
York. Guthrie, who was suffering from chorea and dementia,
symptoms of the debilitating Huntington's disease, was laid up in
the Greystone Park Psychiatric Hospital in Morris Plains. He'd been
there since 1956.

Woody wasn't short of friends or visitors; there was no obvious
reason for him to be touched by the visit of a young, earnest admirer;
he already had plenty of those. But touched he was. Guthrie took
an immediate shine to Dylan, and Dylan in turn was overwhelmed.
He went back to visit him time and again, often three or four times
a week. Visiting the sick is a fundamental Jewish obligation, but it
is not likely that Bob's visits to Guthrie in hospital were driven by
any sort of religious imperative. Though it is, perhaps, possible that
Woody saw it that way. Guthrie's second wife, Marjorie Greenblatt,
was Jewish, as were their four children. One is Arlo Guthrie, a
social commentator like his father, best known for poking fun at
the Vietnam draft in his song and film *Alice's Restaurant*. Ten years or
more before Dylan met him, Woody had started to take an interest
in Judaism, studying its history and stories. He wrote seven songs
about the festival of Hanukkah for his children and the local Jewish
community – more than any Jewish composer has ever written about
Hanukkah. He had no truck, though, with Jewish sentimentality.
Irving Berlin's 'God Bless America' is an uncompromisingly patriotic
song written by an eternally grateful immigrant. Guthrie's riposte,
'This Land Is Your Land', written by a man whose American roots

ran deep, for whom American life and hardship were inseparable, is a world removed from such schmaltz.

It would be stretching a point too far, though, to argue that the Jewish connection was one of the reasons why Bob idolised Woody Guthrie. If he had remained Bobby Zimmerman, maybe. But not as Bob Dylan, earnestly trying to discard his Jewish persona (years later, he would discover that it just can't be done). Bob Dylan's hospital visits to see Woody Guthrie were acts of musical devotion, of worship maybe, to the idol who was making such an impression upon him at this formative stage in his career. But Woody's daughter Nora did say that her mother found Bob particularly charming. 'She responded to the Jewish part of him, too. I think that was endearing to her.'[3]

Woody Guthrie was a long-term patient; there was no cure in sight and the hospital could do no more than care for him. Since it made very little difference which bed he lay upon each day, a local couple, Bob and Sidsel Gleason, friends of his, had agreed with the hospital that Woody could leave at weekends to stay with them in their apartment. It allowed those closest to Woody to visit him in a more relaxed and informal atmosphere, rather than all sitting around a hospital bed. Each weekend folk singers, musicians, beatniks and hangers-on would descend on their apartment, to spend time with Guthrie. It was Bob Dylan who seems to have developed the closest relationship with the ageing singer at this time. So much so that at times Woody would ask his hosts whether 'the boy' would be coming that day.

Bob Dylan was changing. Not physically, he still looked frail and vulnerable, like a kid who needed care and affection, a waif looking for someone to mother him. It was a look that worked to his advantage, he was never short of a bed to sleep in or an older woman to offer him a meal. He milked his inbuilt magnetism to maximum effect, with throwaway, cryptic hints about his rootless origins and the extraordinary encounters he'd had, in way-out places, with pioneering singers of folk and the blues. Emotionally though, something was happening to him. In the past the fantasies may have been a defence, to deflect attention from his decidedly unfashionable, middle-class, Jewish origins. Now the fictions that he had treated as essential to his persona were falling away. He was becoming endowed with a new image, one rooted in his talent, ability and creative imagination. His accomplishments, rather than his imaginings, were propelling him towards the recognition his ambition demanded.

He had grown in confidence and stature, both musically and in his own personality. The naive student dropout singing in an adenoidal monotone was evolving into a mature singer. He no longer needed to rail at his audiences for not listening, because now they stopped their chatter when he played. His voice was still nasal, it always would be, but his singing could be loud and assertive, commanding attention. On one early visit to see Guthrie, he sheepishly told the dying man that he had written him a song. He quietly started to play 'A Song to Woody', just loud enough, he thought, for only Woody to hear. But his playing wasn't as soft as he'd imagined. The room went quiet and as he realised that everyone was listening, all trace of sheepishness disappeared from his voice. When he finished Woody Guthrie was ecstatic. 'That boy's got a voice,' he said. 'He's a folk singer all right.'

Some people dispute that account. They say that by the time Bob Dylan visited him Woody was too ill to recognise anybody, that Bob Dylan would have just been another visitor who he couldn't quite make out. But whether or not Woody ever said anything to, or about, Bob doesn't really matter. What does matter is that Dylan had proved that if he wanted something, like meeting Woody, he would be determined enough to achieve it. And that, unlike his fantasy backstories, the tales that Bob was now able to tell about himself were true.

'Song to Woody' is a paean of praise to Dylan's hero. The lyrics are not great, it is not surprising that Guthrie tempered his praise of Dylan's voice with uncertainty about the quality of his writing.

Nor is there anything in the song to give any hint that the name Bob Dylan was soon to become synonymous with the label 'protest singer'; that his compositions would be instrumental in shaping the outlook of a generation and help usher in a decade or more of social change. But like Woody, there were evils and injustices he wanted to expose. A social upheaval was about to engulf the nation. Bob Dylan would make it his own.

Beyond the New York folk scene, beyond the corona of Bob Dylan's rapidly waxing star, momentous things were happening in the world. Space, 'the final frontier', was about to be conquered, man daring, in the words spoken by William Shatner in *Star Trek*, 'to boldly go where no man has gone before'.[4] A chimpanzee had already paved the way, spending 16 minutes beyond the pull of Earth's gravity, just a few weeks after a similar force had impelled Bob Dylan towards New York.

Important things were happening on Earth too. John Kennedy was now President, inspiring his nation with his oratory of hope and optimism, committing America in his inaugural speech to 'pay any price, bear any burden, meet any hardship, support any friend, oppose any foe, in order to assure the survival and success of liberty'.[5]

We know now how that worked out; how Kennedy's first, disastrous escapade in Cuba, his attempt to return 1,400 exiled supporters of the overthrown Batista regime ended in defeat and tragedy at the Bay of Pigs and cemented Fidel Castro in power. It was the first of a succession of foreign military failures over the coming decades, of which Vietnam, Iraq and Afghanistan were just the most notorious. Bob Dylan saw it coming long before most of us, but it would be two years before he could sing about it, about the cynicism of politicians and generals, the immorality of armed conflict. He would record his masterpieces of dissent 'Blowin' in the Wind' and 'Masters of War' on his landmark second album, *The Freewheelin' Bob Dylan*, along with the lesser known 'Oxford Town', of which more soon.

GASLIGHT

Things were beginning to fall into place for Dylan in Greenwich Village. He had achieved his first objective of meeting Woody but as far as the world was concerned he was still unknown. Apart from a few friends it made no difference to anyone that he had sat in the same room as Guthrie and sung a few songs. He teamed up with another young folk singer, Mark Spoelstra. They played onstage together at the Cafe Wha?, taking turns at singing, the coins that landed in their basket augmented by a few dollars here and there from friends, primarily in Bob's case from older women who felt sorry for him. Like Sidsel Gleason, Woody's friend, who Bob soon started calling 'Mom'. Bob probably also got a little money from his parents. Although he denied or at least shrugged off their existence whenever he was asked, there doesn't seem to have been any hostility between the Zimmermans and their wayward son.

Gradually Bob managed to get himself onstage at some of the other Village venues. The most important, to him anyway, was Gerde's Folk City, run by an Italian immigrant, Mike Porco. When a friend told Porco he should hire Bob he vacillated, concerned that he was too young. Eventually he offered him a two-week slot backing the renowned blues player John Lee Hooker. Porco told Bob that he had to get some decent clothes to play in, and would need to join the Musicians' Union. One of the older women who mothered him, Camilla Adams, found Bob a pair of dungarees, and Porco gave him some of his own children's cast-offs. Then he took him to the Musicians' Union to register.

At the Union, Bob was told that, since he was under 21, his application would need to be countersigned by his parents. Bob, still able to slip into his fantasises when he needed to, said that he didn't have any. Mike Porco, thinking that Bob was a runaway, signed on his behalf, as his guardian.

Dylan was thrilled to be playing as a warm-up for John Lee Hooker, and despite the age difference, the bluesman was delighted to have Dylan as a friend. Dylan would go up to Hooker's hotel room with his guitar and sometimes a few friends after they had finished playing. Hooker, nearly 25 years older than Dylan, would complain that they kept him awake. It didn't stop him from welcoming them.

Dave Van Ronk first heard Bob Dylan play one evening when he went with his fellow folk singer Tom Paxton, to Gerde's Folk City. Van Ronk, a six-foot-five-inch, 17-stone blues singer with an astonishing voice that could switch from a growl to a wail and back, all on the same chord, was a long-established performer in Greenwich Village. Physically imposing, and with a personality to match, had the musicians in the Village ever gathered together to appoint a leader for themselves, the 25-year-old former merchant sailor Van Ronk would have been their choice. They nicknamed him 'The Mayor of MacDougal Street'; it later became the title of the memoir he wrote with the musician and author Elijah Wald.[6] First recorded by Moses Asch for the Folkways label in 1957, and allegedly the inspiration for the Coen Brothers 2013 film, *Inside Llewyn Davis*, Van Ronk had been one of Dylan's musical heroes even before Bob arrived in the Village. The first time their paths crossed, Dylan was too shy even to open a conversation.

Van Ronk was playing regularly at the Gaslight, a renowned basement café on MacDougal Street. The Gaslight had been a speakeasy during the 1920s and 1930s, the years of Prohibition, and was now the most popular of all the music venues in the Village, the coffee house where Dylan most wanted to play. Describing itself as 'world famous for entertainment in the Village' it was no basket house. The Gaslight paid proper money, hosting young, up-and-coming musicians and comics of the calibre of Len Chandler, Tom Paxton, Peter, Paul and Mary, and Woody Allen. After its speakeasy days it had reopened in 1958 as a poetry venue, with the Beat poets Allen Ginsberg, Jack Kerouac and Gregory Corso among those who read their work there. The Gaslight was given a fictional revival in 2017 in the TV show *The Marvelous Mrs. Maisel* when it became the setting for the eponymous star's debut.

When he bumped into Van Ronk a second time and summoned enough courage to speak to him, Dylan unaffectedly dived straight into the conversation with a direct question. He asked Van Ronk how he could get to play at the Gaslight. He played him a couple of songs – he always found it easier to play to people than speak to them – and Van Ronk told him that if he came down to the Gaslight one evening, he could play a couple of numbers in his set.

Dave Van Ronk became something of a mentor to young Bob Dylan. He and his wife would put him up in their apartment and Dylan would regularly play with him at the Gaslight, until he grew big and popular enough to be hired in his own right as a solo act.

It was through the Gaslight that Bob Dylan had his first encounters with the Beats. The Gaslight itself had been transformed from a poetry venue to a folk club in 1961 but the Beat ethos remained, there and across the Village. Poetry readings could be heard, often accompanied by jazz, at any one of half a dozen venues along MacDougal Street, the Village's main cultural highway. Dylan had read Ginsberg's landmark poem 'Howl' before he arrived in New York, and had devoured Ferlinghetti and Kerouac, giving the lie to the tale that he didn't read anything in Minnesota. A couple of years later he would meet Ginsberg and begin a friendship that would last until the older man's death in 1997.

Like his fascination with Woody, Dylan's interest in the Beats was both artistic and political; he admired their use of language, their transcendent imagery, their disaffiliation from mainstream society. He told the filmmaker Cameron Crowe, 'I came out of the wilderness and just naturally fell in with the Beat Scene, it was all pretty much connected . . . I got in at the tail end and it was magic . . . it had just as big an impact on me as Elvis Presley.'[7] The influence of the Beats on Dylan's work is unmistakable in the two albums he released in 1965, *Bringing It All Back Home* and *Highway 61 Revisited*.

Dylan rapidly became part of the Gaslight scene, sitting at its tables and conversing with other performers backstage. For a while he shared a flat above the Gaslight with the venue's entertainment director, the Beat poet and comic Hugh Romney, also known as Wavy Gravy. When Bob Dylan first stepped onto the Gaslight stage, Romney grabbed the microphone and announced 'Here he is! The legend in his lifetime', then whispered, 'What's your name, kid?'[8]

Dylan's cultural horizons were broadening. Or, in another version of his history, they were already broad and it was only now that he was owning up to them. When Van Ronk asked Dylan if he had heard of Arthur Rimbaud or Guillaume Apollinaire, Dylan asked who they were. Upon hearing that they were nineteenth-century French poets, he just shrugged and exhibited no interest. Shortly after, Van Ronk found a well-thumbed book of French poems on Dylan's shelf, including several by Rimbaud. He had probably known who he was all along. Either that or he found a well-thumbed book in a second-hand store. Dylan himself wrote that it was his girlfriend Suze Rotolo who introduced him to Rimbaud. One way or another, both the Beats and Rimbaud have been huge influences on Dylan's work. He mentioned both Rimbaud and his contemporary Paul Verlaine in 'You're Gonna Make Me Lonesome When You Go' on *Blood on the Tracks* in 1975.

He was reading too. For education, not just for fun. Classic poetry: Shelley and Longfellow, Coleridge's 'Kubla Khan' and Byron's 'Don Juan'. Long poems often, trying always to keep the beginning in his memory as he reached the end. Other works too, Faulkner showing him how to translate deep feelings into words. At a friend's house he dipped into Albertus Magnus, the thirteenth-century German philosopher and theologian, the scholastic who looked at his surroundings through the eyes of an empirical scientist, who perceived poetry in the natural world. Dylan's friends in Minnesota had said he read nothing, that he just concentrated on his music. Well, maybe he wasn't reading at that moment in his life, but Dylan was no dunce. He'd grown up in a Jewish home and Jews read, that's what they do, whether they like it or not. They have a relationship with books that goes back to the birth of their history. Dylan may not have been academic at school, but that means nothing, the classroom environment doesn't suit everybody, exams are no way to test the power of a creative mind.

The book that seems to have shaped his early thinking more than any other was Jack Kerouac's *On the Road*. A stream-of-consciousness travelogue, relating the journeys across America of young men, 'sordid hipsters' in the narrator's words,[9] in search of life, knowledge, thrills and inspiration. The book came to define, in the public mind at least, the curious phenomenon of America's Beats.

The 26-year-old John Clellon Holmes, writing in 1952, gave the Beat Generation its name, though he said it came from Kerouac. A close friend of Kerouac, Clellon Holmes's book *Go* is often said to have been the first Beat novel, written five years before *On the Road*. Now he was explaining to readers of the *New York Times* why his contemporaries were 'beat':

> The origins of the word 'beat' are obscure but the meaning is only too clear to most Americans. More than mere weariness, it implies the feeling of having been used, of being raw. It involves a sort of nakedness of mind, and, ultimately, of soul; a feeling of being reduced to the bedrock of consciousness. In short it means being undramatically pushed up against the wall of oneself. A man is beat whenever he goes for broke and wagers the sum of his resources on a single number; and the young generation has done that continually from early youth.

His generation was 'beat', Holmes wrote, as a result of the world they had grown up in. Born in the wake of far-off World War I, 'brought up in the circumstances of a dreary depression, weaned during the uprooting of a global war', a war in which those who were older had fought. 'Their brothers, husbands, fathers or boyfriends turned up dead one day at the end of a telegram.' Now they lived in the shadow of nuclear confrontation. Their vast, overwhelming country was riven by racial conflict, terrified of communism, and dominated by public figures who were obsessed with witch-hunts, religion and conformity. They were a generation whose members had an 'instinctive individuality', whose only complaint seemed to be 'Why don't people leave us alone.'[10]

Not every member of Holmes's generation could be categorised as 'beat'; those whom he attributed with instinctive individuality were very much a minority among their peers. All their contemporaries had lived through the same destabilising events, they had all experienced the same traumas. What set the Beat Generation apart from everyone else was their response to those traumas, an experiential curiosity that led them to reject the safe, accepting conventionalism of their peers.

Even so, the rift between the Beat Generation and their contemporaries was shallow in places. Kerouac's anti-heroes in *On the Road* were still turned on by the creature comforts of Middle America, by offers of apple pie and ice cream. And despite their opposition to race discrimination, none of the Beat fraternity seem to have woken up to the inequalities between the sexes. Overwhelmingly educated and middle class, sufficiently adventurous to forgo conventional aspirations for the sake of an intellectual or sensory quest, their enduring social influence was vastly disproportionate to their number. Bob Dylan was born at the nexus between the Beat Generation and those who followed in their wake.

Writing about the life he had lived before arriving in New York, Dylan said that *On the Road* had been 'like a bible' to him.[11] It had opened his eyes, the eyes of a young, small-town Jewish boy to a different sort of America, where one could live a freer, less constrained life, the romance of an existence in which every moment was part of a story, each episode an adventure.

A bible it may have been to him but after Dylan's first few months in New York he was already losing interest; disillusioned with the 'hungry for kicks, hipster vision' of its lead character, Dean Moriarty.[12] Perhaps when Dylan first read *On the Road* he had wanted to live a travelling, unfettered, Beat life, to be his generation's Kerouac or Neal Cassady (the model for Dean Moriarty). But a rootless existence, living for kicks, taking each day as it comes, is no recipe for life for an ambitious young Jewish boy from a small town, hungry for recognition and fame. Such a life sounded attractive as a dream but it would not get him where he wanted to go. It was a life he didn't want. But it was still a life he wanted to have come from.

ADNOPOZ

Happily believing himself to now be a part of Woody Guthrie's orbit, even if the great man was too ill to recognise him as such, Bob was gradually meeting his hero's closest friends and entourage. Chief among them was Ramblin' Jack Elliott. A cowboy folk singer a few years older than Bob Dylan, Jack Elliott's mother had bought him a guitar when he was 13. Within a couple of years he was hanging out in Greenwich Village, playing guitar in the park, mixing with the small folk crowd until one day a friend gave him Woody Guthrie's telephone number, suggesting he give him a call. With impeccable timing Elliott rang Woody just as he was being admitted to hospital with a ruptured appendix. Elliott picked up his guitar, headed for the hospital and – just as Dylan would do 10 years later – first met Woody Guthrie while he was lying in an infirmary bed.

Jack Elliott has been described as Guthrie's first disciple, living with him between 1951 and 1952, watching him play and learning as much as he could, playing with him onstage just once. By the time that Bob Dylan met him, Jack Elliott had been following and imitating Guthrie for so long that he had picked up much of his style and mannerisms. As Bob Dylan drew closer to Ramblin' Jack, he in turn acquired some of the same characteristics.[13]

It was not just Woody Guthrie's characteristics that Dylan and Elliott shared. The story goes that when Ramblin' Jack was ill, some of his relatives came to the Village to visit him. They were Jews from

Brooklyn and his friends discovered that, rather than him being, as they believed, a wandering cowboy from out west, Ramblin' Jack Elliott's real name was Elliott Adnopoz. He was the son of a Jewish doctor from Flatbush, Brooklyn.

The first that Bob Dylan heard of this was when he was sitting in a club one evening with a couple of friends. The name Adnopoz came up and Dylan asked 'Who?'. When he was told Ramblin' Jack's real name, Dylan fell on the floor, rolling around with laughter. He couldn't stop; he kept repeating the name Adnopoz, over and over.

It was a cathartic moment for Dylan. A few weeks earlier, while trying to get a gig at Gerde's Folk City, he'd been asked to show proof of his age. He had produced a document with the name Robert Zimmerman on it. Word had got out that this was Dylan's real name, that he hadn't been raised in an orphanage in New Mexico, or whatever story he was peddling that week, that in fact he was a Jew named Robert Zimmerman. But nobody was really sure if the rumour was true and nobody was willing to go out on a limb and challenge his origin stories; he was still too young and appeared too vulnerable to be confronted as an imposter. As soon as he collapsed in hysterics upon hearing Jack Elliott's real name, the game was up. It was obvious to everyone that his reaction was because he'd discovered that he and Jack had something in common. Just like him, it seemed as if Ramblin' Jack had fantasised an origin story for himself to cover up his identity as a Jew from a middle-class home. Dylan had discovered he wasn't alone, and the suspicions of his friends had been confirmed; Bob Dylan was Jewish. And, of course, it didn't matter a bit. That's the funny thing about being Jewish. The antisemites hate you, the philosemites want to be like you, and nobody else gives a damn. It's a lesson that every Jew with a crisis of identity learns eventually. To stop being so self-conscious and accept the reality of who you are.

In fact, Ramblin' Jack wasn't trying to cover up his Jewish identity in the way that Dylan was. At his very first concert in New

York he told the audience that he was Elliott Charles Adnopoz, a
doctor's son from Brooklyn. His parents Abe and Flossie were in
the audience that evening. It was his relationship with his parents,
rather than a Dylanesque attempt to cover up his origins, that drew
him to a cowboy lifestyle. In a radio interview, Jack said that his
father Abe Adnopoz, who had grown up on a farm in Connecticut,
'told me lots of stories about the farm and we'd go out and visit the
farm a lot of times, see cows and chickens and people that were
more slowed down, so I was starting to fall in love with the country
and America'.[14] Jack's childhood was not an easy one; the oldest of
two boys, his younger brother David said that he didn't remember
a lot of joy or happiness in the family as they were growing up.
Their father was hard-working, distant and aloof, and their
mother's sister said that Flossie, an elementary schoolteacher, was
'always nasty, she always did terrible things, nobody liked her'. His
parents wanted Elliott to become a doctor. A professional career
is an ambition many Jewish parents have for their children, not
so much for wealth as for security, but it is not an ambition many
creative or adventurous children share. Elliott's escape, according
to his daughter, was to immerse himself in a fantasy world. He
internalised adventures, watched every western he could, imagined
himself as a cowboy, and listened in bed to the Grand Ole Opry, a
country-music radio show from Nashville where he heard his first
musical heroes. He saw his first real cowboys when his parents took
him to the rodeo at Madison Square Gardens. He would try to get
away from them and sneak into the backstage area, to get close to
the horses and bulls. When he eventually ran away from home he
got a job at a rodeo in Washington, and from that moment on he was
a cowboy. Elliott Adnopoz adopted his cowboy identity, not because
he was embarrassed about being Jewish, but because, culturally, he
was born into the wrong world. It can happen to anybody, not just
a Jewish boy from Brooklyn.

When they first met, Bob told Ramblin' Jack that he was a fan,
that he had all five of his records, naming the tracks he liked the

best. Jack said that the first time he heard Bob perform, 'people in the audience poked me saying, "He's doing your stuff. He sounds just like you." He sounded good, but I didn't think he sounded like me at all.' He and Bob played a few gigs together at Gerde's Folk City, where Bob was jokingly billed as 'Son of Jack Elliott'. They both strapped harmonicas around their necks, in a tribute to Woody Guthrie, until Ramblin' Jack became fed up with it. He wore his harmonica in such a way that it kept scratching the varnish off his guitar. Eventually he told Bob, '"We sound like the Harmonica Brothers, and anyway I'm tired of scratching my guitar." That's when I officially stopped playing harmonica in my shows in order to get rid of that copycat element.'[15]

Bob was now playing regularly at the Gaslight, hanging around with other performers, always watching, learning and developing his own distinctive style. He was no longer a conventional folk singer, a purist carefully preserving the melodies of lost communities and vanished ethnicities. He was loud, assertive, formidable; his guitar, harmonica and voice, not necessarily all in harmony but each making its presence known. Even at this early stage in his career, all one had to do was walk into the room to know it was Bob Dylan playing. You either loved hearing him, or you hated it. It was as simple as that, and it wouldn't change for the rest of his career.

He was spending time hanging out with Len Chandler, a classically trained oboist who had moved to Greenwich Village, taken up the guitar, and was now writing topical songs. Chandler took stories from the newspapers: crimes, tragedies, and odd events that he would fashion into lyrics and set to music, typically old folk melodies. Nearly everyone in the folk world recycled old tunes, or even occasionally 'borrowed' newer melodies written by a fellow singer. It wasn't theft, it was the way that things were done.

Len Chandler taught Dylan two important lessons. One was how to bluff at poker, a game they played a lot, albeit for tiny stakes. The other was to look beyond the standard folk-music catalogue

for his repertoire. Woody Guthrie had inspired Dylan to write his
own material and now he was following Len's lead, looking for
stories to write about. Noel Stookey, who was better known as
Paul of Peter, Paul and Mary, pointed him to a story he had read
in the paper, about a social club that had planned a boat trip to
Bear Mountain, where they would have a picnic. It was a nice idea
but it had gone horribly wrong. The boat had arrived very late
and when it did finally dock at the landing stage, everyone rushed
towards it at once. The crush of people trying to clamber aboard,
all pushing, shoving and fighting, caused the vessel to list and then
sink. Bob took the story, set it to a melody, and called it 'Talkin'
Bear Mountain Picnic Massacre Blues'. A comic song in which
the singer imagines himself as a passenger on the ill-fated boat.
Rhyming 'casket' with 'basket', 'pushed around' with 'a screaming
sound', the humour is in the poetry as much as the story he is
telling. 'Talkin' Bear Mountain Picnic Massacre Blues' is not one
of Dylan's best-known numbers. He played it a few times in
the Village and once a couple of years later at the Brandeis Folk
Festival. It was eventually issued years later, on Volume One of
the 1991 *Bootleg Series*, sounding musically indistinguishable from
'Talkin' New York', and again in 2010, as a recording of his 1963
Brandeis concert.

Dylan performed all three of his talkin' blues songs: 'Hava
Negilah', 'Talkin' New York' and 'Bear Mountain Picnic Massacre'
at Gerde's Folk City on 25 September 1961. It was the first night of
a two-week stint he had been offered at the venue. In the audience
was a young reporter, Robert Shelton. Shelton had heard Dylan
play a few times and had promised him that when he got himself
a serious gig he would write a review. The Gerde's Folk City
residency, Shelton deemed, was the serious gig and now was the
time for the review. Just 400 words long, Shelton's piece appeared
in the *New York Times* four days later. Calling Dylan a 'bright new
face in folk music', describing his voice as 'anything but pretty' and
predicting that his prospects were 'going straight up', Shelton's

review has always been considered the single most consequential event in Dylan's early career trajectory. It launched him onto the national stage and granted him an entry ticket, should he care to use it, into posterity.[16]

Big things were happening in Bob Dylan's life. A few weeks earlier he had fallen in love. It was as sudden as that. He had been backstage at the Gaslight, chatting with a young woman he knew. She introduced him to her seventeen-year-old sister and Bob was instantly smitten. Her name was Suze Rotolo. She came from a cultured, politically aware, left-wing Italian family, an artist and designer who worked in the theatre and was active in the civil rights movement. Highly intelligent, she introduced Bob to art and the theatre, encouraging him to spread his already broadening horizons even further. It was under Suze's tutelage that the many disparate influences which Bob Dylan had been soaking up since his arrival in New York began to coalesce, shaping his outlook and self-image, forcing him to confront the reality of a life that included other people. Like most young men, at no point in his life so far had he been obliged to commit to anyone else; all his friendships had been passing familiarities, his single focus had always been on his musical ambitions. Unlike many young men he displayed no desire to enter a stable relationship, he probably wasn't thinking of falling in love when he met Suze, and he probably had no inkling of how hard he would be smitten. A serious romance was an experience that had figured nowhere in his plans.

By many accounts Bob and Suze's relationship was intense and often dark, impeded and possibly fatally undermined by her mother Mary's dislike and distrust of him. She didn't display the same maternal feelings towards him as the other older women who had mothered Bob when he first arrived in New York; but that was bound to be so, he wasn't *shtupping* their 17-year-old daughters. Mary Rotolo saw Bob Dylan as a scruffy, penniless beatnik leading her daughter astray, taking advantage of her. Suze doesn't look like she's being taken advantage of in the photograph that appears on the cover of his second album, *The Freewheelin' Bob Dylan*. Two young people, in love, walking together; cuddling into him, she looks happy. He is harder to read, hunched over in the freezing New York winter, his head turned low, withdrawn in contemplation or in shelter from the cold. The album itself belies the romantic bliss portrayed on the cover. The landmark track 'Don't Think Twice, It's All Right' is a bitter song that Dylan wrote when Suze left him and New York for a few months, to study art in Italy. It is one of several songs he wrote about her. Caustically ironic, it is a masterwork in young male petulance. In real life she had left him, albeit temporarily. In the song he has left her, for good. And it's her fault. If the lyrics of the song are anything to go by, it doesn't seem that, deep down, they had an easy relationship. Joan Baez sang the song on the Newport stage in 1963, introducing the number as 'a song about a love affair that has gone on too long'.[17] Suze, who had been back from Italy for some months, was in the audience. Baez had introduced the song in that way to humiliate her.

On the day that Shelton's review was published, Bob Dylan was playing harmonica at a recording session at the studio of Columbia Records. A young folk singer, Carolyn Hester, making her first album for the company, had asked him to back her on a few tracks. She would later say that Dylan's new sound was liberating her as a folk singer. When he heard this he replied, 'tell her she can come around and see me any time now that she's liberated'.[18]

Hester's session was being produced by John Hammond, a legendary jazz producer who had worked in the past with stars like Billie Holiday, Count Basie and Benny Goodman. Hammond had only recently joined Columbia and was on the lookout for young talent; he was concerned that the label had not been paying enough attention to what was going on in the folk world. He had already signed Pete Seeger, wilfully paying no attention to the fact

that he was still under indictment, due to go on trial for contempt
of Congress.

Hammond had probably already made up his mind to sign Dylan.
He'd heard him play a few weeks earlier while Carolyn Hester was
rehearsing, and his son John Jr was raving about the impact Dylan
was having in the Village folk clubs. Dylan, who was thrilled with
Shelton's review, took it with him to show Hammond. By the end of
the session Hammond had offered Dylan a contract; he would make
an album immediately, and another one each year for the next four
years. A five-year contract for an unknown singer had never been
heard of in the Village. Dylan was over the moon.

3

PROTESTIN'

OXFORD TOWN

Throughout his long career Woody Guthrie had sung about civil rights, about people of all colours working and marching together. When he started singing, the idea of racial equality was still a far-off dream; lynchings were common, segregation was ubiquitous in the Southern states. Now, however, civil rights campaigners were growing in prominence and daring, determined to force through change. In 1961, at the Congress of Racial Equality, a group known as the Freedom Riders were finalising their plans to travel on buses from Washington DC to New Orleans, black and white activists occupying seats alongside each other, using the same restrooms and sitting at the same tables in terminal dining areas. They were testing a Supreme Court ruling a few months earlier, in the case of Boynton v. Virginia, that had extended the earlier rulings against segregation on buses by declaring separation of the races in bus terminals illegal.

In 1962 the black student James Meredith found himself forced to fight to take up the place he had been awarded at the whites-only University of Mississippi. Backed by the National Association for the Advancement of Colored People, he won a lawsuit against the university, but riots broke out at the very end of September when he went to register as a student. Meredith's fight would become the subject of 'Oxford Town', Dylan's first overtly political song. He didn't mention Meredith by name but Oxford was the site of the university campus and the lyrics made it patently clear who he was singing about. The author William Faulkner, who had spent most of his life in Oxford, Mississippi, had died in the town in early July, just two months before the trouble flared up.

For the young Bob Dylan, seemingly taking an active interest in politics for the first time, the struggle for civil rights was a topic with emotional heft. Nobody growing up in a Jewish home, no matter how far they tried to distance themselves from their roots, could be ignorant of the evils of racial persecution. Every family had stories: of relatives long ago murdered in pogroms, of young boys conscripted to serve for decades in the Russian Army solely for the crime of having been born Jewish. Of family members fleeing the racial laws in Nazi Germany, of impoverished Jewish immigrants to the New World unable to find work or accommodation due to their race. Rumours first, and then news reports, of unimaginable numbers of Jews being slaughtered in Europe during the 1940s, while boys like Bobby Zimmerman were growing up safely in the United States. And now in the early 1960s horror stories, worse than fiction, were beginning to emerge of what had really been done to the Jews of Europe by the Nazis and their lackeys. Events so harrowing, so shocking that it had taken the survivors this long even to begin to talk about them. It is little wonder that the persecution of James Meredith resonated with Bob Dylan.

The Jewish experience was one motivation for a topical song condemning racial inequality. Perhaps more importantly for Bob Dylan, a young man rooted in the present not the past, the struggle for civil rights was the overriding political issue of concern in the folk-music community. The new and already influential Greenwich Village folk magazine, *Broadside*, devoted a front page to James Meredith and the events at Mississippi University. The editors told their readers that they were 'waiting for a song about one of the most important events of this year – the enrolment of James Meredith in the University of Mississippi. His courage is as deserving of the Distinguished Service Cross as any soldier's bravery on the battlefield. Perhaps more so since he stands alone. The least tribute we could pay him would be a good lasting song in his honour.'[1]

'Oxford Town' doesn't seem to have been a direct response to *Broadside*'s call. It was another Jewish folk singer, Phil Ochs, who took up the challenge. *Broadside* printed his words and music to 'Ballad of Oxford, Mississippi' on the front page of their next issue, in November 1962.

The Jewish experience and the folk community were both instrumental in steering Dylan towards 'Oxford Town'. The sanction, however, for him to protest through music came of course from Woody Guthrie. The unshakeable imperatives of racial equality and civil rights for all were a staple of Woody Guthrie's repertoire. His 'The Blinding of Isaac Woodard' is a distressing, true story of a black soldier who, in 1946, three hours after having been honourably discharged from the US Army, while still in uniform and having committed no offence, was falsely denounced by a bus driver in South Carolina. The driver called the police who gratuitously beat Woodard, leaving him permanently blind. The case caused an outcry, President Truman demanded an inquiry, the police chief who had blinded Woodard was put on trial but, as happened so often in those unjust days, was acquitted by an all-white jury.

Dylan recorded 'Oxford Town' on his second album, *The Freewheelin' Bob Dylan*, issued in 1963, two years after he first met Woody Guthrie. It is a song in the same vein as 'The Blinding of Isaac Woodard' though with less rage; Woody was always far more ideological in his politics than Dylan would ever be. Woody's songs were his weapons. During World War II he stuck a label on his guitar reading 'This Machine Kills Fascists'. He had warned racists the previous year, in his song 'All You Fascists', that people of every colour would march together across a field where one million fascists had died, to rid the world of slavery.

Nor did Woody confine himself to condemning prejudices or singing about high-profile racist crimes that had hit the headlines. His

accusations were personal too. 'Old Man Trump' is an indictment
of Guthrie's landlord Fred Trump, father of the felonious Donald.
Trump had instituted a no-blacks policy at his Beach Haven housing
project in Brooklyn, close to Coney Island beach, where Guthrie
lived for two years. We have to assume that Guthrie did not know
about the racial discrimination when he moved into his Beach
Haven apartment; though the very fact that his signature appears
on the same lease as Trump's has disturbed several commentators.[2]
For Woody Guthrie, hatred and prejudice were personal. Whether
they were directed towards the underprivileged, or whether it was
himself who had been sucked into their orbit.

EVOLVIN'

Bob Dylan's first album was released on 19 March 1962. It appeared
to no great acclaim, selling only 5,000 copies in its first year, just
enough for Columbia to recoup the astonishingly low sum of $402
that they had spent producing it.

Simply called *Bob Dylan* the album had been recorded the previous
November, in just three sessions. A wait of four months until release
was a long and frustrating gap for an artist whose style and output
seemed to be evolving and maturing almost by the hour. By the time
the album was issued he had moved far beyond the reworked folk,
blues and spiritual classics that dominate the disc. On hearing it,
Dylan was disappointed, he did not believe that the album showed
him at his best. He said that the notes on the record's liner were
better than the recording. 'Song to Woody' and 'Talkin' New York'
are the only tracks on the album that he composed himself, though
listening to 'Man of Constant Sorrow' with its exuberant harmonica
interludes between verses and his elongated vowels, one can hear
Bob Dylan's distinctive style in the making.

Nevertheless, we only need to compare the tracks on his first
album with those he recorded for *The Freewheelin' Bob Dylan*, released
just over a year later, to appreciate the extent of his evolution during

1962. He'd come a long way already, he was still only 21 and in less than three years had graduated from a novice who couldn't hold the attention of a Minneapolis café audience, to a recognised performer in the vibrant and creative Village music scene. Given his talent and ambition he could not help but grow further.

He had caught the attention of the media as well, largely due to Robert Shelton's *New York Times* article. In the month that his initial album came out he made his first radio broadcast, for New York's WBAI-FM station, on their programme *Folksinger's Choice*.[3] He played 11 songs and was interviewed between each one by Cynthia Gooding, a traditional folk singer well known in Village circles. He told her a few tall stories about his origins, giving her his usual *shpiel* about travelling with the carnival for six years, working on the Ferris wheel, about playing guitar and singing with Howlin' Wolf. She swallowed it all, or at least pretended to. He told her that he had stolen the melody for 'The Death of Emmett Till' – a song he had written a few weeks earlier about the black youth murdered by two white men in Mississippi – from his friend Len Chandler.

The recording of the interview includes Dylan playing a few traditional songs, like 'Smokestack Lightning' and 'Fixin' to Die', along with several of his own compositions. Somewhat older than him and considerably more experienced, it was clear to Cynthia Gooding that he hadn't been playing the harmonica for long, and she told him so. He denied it vehemently.

Dylan was developing fast but his was not simply the growth of a musician or performer who was getting better. He was maturing commercially too, developing a better understanding of how to leverage his talent, how to position himself to take advantage of the opportunities that New York offered. The world of music was changing. New York, for now, was at the forefront of those changes, and his ambition was telling him that if he was to succeed, he needed to make those changes his own. Bob Dylan was not one to swim with the tide. His choice was to swim ahead of it.

If we view his trajectory objectively, Dylan's is the classic Jewish immigrant success story. He wasn't an immigrant of course, but he had remade himself as one, with a new persona and a fantasised origin; living with the circus, working in the carnival, playing with the great blues and folk singers. Had he remained Robert Zimmerman his destiny would most likely have been that of his erstwhile Minneapolis frat buddies; settling down to live a comfortable professional or commercial life. But as Bob Dylan the itinerant free spirit, his options were unconstrained. Like the immigrants he had arrived in New York unknown and with nothing. Like Goldman, Guggenheim, the Lehmans and Levi Strauss, immigrants all, he would go all the way.

RIOTIN'

Change was everywhere. In Illinois it was now legal to be gay, the first state in the Union to permit homosexuality. Marilyn Monroe was dead from an overdose, The Beatles had issued their first single, men had flown into space, orbited the earth and returned safely. The University of Mississippi had finally admitted James Meredith, but only after the army had been sent in to quell the riots. Meanwhile, Martin Luther King was teaching the world the meaning of non-violent resistance; when a Nazi sympathiser hurled punches at him at a rally, he placed his arms around the man and held him close. His attacker burst into tears. There was no such reconciliation for the Soviet Union and the United States, still squaring up to each other. Six weeks after the Bay of Pigs, Presidents Kennedy and Khrushchev held a summit in Vienna. Kennedy, young and inexperienced, was outmanoeuvred by the seasoned Soviet dictator. The American President described it as the worst moment in his life. He went home, calling for a build-up of troops and a massive increase in military spending. It was a complicated time to be alive. Particularly if you were young.

Change was rarely achieved easily; when it came it was often in tandem with confrontation. Greenwich Village had experienced a taste of it, not long after Dylan first arrived in town. Since this was the Village the confrontation naturally involved music, but it was far more than just a squabble over quality, style, originality, or any of the many other things musical devotees argue about. Lying beneath the confrontation was a conflict of generational values. Young against old. Free spirits confronting authority. Fun versus tedium.

The clash took place in Washington Square, a 10-acre park at the foot of New York's Fifth Avenue, in the heart of Greenwich Village.

Washington Square was more than a park; it had long been an informal cultural centre, a gathering place both for local residents and those from afar. They came to relax, play, and do what people do in parks, while soaking up the sounds and bohemian atmosphere of New York's most creative and radical neighbourhood. Washington Square Park was a special place, a tolerant haven in the middle of a tough, noisy city, where people of all ages, colours and orientations felt safe mixing together, where it was easy to feel at home.

The Park buzzed at the best of times, and especially so on Sunday afternoons. That was when the local folk artists were joined by aspiring and wannabe musicians, singing, jamming, having fun, and maybe hoping to catch the eye of someone who might launch or advance their career. They had been doing this since the 1940s; playing music in Washington Square Park on a Sunday afternoon was a long-established New York tradition. The City insisted that a permit would need to be obtained to play music in the park, but Israel 'Izzy' Young, the proprietor of the Folklore Center on MacDougal Street, took care of that. He applied to the Parks Department every month, for a licence to play music during the coming period. Ever since the 1940s, whenever they received a request for a permit, the Parks Department had not demurred.

By the 1960s though, with the flowering of the Village folk scene, more and more people had begun to turn up at the Sunday gatherings.

Many came from elsewhere in the city, to gawp at the strange antics of the Village weirdos. The Parks Department officials, backed up by some of the local residents, were growing concerned. There was more noise than in the past, larger crowds, and some of the people, particularly the beatniks, appeared decidedly undesirable. So in April 1961, when Izzy Young applied for his customary monthly permit, the Parks Commissioner said 'No'.

Pictures of Izzy Young at the time show a soberly dressed, clean-cut and earnest-looking Jewish man in his mid-thirties. He happened to have a passion for folk music but he didn't look like a troublemaker. Still, once he was denied the permit, what else could he do? Handwritten signs appeared across the Village, announcing a protest rally to take place at the Fountain in Washington Square the following Sunday at 2 p.m., to complain about the Park Commissioner's 'capricious revoking' of the right to sing folk songs. The fact that the rally was expected to take place at the small Square's iconic Fountain suggests that expectations of a large turnout were muted.

Nevertheless, the word went out around the Village and, to some surprise, 1,500 people turned up. Musicians brought their instruments, lovers brought their sweethearts, parents brought their kids. The children ran to the playground and swung on the swings. The adults played music, sang songs, and waved placards extolling freedom and tolerance. It was a festival, not a confrontation, even though they were deliberately flouting the Park Commissioner's ban.

The police turned up too, just a few at first. Izzy Young and a couple of others got into a polite and respectful discussion with the senior police officer; he spoke about the law, they asserted their rights. Slowly the watching throng grew impatient. The discussion with the police was going nowhere. Someone began strumming a guitar, one or two voices broke into song. The very act the Commissioner's ban was supposed to prevent, the singing of folk songs, was taking place.

Meanwhile the crowd was expanding, more police were arriving, very gradually and then all of a sudden the atmosphere became confrontational. At Izzy Young's suggestion a group of protesters began to sing 'The Star-Spangled Banner'; Young had reasoned that they would not be prevented from singing the national anthem. The police disagreed. They arrested a few protesters, harassed a couple of dozen more. A few sat in the Fountain and sang 'We Shall Not Be Moved'. They were. The crowd waved their placards and sang Woody Guthrie's 'This Land Is Your Land'. The police moved in, pushed, shoved, grabbed and arrested. Pretty soon they had cleared the area.

The events of that Sunday have become known as The Beatnik Riot. It may well count as the earliest indication of the burgeoning generational rift, a mutual intolerance, that would come to characterise the 1960s. It may even have been the event that initiated the movement which would soon become known as the 'counterculture' or 'underground'. It was certainly the moment when the pioneering movement first stood up to mainstream authority. The events were preserved by the filmmaker Dan Drasin, who was there with his camera. His 17-minute movie *Sunday* can still be viewed online.[4]

Bob Dylan was probably in the Park that April day in 1961. He had only been in the Village for a few months but, given the urgency with which he set about establishing himself in the area, it is hard to imagine him not being there. He is not known to have played any part in the events, but as the artist who, more than anyone else at that time, caught and propagated the shifting mood of his generation, he could not have failed to appreciate the historic significance of that afternoon's events. Today, anyone can legally play music in Washington Square Park, and it is widely accepted that it was the Beatnik Riot which initiated the policy change. In 2011, in a letter, New York Mayor Michael Bloomberg wrote to the organisers of the riot's 50th anniversary celebrations saying how pleased he was to join them in 'applauding the folk performers who changed music, our city and our world beginning half a century ago'.[5]

Dylan remained silent about the riot of April 1961. But by the following year, by the time he recorded his first album he too had changed. He was taking a greater interest in politics. Woody Guthrie had built his career singing about the topics that mattered in his day; Dylan was now taking an interest in the issues that were important in his, issues that were frequently on the lips of the two people in the Village he was closest to, Suze Rotolo and Dave Van Ronk. Each in their own way was helping him to shape his thinking. And in so doing, they were drawing him to the attention of those whose duty it was to stop America turning Red.

SURVEILLIN'

If you had wanted to find Dave Van Ronk on a Sunday afternoon the best place to look would have been Washington Square Park. The same went for most of the Village folk singers, Washington Square was where they hung out on a warm Sunday, Park Commissioner or not. But Dave Van Ronk stood out from the crowd, in more ways than one. He was big and easy to spot. And if you followed the gaze of the other man who stood out in the crowd in Dan Drasin's video, the guy who had 'FBI Agent' plastered across his face, you would see that he was most likely searching out, or even staring at, Dave Van Ronk. Because, while nearly everyone in the Village folk scene had radical left-wing leanings, Dave Van Ronk was one of the very few who belonged to an organised socialist group.

Van Ronk's name first appeared in the FBI files in 1958, as a member of the Young Socialist League. He left the League to join the Trotskyite Socialist Workers' Party but was expelled for contending that they were not sufficiently radical. He then joined the pretentiously named American Committee for the Fourth International, which later became the blandly monikered Workers' League.[6] His file records his journey through a maze of left-wing factions and counter-factions. As a folk singer he wasn't as famous as Woody Guthrie or Pete Seeger, the two standard-bearers of the troubadour left, but the FBI knew that a singer did not need to be famous to constitute a threat to the American Way of Life.

In Martin Scorsese's film *No Direction Home*, Van Ronk talks about trying to recruit Bob Dylan into the Socialist movement. He says that Bob was not interested, that he came across, in Van Ronk's assessment, as politically naive:

> Oh, of course, I was always trying to recruit him. But Bobby was not really a political person. He was thought of as being a political person and a man of the left and in a general sort of way, yes he was. But he was not interested in the true nature of the Soviet Union or any of that crap. We thought he was hopelessly, politically naive, but in retrospect, I think he may have been more sophisticated than we were! Really, no protest song changed anyone's politics. Essentially, it's preaching to the choir.[7]

It is true that when Bob Dylan started singing protest songs they rarely related to political ideologies or to national politics. His protests were mainly about injustice, about the actions of abusers like the bullying aristocrat William Zantzinger, born into privilege in Charles County, Maryland, a man with influential connections among local politicians. Zantzinger's casual murder of a 51-year-old kitchen maid, the mother of ten children, and his walking away with a six-month jail sentence, is chronicled in 'The Lonesome Death of Hattie Carroll', the song Dylan recorded on *The Times They Are A-Changin'*.

When Dylan wasn't protesting at specific examples of injustice, he was pointing a finger at the invisible elites corrupted by power. Like the 'Masters of War' on *Freewheelin'*, who prepare the weaponry then sit back, watching, as the death toll rises. Concerns such as those that Dylan aired didn't stem from the revolutionary socialism discussed in the Van Ronk household. He inherited them from

Woody Guthrie and had them reinforced by Suze Rotolo. Radically
left-wing, with an FBI file of her own, Suze was no theoretical
ideologue. Her political activism was rooted in the here and now,
rather than in the nature of capitalism or the class struggle, the
exploitation of workers or the true meaning of the Soviet Union.
She had grown up in a politically idealistic home; her parents had
both been members of the Communist Party and she fought for
the values they taught her. Active in the civil rights movement,
she worked as a volunteer for the Congress of Racial Equality, and
spent her Saturdays picketing Woolworths stores in New York, in
support of the black students in North Carolina protesting and
sitting in at the company's segregated lunch counters there. When
Suze volunteered as an usher at a rally of the Committee for a Sane
Nuclear Policy, she was invited backstage to meet the former First
Lady, Eleanor Roosevelt. Her teenage friend Susan Green recalled
it as an 'unforgettable moment of personal history'.[8]

It was through Suze that Dylan came to know some of the
activists in the SNCC, the Student Nonviolent Coordinating
Committee. He struck up a friendship with two of them, Bernice
Johnson and Cordell Reagon. Bernice had been a music student
at Albany State College in 1960 when the sit-in movement in
support of the four young black Greensboro students erupted.
She met Cordell Reagon, who she later married, when he came
to the college in 1961, to recruit members for the newly formed
SNCC. She was arrested during a protest march, suspended from
college and, at Pete Seeger's suggestion, founded the Freedom
Singers, along with Cordell Reagon, Rutha Mae Harris and Charles
Neblett. They sang at political meetings, rallies and churches,
encouraging audiences to join the struggle for civil rights, raising
awareness of the SNCC and much-needed funds. She appeared on
the same bill as Dylan at Carnegie Hall in 1962, before the largest
audience that either of them had ever faced. Steeped in the African
American musical tradition, she obtained a doctorate in history
in 1975 and embarked on an academic career, in tandem with her

political activism. Bernice ended her working life as Distinguished Professor of History at American University and Curator Emerita at the Smithsonian Institute.

Dylan counted Bernice and Cordell among his closest friends, performing at fundraisers for them and attending some of their protests. He considered their music, rooted in their African American heritage and their experiences as young black activists, to be far more potent than the topical folk songs coming out of the largely white community in Greenwich Village. 'It's all right there in their back yards. They aren't singing about tomorrow or yesterday. They are singing about themselves and the kind of lives they're leading.'[9]

Suze Rotolo's connection with the SNCC came through her work with the Congress for Racial Equality, but her FBI file ostensibly dated back to a much earlier point in her life. She had been known to the Bureau since 1958, when she was 14, because of her parents' membership of the Communist Party.

Her FBI file states that in 1958 she attended Camp Kinderland, described by the Bureau as a 'Communist-managed camp'. Maybe the managers in 1958 were communists, but politics was not the raison d'être for Camp Kinderland. Established in 1923 and still running today, Kinderland is a Jewish summer facility, catering in those days for children from poor working-class backgrounds. It's true that it was left-leaning in terms of its values, but it did not aspire to habituate its children to a political ideology. It leaned to the left because of the demographic and social profile of its client children, and its staff. Nor, despite its Jewish origins, was it exclusively Jewish. Suze came from a Catholic Italian family but she had been born in Brooklyn Jewish Hospital and grew up in a mixed Jewish-Italian neighbourhood. Her parents sent her to Camp Kinderland because of its egalitarian, socialist values.

Anxious to surveil anyone whose political opinions might diverge from the acceptable norm, the Bureau wanted to know everything it deemed important to know about Suze: her family, her politics and even her personal life. Her file states that in 1959 she'd had a boyfriend who was the son of the Communist Party's National Secretary. It also states, unsurprisingly, that she had been involved with Bob Dylan. Surprisingly though, the entry is dated 1964, quite some time after he and Suze had broken up. The Bureau seems not to have had a mole in the Village in 1962 capable of blowing the whistle on Bob and Suze's liaison. His name only appears in her file because of an FBI Special Agent who claimed that his wife had known Suze in 1956, that they had heard 'through family channels' that she had been dating Bob Dylan, and that the relationship had now been broken off. [10]

Maybe the FBI did know that Bob and Suze were involved and hadn't considered it important. They had other ways of gathering information about him. They had been sniffing around him for a while. A few days after Robert Shelton's 1961 article appeared in the *New York Times*, Bob was playing a gig at Gerde's Folk City. At the bar was a well-dressed, smiling man in his fifties, offering drinks to some of Dylan's friends. He wouldn't say who he was, but Dylan reported that he knew the man was from the police, and that they had been following him. It wasn't one of his fantasies. The FBI files do show that they visited Gerde's Folk City, though there is no record of them being there on the day the smiling man turned up.

BROADSIDE

In February 1962 the first edition of *Broadside* appeared. A small magazine, no more than four sheets of paper initially, produced on a typewriter and duplicated by hand, it was little more than a pamphlet really. Edited by the activist and former member of The Almanac Singers, Sis Cunningham, and her husband Gordon Friesen, like so much else at the intersection of the civil rights and folk movements, the impetus for *Broadside* had come from Pete Seeger. He had recently returned from a tour of England where a new genre of protest music was emerging. It was a movement that didn't gain much traction, soon to be eclipsed by The Beatles and the pop revolution. But while it lasted, folk singers sang to small crowds anywhere they could hire a venue cheaply. In pubs, clubs, church halls, even out in the open air, on the village green. Artists were, in Sis Cunningham's words, 'singing commentaries on the times, mixing satire, humour and often deep, probing insight . . . Pete heard songs demanding an end to atom bomb insanity, songs scandalizing corrupt politicians, songs frankly telling Uncle Sam to take his nuclear submarines out of the Clyde and stick 'em.'[11]

Among the leading figures of the British folk-protest movement were the Liverpudlian folk singer Stan Kelly and Leon Rosselson, the son of Jewish immigrants from Russia. In 1961 the two men collaborated on an Extended Play record – a 7-inch , 45 rpm, vinyl disc pitched midway between a single and an LP. The same size as a single and typically containing two tracks on each side, EPs, as they were called, were more affordable than albums but more or less disappeared during the 1960s as bands discovered that LPs could showcase them better.

The title of Kelly and Rosselson's EP, *Songs for Swinging Landlords To*, was a spoof on Frank Sinatra's hugely successful album *Songs for Swinging Lovers*. The four tracks on the disc, all unashamedly partisan in their politics, were 'Greedy Landlord', 'Oakey Evictions', 'The Man Who Waters the Workers' Beer' and 'Pity the Downtrodden Landlord'.

The lyrics to all four tracks were composed by staunchly left-wing British poets. Among them the acclaimed scientist Barnet Woolf, who like Rosselson was the son of Jewish immigrants, and Karl Frederick Dallas, whose name tells us all about his parents' politics; they named him after both Karl Marx and Frederick (Friedrich) Engels. His best-known composition, 'The Family of Man', a hymn to universal brotherhood, was recorded by The Spinners, translated into 13 languages, and appeared in songbooks and hymnals. Pete Seeger heard Kelly and Rosselson's work, took note of what was happening in Britain's left-wing music scene and returned to the United States, determined to give a voice to America's growing number of radical poets and lyricists. *Broadside* was the result.

The eight-page first edition appeared in February 1962. It was headlined *Broadside – A Handful of Songs About Our Times.* Comprising articles, poems, clippings from other journals, lyrics and musical scores, the songs the paper included were siren calls or laments about the day's pressing issues: civil rights, nuclear weapons, worker exploitation and political witch-hunts. Early 1960s protest singers were rarely short of things to sing about.

Broadside had a rather subdued view of its own importance. Rather than presenting itself as an ambassador of the new folk revival, its flagship publication, bringing the best of the new music to as many people as possible, the front page simply explained: 'Many people throughout the country today are writing topical songs, and the only way to find out if a song is good is to give it wide circulation and let the singers and listeners decide for themselves. *Broadside*'s aim is not so much to select and decide, as to circulate as many songs as possible and get them out as quickly as possible.' The journal didn't explain how people who couldn't read music and hadn't heard a song might be able to assess from its appearance on paper whether it was any good or not.[12]

On page three of *Broadside*'s inaugural issue were the lyrics to 'Talkin' John Birch', Bob Dylan's first explicitly political song. The magazine didn't tell its readers who Dylan was, though its editors must have known, but in the next issue they described him as a 'young new songwriter and singer out of New Mexico'.[13] As far as the editors of *Broadside* knew, Bob Dylan's fantasised origins were true.

As the title suggests, the target of Dylan's ire was The John Birch Society. Founded in 1958 as an avowedly anti-communist, membership group, it had chapters across the country. An extremist, far-right organisation, it was particularly vocal in the late 1950s and early 1960s when the campaigns for civil rights were high on the political agenda. Dylan's song takes the mickey out of a fictional member of the Society who looks for communists everywhere, even up the chimney and behind his TV set. He even looked in the bowl of his toilet, but they had disappeared.

The song does not appear on any of his studio albums, but renamed as 'Talkin' John Birch Paranoid Blues' it was released in four different versions, as part of the extensive series of Bootleg Dylan albums. One was a demo version, the other three were recorded at gigs he played between 1962 and 1964. He played the song for the last time in 1965.

Bob Dylan became one of *Broadside*'s most prolific contributors. He recorded a radio interview with Pete Seeger in 1962, telling him 'I don't even consider writing songs; even when I've written it I don't even consider that I wrote it . . . the song was there before me, before I came along, I just sorta came along and took it down in pencil, but it was all there before I came around.'[14]

The third issue of *Broadside* flagged the release of his first album, *Bob Dylan*, not giving the title, just saying simply that it was released recently. They printed the music and lyrics to a new song he had written; an anti-war protest. *Broadside* gave it the title of its first line, 'I will not go down under the ground'. When it was finally released, in the Bootleg Series, it was catalogued as 'Let Me Die in My Footsteps'.[15]

Bob Dylan sent *Broadside* the words and music to 'Blowin' in the Wind' a year before its release on *The Freewheelin' Bob Dylan*. The editors placed the song on the front page of issue 6, appearing in May 1962, suggesting that an alternative title might be 'How Many Roads'. They told their readers it was the third of his songs that they had published: 'Only 20 years old, some consider him to be the nearest composer we have had to Woody Guthrie in recent years. He has an album out of his songs and he is scheduled to bring out his song-book soon.'[16]

Dylan carried on submitting material to *Broadside* for 16 years, until 1978, long after he became famous. They printed a total of 26 of his songs altogether, the last one being 'Changing of the Guards' from Dylan's *Street Legal* album. Alongside the lyrics the editors of *Broadside* wrote:

> When he starts with the phrase 'Sixteen years', we recognize that he is referring to the period of time his career had covered . . . More importantly. when he says, 'Sixteen banners united over the field', he is telling us that there is a unity running throughout his work, beginning with his earliest explicit protest songs such as 'With God on Our Side', 'Masters of War', and continuing with his profoundly poetic 'Sad-Eyed Lady', 'Desolation Row', on to 'Idiot Wind' and 'Changing of the Guards'.[7]

'Talkin' John Birch' marked the beginning of Dylan's career as a protest singer. It was a strong, no-nonsense satire and it caused him no end of aggravation. He was now in the public eye, thanks to Robert Shelton's review, had begun to work on his second album — and he had a new manager too. It was being taken on by his new manager that lay at the root of the aggravation.

Up to now Bob had been managed by Dave Van Ronk's wife Terri. But she wasn't a full-time manager and didn't have the resources of an established, professional team. All she could really do was to book him into gigs in small venues, for little or no fee. Meanwhile he had caught the eye of Albert Grossman, a smart and well-connected manager with a good eye for talent. Fifteen years older than Dylan, born in Chicago to Jewish immigrant parents, he had worked in a clerical job until the mid-1950s, when he opened the Gate of Horn, one of Chicago's earliest folk clubs. Commercially astute, he offered to manage some of the up-and-coming folk artists who he had booked to play in his club, chief among them Joan Baez and the inspirational Odetta, the apotheosis of towering, unafraid, black civil rights champions, crowned by

Martin Luther King as the Queen of American Folk Music. Soon Grossman would add Janis Joplin, Jimi Hendrix, and of course Bob Dylan to his prestigious stable.

Quick to spot the commercial potential of the burgeoning, new folk revival, Grossman looked beyond Chicago, travelling to New York and hanging around the Village clubs, talent spotting. He had recently put together a trio of young folk singers who were already well on the way to becoming one of the most popular acts of the early 1960s. One of the trio was called Peter, another was Mary, and the third was Noel. Grossman renamed him with his middle name of Paul. As Peter, Paul and Mary their success helped to propel the Village folk scene to the forefront of the global music industry.

Albert Grossman had ambitions for Dylan that the young artist couldn't even contemplate. Dylan knew he wanted success, but he had no idea, at his young age, of what that looked like. When Grossman told him that he only took on artists capable of earning at least $50,000 a year, Bob was overwhelmed. As tremendous as Dylan's talent was, it was only under Grossman's tutelage that he became a star. On his own, as a singer and poet with very little commercial nous, despite his ambition, he may never have broken out of the Village – suffering the same fate as Dave Van Ronk, Phil Ochs and so many others, highly respected musicians and singers whose names and talent were only really known to serious folk-music aficionados. The fact that both Dylan and Grossman were each blessed with temperamental Jewish volatility would tear their relationship apart in due course. But at this stage their cultural background probably helped to create a chemistry, a shared ambition for success.

On the strength of Robert Shelton's review and with the prospect of a forthcoming second album, Grossman had managed to get a booking for Dylan to appear in May 1963 on the phenomenally popular *Ed Sullivan Show*. The TV variety programme, produced by CBS and compered by Sullivan, had run non-stop on peak time, Sunday evenings from 8 to 9 p.m., since 1948, eventually chalking up more than 20 years. For any up-and-coming artist, being offered a slot on the show was huge. For a relatively unknown, adenoidal, young folk singer, there was no better way to rocket-launch his career than by making an appearance on *The Ed Sullivan Show*.

Bob Dylan turned up at the dress rehearsal and sang 'Talkin' John Birch', which now had the words 'Paranoid Blues' appended to its title. The rehearsal went well, everyone was happy, both Sullivan and his producer liked Dylan, and they liked his song. But immediately afterwards senior CBS executives told Grossman that 'Talkin' John Birch Paranoid Blues' could not be used; they were worried that it might be construed as libellous. When asked to explain they pointed to the third verse, suggesting that the white supremacist in the song agreed with Hitler. They were concerned that CBS ran the risk of being sued by any member of the John Birch Society. The fact that the song was clearly satirical and that leading politicians were regularly satirised on American TV cut no ice with the CBS management. Dylan was not allowed to perform the song on the show. They asked him to choose another.

Dylan was furious. He refused to sing anything else. If he couldn't sing 'Talkin' John Birch Paranoid Blues' then he would not sing at all; he would not even go on the show. Ironically, Dylan's first protest song itself became the subject of Dylan's first public protest. The row even made it into the *New York Times*. CBS executives refused to give the newspaper a comment, but Ed Sullivan himself told the rival *New York Post* that he believed the TV company's decision was wrong.

That wasn't the end of the row. Dylan had recorded 'Talkin' John Birch Paranoid Blues' for his forthcoming second album, *The Freewheelin' Bob Dylan*, due to be released that month. When Columbia got wind of what had happened on *The Ed Sullivan Show* they took fright. They refused to issue the album with the track on it. The album had already been pressed and was on the point of being distributed when they forced the producer John Hammond to remove the song. As a result the album's full release was delayed by two months. Nevertheless, 300 copies of the album's original pressing, with 'Talkin' John Birch Paranoid Blues' on it, slipped through the net. They were released by mistake and are now collectors' items.

SUCCEEDIN'

The original pressing of *The Freewheelin' Bob Dylan* slipped out on 27 May 1963; the redacted version was finally released in July. The album was an instant success, with sales reaching 10,000 copies a month almost from the moment it came out. Dylan was finally earning good money and becoming known as a rising star. *Billboard* declared that of all the emerging artists on the folk-pop scene, he was one of those making the heftiest impact. 'Though his first album has yet to break through in any major way, there's a good possibility this one will . . . the performances and concepts are striking. Watch this one.'[18]

The Freewheelin' Bob Dylan cemented him as a songwriter and performer who had something important to say, and, it was assumed by many older people, he was saying it on behalf of his own generation. He was 22 years old and had written 12 of the 13 tracks on the album himself, each one dealing with an issue or topic of overwhelming importance to those trying to make sense of the rapidly changing world in which they lived. The only track he didn't write was the old blues number 'Corrina, Corrina'.

Freewheelin' was remarkable both for the range of topics Dylan covered and for his musical versatility. He was a balladeer when he sang the romantic 'Girl from the North Country' and 'Corinna, Corinna', paid homage to the blues in 'Down the Highway' and 'Bob Dylan's Dream', and displayed his sense of comic timing in the humorous, surrealistic 'Talkin' World War III Blues'. He wore his heart on his sleeve too, with 'Don't Think Twice, It's All Right', directed, as we have seen, at Suze Rotolo who, much against his wishes, was spending several months studying art in Italy.

Every track on the album was memorable, but the song that had the greatest impact, the one that became an instant classic, was 'Blowin' in the Wind'. Made up of three verses, each containing three speculative questions about war and peace, oppression and human intransigence, the answer is, as the song title implies, blowin' in the wind. The power of the lyrics lies in the imponderability, yet apparent reasonableness, of the questions, and the shadowy certainty that there are answers, even if they are unattainable, merely blowin' in the wind. The hook, the reason why the words catch the listener's ear, is that they are being addressed to a person, 'my friend'. But what made the song unusual, for a Dylan number, is his voice. Unlike the harmonious version released by Peter, Paul and Mary, and noticeably different from his typical rasping, adenoidal vocals, Dylan sings 'Blowin' in the Wind' in a clear, authoritative voice. Sounding far older than his 22 years, this is a serious man asking serious questions of the world. And unlike Peter, Paul and Mary's version, Dylan introduced the second and third questions of each verse with the word 'yes', emphasising and elevating each query over its predecessor. A poem about the imponderability of life, about the unknowability of everything, 'Blowin' in the Wind' is an Ecclesiastes for our age. It is sometimes suggested that the Scottish folk singer Donovan, often dismissed as a British imitation of Dylan, responded to the song with his 1965 recording, 'Catch the Wind'. However, Donovan's is a love song that, on the face of it, does nothing to respond to Dylan's existential questions.

Almost as soon as 'Blowin' in the Wind' was issued it was adopted as an anthem by civil rights campaigners, spiritual seekers and folk enthusiasts alike. Albert Grossman appreciated its commercial potential the moment he heard it. He played a demo to Peter, Paul and Mary, who jumped at the opportunity of recording it, releasing it as a single three weeks before *The*

Freewheelin' Bob Dylan was released. It reached number 2 in the *Billboard* Hot 100 on 24 August 1963. For his part, Dylan was dismissive of it, calling it a lucky, one-dimensional song with which he was never satisfied. He said he wrote it in about ten minutes, sitting in a café opposite the Gaslight.

'Blowin' in the Wind' quickly achieved cult status, but it wasn't the only song to earn Dylan the image of prophet, the stern ethical voice of the most radical era of modern times. Like an Amos or an Isaiah he pointed a finger of unrelenting rebuke, reproaching evil, exposing the unarticulated fears of a generation who knew but had not yet spoken, who felt but knew not how to act, pronouncing the words they could not find, yet that made perfect sense to them, as soon as they heard them.

'Masters of War', the third song on *The Freewheelin' Bob Dylan*, is a merciless indictment of the generals and politicians who use the world as their military plaything. They cower, devoid of conscience, in their mansions and behind their desks while despatching their pawns to slaughter, bomb and obliterate the world. It was a timely composition. War was very much on people's minds when *Freewheelin'* came out. Only a few months had passed since the Cuban Missile Crisis, when the world had come to the brink of nuclear war. Presidents Kennedy and Khrushchev had faced each other down over the siting of Russian nuclear missiles on Cuba, and the Soviet response to American atomic weapons already installed in Turkey and Italy. The crisis had been resolved but only after a terrifying round of brinksmanship, and now a further military clash was looming. America was becoming ever more deeply involved in the civil war in Vietnam, another, this time far more disastrous confrontation, between East and West. There were already 11,000 American military personnel in the tiny Southeast Asian country, sent there to support President Diem's regime in its ultimately futile opposition to the Vietcong, Ho Chi Minh's communist forces in the North. Nobody could yet foresee that the Vietnam debacle would become America's greatest ever foreign-policy failure. Nor was there any inkling that the war would escalate far beyond its current level, sucking in nearly two million young American draftees, becoming a totem for their generation's rebellion against the mores and conventions of the society they had been born into. Bob Dylan may not have foreseen the details of the Vietnam catastrophe either, but he could sense, more than most, the depth of what was wrong. And he had the words, far more than others, to articulate the evils and immorality of unbridled militarism and the capricious futility of political posturing. Not as a journalist or commentator, pointing out everything that was wrong, but as a poet, using verbal images to convey insights and transmit emotions in a manner that prose can rarely achieve, and as a musician, using the power of melody to implant his lyrics into the hearts of his listeners.

Dylan was always one step ahead of his generation. When the teens and twenties of 1960s America finally woke up to what was wrong with the world, they found that Bob Dylan had already spelt it out for them, in words they could echo and melodies they could sing along to. And not just American youth. *The Freewheelin' Bob Dylan* hit number 1 in Britain and reached number 27 in the French charts.

In the final verse of 'Masters of War' Dylan told the generals to whom the song was addressed that Jesus would not forgive the things they do. Some commentators have suggested that this was an early indication of the interest in Christianity that would be fully awakened in him in the late 1970s. It is an unlikely presumption. Dylan may have been a Jew but he lived in America, a strongly Christian society. Whatever their personal faith, everyone growing up in Western society is familiar with Jesus. Invoking his name as a conduit to forgiveness was a cultural, not a religious, statement. Dylan also mentioned Jesus in 'With God on Our Side' on the forthcoming albums *The Times They Are A-Changin'* and in 'Bob Dylan's 115th Dream' on *Bringing It All Back Home*. There is no religious connotation in either case. When

Dylan did eventually turn briefly to Christianity in 1978 he was almost evangelical in portraying his beliefs. He is unlikely to have deemed the passing reference he made in 'Masters of War' as appropriately respectful.

In the album's sixth song, Dylan turned his attention from warlords to their weapons, addressing the threat of nuclear conflict through the apocalyptic lament of 'A Hard Rain's A-Gonna Fall'. Written as a dialogue between an unknown parent and a young man wandering in the aftermath of a nuclear holocaust, we hear of the surreal visions he has seen and his terrifying encounters. With echoes of Lorca and Rimbaud, 'A Hard Rain' lyrically entwines Picasso's *Guernica* and Salvador Dalí's *Metamorphosis of Narcissus*.

The 'Hard Rain' of which Dylan warns sounds as if it is the poisonous deluge about to descend from an overhanging radiation cloud. Dylan denied this, however, telling Studs Terkel in a 1963 radio interview that it was 'not atomic rain at all . . . it's some sort of end that's just gotta happen'.[19] Metaphorically, 'Hard Rain', like 'Blowin' in the Wind', resembles Ecclesiastes but this time the negativity is pronounced, symbolising an age where all is emptiness and nullity, where futility reigns and nothing has a purpose.

Perhaps the most powerful of all Dylan's songs in the starkness of its imagery, Allen Ginsberg said that he wept with joy when he heard it, because 'it seemed that the torch had been passed to another generation'.[20] A little more thoughtfully than in his comment to Studs Terkel, ramping up the immediacy of the song's portents, Dylan, also said, 'Every line in it is actually the start of a whole new song. But when I wrote it, I thought I wouldn't have enough time alive to write all those songs so I put all I could into this one.'[21]

It is all very well to protest against the universal evils of war and global destruction, but one cannot ignore the iniquities lying closer to hand. *Freewheelin'* is the album on which 'Oxford Town' appears, his musically cheerful but lyrically depressing commentary on James Meredith's solo struggle to enrol at the University of Mississippi and the riots that ensued in the wake of his efforts. The tactic of drawing attention to injustice by highlighting the cases of individual victims is one that Dylan would carry forward into subsequent albums, with songs like 'The Ballad of Hollis Brown', 'The Lonesome Death of Hattie Carroll', 'Hurricane' and 'Joey'. Masterfully telling stories of personal suffering and institutional wrongdoing, encapsulating the entirety of America's ongoing racial crisis, Dylan's lyrics had far more emotional impact and political consequence than any number of pamphlets, broadsheets or speeches could hope to achieve.

4

FREEWHEELIN'

NEWPORT

In 1959 George Wein took a gamble. It wasn't the first gamble he had taken; he had acted similarly when he invested his life savings in opening a jazz club in Boston, gambled again when he founded the Storyville record label, and rolled the dice once more in 1954 when, encouraged by an habitué of his club, the wealthy Elaine Lorillard, he founded the Newport Jazz Festival. Never a man to do things by halves, for the first festival, George Wein booked, among others, Oscar Peterson, Dizzie Gillespie and Billie Holiday. In 1959 he was ready to gamble once more, creating the Newport Folk Festival.

George Wein was born in 1925, to secular, Jewish parents in Massachusetts. His father Barnet was a dentist turned ear, nose and throat surgeon with a betting habit that probably inspired George's penchant for taking chances in business. When it came to making a first career choice though, George did not take a chance. He followed his piano-playing mother, becoming, for a short while, a professional jazz pianist. His fame rests on the Newport Jazz and Folk festivals he founded but his accomplishments went far beyond Rhode Island. As his business grew he set up and ran music festivals across the world, eventually running over 50 major events a year, attracting hundreds of thousands of fans and providing work for more musicians than anyone else in the industry. He is regarded as the creator of the modern music festival and, although hardly any festivalgoer today has heard his name, without George Wein and

Newport Jazz there would have been no Woodstock, Glastonbury or even the Donauinselfest, a festival held on an artificial island in Vienna and attracting over two million visitors each year.

Festival goers are not the only ones who owe a debt to the invisible hand of George Wein. So too do the fans of dozens of artists whose careers he launched or revived. Duke Ellington's career, which had reached its heyday in the 1930s, had hit a brick wall by the early 1950s; he believed that as a jazz musician he was finished. Then he appeared at the 1956 Newport Jazz Festival. Coming on at midnight to perform just two numbers, the crowd went wild. Every time George Wein tried to bring the set to an end, citing the curfew that had been agreed with the local authorities, the audience insisted that Ellington carry on. Six weeks later Ellington's picture appeared on the cover of *Time* magazine, as great an accolade as any musician could hope for. Duke Ellington himself proclaimed that 'I was born at Newport in 1956.'[1]

The Newport Folk Festival followed hard on the heels of the Jazz Festival. Odetta had been the catalyst, as Wein had negotiated her appearance with her manager, Albert Grossman, initially thinking she would headline a folk set at the Jazz Festival. Albert Grossman had bigger ideas. By the time Wein had finished speaking with Grossman he'd realised there was too much folk talent out there to simply append folk music to the jazz event. The folk event needed to be a festival in its own right. Wein hired Grossman to assemble the programme and although Wein has gone down in history as the Newport Folk Festival's founder, it was Grossman who gave the event its shape. He put together a folk line-up that included Pete Seeger, Odetta, Joan Baez, Cynthia Gooding, New Lost City Ramblers and The Kingston Trio, who had also appeared that year at the Jazz Festival. Grossman complemented the folk performers with a blues contingent, headlined by Bo Diddley, Sonny Terry & Brownie McGhee, and Memphis Slim. The Folk Festival ran over two days, Saturday and Sunday, 11 and 12 July 1959. George Wein later wrote that 'there were more

different sounds and styles in one place than you could absorb.
But it was all a part of the same idea, part of the folk movement.
An unspoken feeling was in the air, a sense that folk music was
approaching a threshold.'[2]

Joan Baez was just eighteen years old when she took to the stage
at Newport that year. Her name doesn't appear on the bill; a late
addition, she had been playing in The Gate of Horn, Grossman's
club in Chicago, where she met the singer Bob Gibson. He invited
her to Newport and introduced her to the 13,000-strong crowd.
She played two numbers with Gibson, 'Virgin Mary Had One Son'
and 'Jordan River', remarking in her memoirs that she descended
from the stage to an 'exorbitant amount of fuss . . . Into one tent and
out of another. Newspapers, student press, foreign correspondents,
and, of course, *Time* magazine. I gave *Time* a long explanation of
the pronunciation of my name which came out wrong, was printed
wrong in *Time* magazine, and has been pronounced wrong ever
since.'[3] Unknown before she reached Newport, the appearance
launched her career.

Bob Dylan did not see Joan Baez make her Newport debut. He
was in Hibbing, getting ready to embark on his brief university
career. Four years later, in the summer of 1963, when they both
played at Newport, he and Baez were rumoured to be a couple. On
the Newport stage that year Joan sang 'Don't Think Twice, It's All
Right', the song that was Dylan's unapologetic complaint to Suze
Rotolo at the beginning of their break-up.

Dylan and Baez had known each other for some while, and despite
Dylan confessing in his biography that he had been entranced by
her the first time he saw her on TV, they had only finally shown an
interest in each other a couple of months earlier, when they both
played at the first Monterey Folk Festival on 18 May, Dylan's initial
West Coast appearance.

By the time he first appeared at Newport in 1963, the festival was
already well established as an influential event in the music calendar,
a venue where top folk artists wanted to be seen, where important

statements, both musical and political, were often made. It was
only the third time the festival had been held, it didn't run in 1961
or 1962. Yet it had grown substantially; now spanning three days,
with over 50 performers on the bill including Pete Seeger, Dave Van
Ronk, Peter, Paul and Mary, Judy Collins and John Lee Hooker. Bob
Dylan played on each of the three days. The festival was now more
than just a series of performances, there were dozens of educational
workshops and panels covering everything from Old Banjo Styles,
Bluegrass and Gospel Music to Copyright Law and a session called
'Whither Folk Music?' hosted by Theodore Bikel.

Larger than life, Theo Bikel was arguably the most enigmatic
of the Newport clique. One of the founders of the festival, his
involvement in folk music was part of a long, variegated journey
that had begun when he was a teenager, when his Austrian Jewish
family was forced to flee from the Nazis. Coming from a passionately
Zionist background (his father had named him after Theodor Herzl,
the founder of Zionism), they managed to circumvent the British
restrictions on entry into Palestine, settling on a kibbutz. Theo took
up acting, appeared in a few stage roles in Tel Aviv, including the
first production of the play that would evolve into *Fiddler on the
Roof*, and in 1946 went to London to study at the Royal Academy of
Dramatic Art. He acted in several roles on the London stage, before
moving to the United States where he appeared in many Hollywood
movies and TV programmes. He created the role of Captain von
Trapp in the original stage version of *The Sound of Music* and played
Tevye the milkman in *Fiddler on the Roof* over 2,000 times in venues
across America. In 1957, while working in Hollywood, he brought
folk music to Los Angeles, opening the Unicorn Folk Club on
Sunset Strip. He was as prolific a singer as he was an actor, making
over 40 albums, mainly of Jewish and Russian folk songs. He once
said that music was 'one of the few answers to the chaos that we
have', putting the principle into practice through his involvement
in the civil rights movement.[4] It was Bikel who had first steered
Bob Dylan towards practical civil rights activism by quietly paying

his plane fare to travel and play at a voter-registration campaign in Mississippi.

Dylan had flown to Mississippi a few weeks before the 1963 Newport Festival, in the company of Bikel and Pete Seeger. They had gone, along with Cordell Reagon and Bernice Johnson's Freedom Singers, to play to a small gathering of black farmers, aiming to get national publicity for the voter-registration campaign being conducted by the Student Nonviolent Coordinating Committee. It was not Dylan's idea to go, indeed when Theo Bikel suggested he went, Albert Grossman told him that he wouldn't be able to afford the plane fare. Bikel told Grossman that he would pay it, and that Dylan wasn't to know.

Dylan took the flight and spent three days with Bikel and Seeger, playing on a makeshift stage in a cotton field in Greenwood, Mississippi, with Bob learning the practical realities of a struggle that up to now he'd only known from a distance.

Dylan may not have realised at the time how significant his presence in Greenwood was to the success of the voter-registration campaign. He was on the threshold of becoming a public figure, albeit still a minor celebrity but one whose fame and reputation were growing. Peter, Paul and Mary's version of 'Blowin' in the Wind' was rising in the charts, *Freewheelin'* was selling well, and his musical success made him a subject of interest to the media. Because of Dylan they paid more attention to the Greenwood event than they would have done had the performers been Seeger and Bikel alone. Their political position was already widely known, their presence at the campaign was no surprise.

Dylan played the Greenwood farmers 'Only a Pawn in Their Game', a song he had finished only a few weeks earlier about the murder of Medgar Evers, one of the leaders of the National Association for the Advancement of Colored People. He followed it up with 'Blowin' in the Wind'. It was good publicity for the campaign and an opportunity for Dylan to experience activism on the ground. Dylan's political activism, at the beginning of what turned out to be his very short-lived protest phase, was as much commentary as campaign; writing and playing songs to expose hatred and injustice. Raising awareness and stirring up outrage. Just as Woody had done.

The biggest names at Newport in 1963 were those of Peter, Paul and Mary. They'd already had two national chart-topping hits, and a handful of other well-known releases. There was something about their harmonious, almost naive style that appealed to audiences across the musical spectrum, and their content range was diverse. They sang children's songs like 'Puff, the Magic Dragon' – a charming fairy tale about a magic creature who lived by the sea, who was left distraught when the child he frolicked with grew up. 'Puff' peaked at number 2 on the *Billboard* charts in April 1963. They followed it at Newport with their version of 'Blowin' in the Wind', lyrically as far removed from a fairy tale as one can imagine. Their gentle harmonies overpowered the urgency of the questions, turning the song, on first hearing anyway, from an anthem of quizzical despair to a sing-along ditty in which the questions hardly mattered. Answers that blow in the wind are presented as no more fantastical than magic dragons who frolic by the sea. That is not to say the trio were deaf to the song's message; they were as conflicted as anyone else in the left-leaning folk world about the existential crises facing humanity. They just chose to put the message across in a way that encouraged people to hum along to it; to absorb the lyrics by osmosis. It is an interesting question as to which approach to 'Blowin' in the Wind' had the greater impact on the hearts and minds of those who heard it – Bob Dylan's or Peter, Paul and Mary's.

Because of their chart hits, Peter, Paul and Mary were probably the act most familiar to those without a particular penchant for folk music. But all the folk staples were at Newport: Pete Seeger of course, Ramblin' Jack Elliott, Dave Van Ronk and Tom Paxton. A small but strong blues contingent represented by John Lee Hooker and Sonny Terry & Brownie McGhee added some variety to the sounds coming off the stage. But undoubtedly, Newport

1963 is remembered as Bob Dylan's festival – the moment when he transitioned from a relatively well-known Greenwich Village folk artist to a national figure.

The not-so-invisible hand of Albert Grossman helped with that. He persuaded George Wein that, although Peter, Paul and Mary were the best-known performers at the festival, Dylan should have the stage for the closing set on the first evening. Peter, Paul and Mary would close the first half of the concert and would make a guest appearance alongside Dylan in his closing set. When they launched into 'Blowin' in the Wind', Peter Yarrow told the audience about the young man:

> . . . living today and writing today in very much the same way that Woody Guthrie wrote 30 years ago. His songs are so poignant and so meaningful that we feel, that is Paul and Mary and myself, that he's the most important young folk singer in America today. He's very young, he's only 22. His name is Bob Dylan and this is one of the songs that he's written. [5]

Peter, Paul and Mary paying homage to Bob's talent, and Dylan reciprocating by bringing them onstage, along with Pete Seeger, The Freedom Singers, Theodore Bikel and Joan Baez, had exactly the effect that Grossman had hoped for. They sang 'Blowin' in the Wind' followed by 'We Shall Overcome', the audience went wild, and Dylan emerged from Newport in 1963 a star. Crowned by the folk aristocracy, acclaimed by a 47,000-strong audience comprising some of America's most knowledgeable musical cohorts, and propelled to the summit by a song that he said he'd written in about ten minutes.

Like Joan Baez, Phil Ochs was not listed on the official programme, but he was there. He sang 'Talking Birmingham Jam' about the brutal response in Birmingham, Alabama, a few weeks earlier to an anti-segregation protest conducted by black schoolchildren. The violence directed towards the children shocked the nation, and from the reaction of the crowd when Ochs introduced the song it was clear that the event was still uppermost in the minds of the audience. The growing, violent responses by state and city authorities to civil rights protests were among the reasons why Newport 1963 marks the moment when protest entered the musical mainstream. Postcards were circulating addressed to ABC-TV protesting that their *Hootenanny* TV show had blacklisted Pete Seeger and The Weavers; 2,000 members of the Newport audience signed them. Cries for freedom were everywhere. At the festival, The Freedom Singers sang 'I Woke Up This Morning with My Mind Stayed on Freedom', Joan Baez sang 'Oh Freedom', and was onstage at Dylan's festival finale, singing 'We Shall Overcome'. *Billboard*, never an organ that lent itself to political controversy, cautiously declared that 'the 1963 Newport Folk Festival has written a sterling new chapter in the saga of the folk-pop movement'.[6]

Billboard was also in no doubt that Bob Dylan was the undisputed star of the Newport Festival. The record vendors sold their entire stock of his albums and were left with customers appealing for more; Dylan was the only artist at the festival to so trouble them. He had kept the fires of protest burning, singing 'Talkin' John Birch Paranoid Blues' and two songs from his next album, first the powerful anti-war protest 'With God on Our Side', then, evoking his home town of Hibbing, 'North Country Blues', about the economic decline of the iron-ore mines and the tragedy of a miner's widow, left to raise her three children.

Alongside its report on the festival, *Billboard* painted a picture for its readers of the burgeoning success of the folk movement. In a piece bizarrely titled 'New Folk Breed Spells Meat' the magazine admitted that the movement's commercial champions were Peter, Paul and Mary whose two hits of the past year, 'If I had a Hammer' and 'Blowin' in the Wind', both posed unanswered questions. But Dylan was the artist who was most talked about, perhaps the ultimate influence on the folk scene. Barry Kittleson, the author of the piece, was in no doubt that 'What places Dylan in a class by himself is his absolute commitment to what he believes in . . . [that] his lyrics are riddled with compassion.' He insisted that it would be incorrect to label Dylan and his colleagues as 'merely anti or contrary'. His protests were fundamentally about 'man's inhumanity to man'.[7]

Barry Kittleson had seen Dylan play a solo concert at New York's Town Hall back in late April 1963, where Bob had interrupted his performance to tell the audience he had been asked to write a few words about what Woody Guthrie meant to him, for a forthcoming book. He told them he couldn't do it, all he could manage was a five-page poem. He happened to have the poem with him, by accident he said, and proceeded to read it out. Unlike the protest songs that made him famous, 'Last Thoughts on Woody Guthrie' is a paean to hope, a tirade against trouble and confusion, a recipe for salvation that can only be found in a church or a hospital. God could be found in a church. Woody, Dylan concluded, could be found in Brooklyn State Hospital.

Kittleson had written a glowing review of the Town Hall concert for *Billboard*, headlining Dylan as a 'Legend Under Construction' and prophesying that his talent would be around for a long, long time.[8] In his review of the Newport Festival, Kittleson had referred back to the Town Hall gig, calling it a triumphant performance. In his eyes, Dylan's conquest of the Newport Festival was wholly predictable and richly deserved.

Cash Box, however, then the second-largest trade magazine in the music industry, seemed to have arrived at Newport knowing very little about Dylan. Introducing him as a '22-year-old writer-singer-guitarist-harmonica player from Hibbing, Minnesota . . . who records for Columbia and who is the writer of the current Peter, Paul and Mary hit, *Blowin' in the Wind*', the magazine described him as looking something like a displaced Bowery Boy and noted that he wore the same pair of blue jeans and mustard-stained workshirt for the whole festival. *Cash Box* tipped him as the logical successor to Woody Guthrie as the nation's poet laureate, their apparent new discovery of him implying that until Newport, Dylan's reputation was largely confined to the Greenwich Village cognoscenti and a few aficionados on the wider folk scene.[9]

The success of 'Blowin' in the Wind' marked the moment when contemporary folk music entered mainstream pop culture. Its adoption as an anthem of protest, perhaps as much due to Peter, Paul and Mary as to Dylan, helped the post-war, boomer generation to find its radical voice. It became a litmus test of political affiliation. Like 'We Shall Overcome', those who sang or played it were implicitly declaring their commitment to the campaigns and protests beginning to sweep through the university campuses and wherever young people gathered en masse. The anti-war campaigns, the fights against injustice, the embryonic stirrings of second-wave feminism. And of course, the civil rights movement, which was now accelerating along its own trajectory.

MARCHIN'

One month after Newport, in late August 1963, Bob Dylan and Joan Baez travelled to Washington DC. They were joined by Peter, Paul and Mary, Odetta and a quarter of a million other people. Led by Martin Luther King and the leaders of all six major civil rights organisations, the March on Washington for Freedom and Jobs was the biggest protest the American nation had ever seen. Its stated goals included a comprehensive civil rights bill, the protection of the right to vote, the means of redress when constitutional rights were violated, the desegregation of all public schools, a federal works programme to train the unemployed and place them in jobs, and an Act barring discrimination in all employment.

It was an ambitious set of goals, which eventually only managed to achieve a fraction of the organisers' hopes. Nevertheless, the size of the march and the publicity associated with it were instrumental in the creation and passing of the Civil Rights Act of

1964, which ended segregation in public institutions and forbade job discrimination based on race.

Together with its political impact, the march has acquired an enduring, cultural significance. It was during the March on Washington that Martin Luther King, standing at the Lincoln Memorial, delivered his transformative speech, 'I Have a Dream'. A landmark in twentieth-century political oratory the speech is a rousing indictment of America's failure to live up to Abraham Lincoln's Emancipation Proclamation 'five score years earlier' (1863), that 'all persons held as slaves within any State . . . shall be then, thenceforward, and forever free'.[10] Dr King set out a utopian vision of an Edenic society in which 'little black boys and black girls will be able to join hands with little white boys and white girls as sisters and brothers', in which 'our little children will one day live in a nation where they will not be judged by the colour of their skin but by the content of their character'.

Listening to recordings of Martin Luther King's speech today one can almost hear the attention of the quarter-million-strong crowd throughout his 17-minute oration, their captivated silence only interrupted by outbursts of applause and assent. Quoting Isaiah's messianic prophecies, Dr King declared his faith that 'the jangling discords of our nation' will be transformed 'into a beautiful symphony of brotherhood'.[11] From the poetic perspective of someone like Bob Dylan, the speech was the quintessence of inspirational oratory, the perfection of the use of language in the service of a cause. Over forty years later Dylan said, 'I was up close when King was giving that speech. To this day, it still affects me in a profound way.'[12]

Dr King ended his speech with a call to:

Let freedom ring. And when this happens, and when we allow freedom to ring, when we let it ring from every village and every hamlet, from every state and every city, we will be able to speed up that day when all of God's children, black men and white men, Jews and gentiles, Protestants and Catholics, will be able to join hands and sing in the words of the old Negro spiritual, 'Free at last! Free at last! Thank God Almighty, we are free at last!'

The bells of freedom are a common enough symbol, metaphor and literary trope. But it is surely no coincidence that the following year, when Bob Dylan is often said to have transcended his 'protest phase', he recorded 'Chimes of Freedom', one of his most powerful broadsides against hatred and enmity.

More parochially, the March on Washington was the moment when a handful of folk singers still in their twenties, some there in body, others in spirit, cemented their place at the forefront of the protest movement – setting an example for their generation and paving the way for the youth-led social upheavals that would consume the remainder of the decade. Old videos of the event show Dylan somewhat self-consciously and without much stage presence singing 'Only a Pawn in Their Game' with Joan Baez behind him offering encouragement and support. He was probably overwhelmed by the vast numbers of people and the puzzled, uncomprehending looks from some of the predominantly black crowd. Many of them had never heard New York's brand of folk music before, were not used to adenoidal raspings, and probably couldn't make out much of what he was singing anyway, because of the size of the gathering, the buzz of voices, and the less than adequate public-address system.

Dylan and Joan Baez were now spending a lot of time together. Perhaps not yet a couple, Dylan was still seeing Suze Rotolo, though, in Baez's opinion, as she had proclaimed at Newport, it was an affair that had gone on too long. Meanwhile, over the past few weeks he had repeatedly joined Joan Baez onstage in a ten-venue, East Coast tour that she had commenced straight after Newport. Now, launching into the second song of his set, 'When the Ship Comes In', he looked around anxiously for her. She mounted the platform to join him as he neared the end of the first verse, harmonising by his side. An almost messianic composition, full of biblical imagery about the overthrow of the corrupt, few Dylan songs could have been better suited to the occasion.

Dylan's extravagant poetry could barely have been audible beyond the first few rows of the crowd, let alone intelligible. But at least one line, about the entire world watching, would surely have struck home. 'The whole world is watching' had been heard at civil rights protests for a number of years and would become a mantra at the 1968 National Democratic Convention, chanted over and again as the police tear gassed the demonstrators. Dylan had slipped an extra word in, calling it the whole *wide* world, but his meaning was clear. 'When the Ship Comes In' is more paean than protest, but the line would have resonated, for those who could hear it. It was the first time he'd sung the song in public; he had it written while travelling with Joan Baez on her ten-venue tour. He released it a few months later, on his third album, *The Times They Are A-Changin'*.

ADVERSITY
'I can tell from your applause,' declared the compere at the March on Washington, 'that he needs no further introduction. Mr Bob Dylan.'

The outsider from Hibbing had come far. He was fulfilling his ambitions, his reputation was growing, he had fans, and people were talking about him. At the age of just 22, he was already recognised as a unique performer of considerable talent, a young man setting new standards for the role of popular song in society, remaining musically within tried and tested boundaries but taking his lyrics into political and social arenas where very few had gone before, with the notable exception of Woody Guthrie and his circle. Yet, unlike his hero Guthrie and those early singers of topical folk songs, Dylan had the great advantage of living at the beginning of the communication revolution, in which speech and music were becoming global, in which a song he recorded in New York one day could be heard on the other side of the world in no time at all. Provided only that the

record company operated efficient distribution channels, or that the
broadcast media despatched their tapes promptly.

Communication would become faster and more sophisticated
still, and pop stars would come under much greater media scrutiny
than early Dylan endured, but even in those simple days of the early
1960s fame and fortune did not arrive unchallenged. There had
always been the false friend of the media to contend with. The small
amounts of publicity that Bob had received during the two years
of his career had been overwhelmingly enthusiastic, the highlight
being Robert Shelton's brief but enthusiastic *New York Times* piece.
But Dylan was beginning to discover that the media are every bit
as ready to sting as they are to swoon. Although a performer and
not a businessman, in many ways Dylan's drive to succeed was no
different from that of any aspiring young Jewish entrepreneur. He
would need to learn how to turn media attention to his advantage,
to see it as if it were any other business opportunity. And conversely,
to face down media adversity as surely as if the business climate, or
a competitor, had turned against him. At least until he became a big
enough star to pay them no mind at all. It wouldn't take long.

Bob had experienced his first taste of media antipathy when he'd
played with Joan Baez at the Monterey Folk Festival the previous
year, in May 1964. Ralph Gleason, a respected music critic for the
San Francisco Chronicle, the future founder of the renowned *Rolling
Stone* magazine, and Bob's senior by more than 20 years, did not like
what he had heard. 'It was an old Dylan concert,' he said, 'and I didn't
dig it. The talking Blues stuff is poor imitation Guthrie. He looked
wrong to me and I didn't like his voice.'[13] Gleason's comments were
of the moment, based on Dylan's performance at Monterey. He was
soon to change his mind. A year later Gleason wrote, 'when I first
heard Bob Dylan at Monterey I did not like him. I was deaf. He is
truly a great artist and to judge him by the standards of others is a
total mistake. He is sui generis, a true loner . . . one of the great
warning voices of our time.'[14]

Gleason, who would become one of Dylan's greatest media advocates, had rated him badly on the strength of one gig and was generous enough to admit that he had been wrong. Not so *Time* magazine. In a cutting, supercilious and unsigned piece titled 'Let Us Now Praise Little Men', *Time* described him 'as a dime-store philosopher, a drugstore cowboy, a men's room conversationalist . . . There is something faintly ridiculous about such a citybilly, yet Dylan is the newest hero of an art that has made a fetish out of authenticity . . . His citified fans have an unhappy tendency to drop their g's when praisin' him but only because they cannot resist imitatin' him.' It was a nasty review, even though it did concede he had something unique to say and said it in a way that nobody had bettered since Woody Guthrie. It praised the value of his 'honest complaints' and ended somewhat wistfully with a verse from 'Blowin' in the Wind'. It was almost as if the author would have preferred to praise Dylan, not bury him, but did not have the courage to do so.[15]

The *Time* article wasn't even the worst of it. In November 1963, following Newport and the March on Washington, Dylan was riding the crest of a wave, performing to sold-out crowds and with a hotly anticipated new album about to be released. At the urging of his publicists, *Newsweek*, one of the most widely distributed magazines in the country, ran a cover story. *Newsweek* was a direct competitor of *Time* magazine and no doubt felt duty bound to dismiss Dylan's talents even more comprehensively than the opposition had done. It was even more excoriating than *Time*'s piece, though *Newsweek* did at least give their reporter, Andrea Svedberg, a byline, and she in turn had done her research. Mocking Dylan for pretending to suffer, for being 'without bread, man, without a chick, with twisted wires growing inside him', the article was equally dismissive of his audiences who 'share his pain, and seem jealous because they grew up in conventional homes and conventional schools'. The irony, continued the article, was that Dylan too had grown up in a conventional home, and had gone to conventional schools, shrouding his past in contradictions. Exposing him as Robert Zimmerman, the son of Abe Zimmerman, an appliance dealer from Hibbing, the reporter quoted Dylan as saying that he didn't know his parents, that he had been out of touch with them for years. However, the article revealed, his mother and father were in fact sitting in 'one of New York's motor inns' a few blocks away, holding the tickets he had given them for the concert he was about to play at Carnegie Hall.

Suggesting that he chose to deny his past because it would ruin his image, the paper then repeated an accusation that 'Blowin' in the Wind' had not been written by Dylan but by a Millburn, New Jersey, high-school student named Lorre Wyatt, who had then sold it to him. The accusation had first surfaced the previous year and, in a letter to *Broadside*, the alleged composer had already denied that Dylan was using his song. But in a remarkable example of shoddy journalism, this did not prevent *Newsweek* from both repeating the accusation and denying its truth: 'Dylan says he did write the song and Wyatt denies authorship, but several Milburn students claim they heard the song from Wyatt before Dylan ever sang it.'

Was there a hint of antisemitism in Andrea Svedberg's article, by revealing Dylan's family name and his true relationship with his parents? Would she have written about him in the same way if his name hadn't been Zimmerman, if his father's name wasn't Abe? After all, many performers adopt stage names; unless they are writing an all-embracing profile journalists don't usually waste copy in pointing this out. Yes, Bob Dylan's fantasy origins were absurd and the frequency with which he recounted them verged on the obsessional. But wasn't this why Dylan had changed his name and created an imaginary backstory, because he was embarrassed about his outsider roots and hated his Jewish-sounding name? Was this the best that *Newsweek* could do, to mock him and his fans when there was so much that could have been written about the cultural impact he was making? Would Svedberg have written a similar article if his family name had been Riley, Jones or Patel? Tellingly, *Newsweek* had quoted his 17-year-old brother David as saying, 'He set out to become what he is.' The implication was that Dylan was a fraud.[16]

Some of the blame for the *Newsweek* piece was pinned on Dylan and Albert Grossman themselves. They had backed out of an interview at the last minute, leading Svedberg to travel to Dylan's home town to find out more about him. Then when she threatened to publish local gossip about him, Dylan backed down and gave her a short but grumpy interview. Did that justify an excoriating article, one that was possibly intended to derail his career, or more likely enhance hers? Probably not. But that's showbusiness.[17]

Those who knew him said that the *Newsweek* article had a devastating impact on Dylan. It sent him into a depression, ruined his relations with his family, and gave him a profound distrust of the media. He adopted an evasive, wary tone in interviews, giving jokey or misleading answers to questions, or avoiding them altogether; he did his best to shock or provoke interviewers and generally hedged himself in inscrutability as a protection against journalistic probing.

Woody Guthrie hadn't endured such trials. He'd had a hard time of it for sure, he had been criticised, vilified, castigated, blacklisted and abused. But nobody had ever accused him of falsehood, of pretending to be someone he was not. But then Woody had lived at a different time. A simpler time, when people knew who they were, hungry or prosperous, privileged or cowed. Before the manufacture of celebrity, before persona became something that could be constructed and identity a matter of choice, when authenticity was a shape-shifting marionette. As Sal Paradise explained, in Jack Kerouac's *On the Road*, when waking up from a day-long sleep in an anonymous hotel:

That was the one distinct time in my life, the strangest moment of all, when I didn't know who I was – I was far away from home, haunted and tired with travel, in a cheap hotel room I'd never seen, hearing the hiss of steam outside, and the creak of the old wood of the hotel, and footsteps upstairs, and all the sad sounds, and I looked at the cracked high ceiling and really didn't know who I was for about fifteen strange seconds. I wasn't scared; I was just somebody else, some stranger, and my whole life was a haunted life, the life of a ghost. I was halfway across America, at the dividing line between the East of my youth and the West of my future.[18]

The disorientation from exhaustion that Sal felt is commonplace — the West of his future indicates he would never be the same again.

Perhaps this was Bob Dylan's problem, perhaps this is why the *Newsweek* piece was so devastating to him. The 'West of my future' (actually East, because he had travelled to New York from Minnesota) was modelled on Woody, or so he had told himself. But he could never be Woody. He hadn't endured personal tragedy, suffered through the Great Depression, or seen children die from hunger. Woody had sung for people like himself from his own personal experience, he had become their voice, his songs their comfort and their escape. Dylan too was singing for people like himself, but they weren't the hard-pressed blacks of the Southern states or the starving farmers of the Dust Bowl; they were the well-meaning, social justice-seeking youth of middle-class America. Woody had been one of the people he was singing for, but Dylan, at this stage, was a 22-year-old country boy still trying to find his way in a crowded, chaotic and self-obsessed city. The *Newsweek* piece had exposed him. And he didn't yet have the celebrity experience, or the confidence in who he was, to deal with it.

Anyway, Bob Dylan was moving beyond his hero Woody. Dylan was already a star on a national stage far larger than anything that existed in Woody's day. The media attention was greater, the pressures more intense, and the material rewards far exceeded anything that Woody could have dreamed of, or probably even wanted. Dylan may not have known it yet, but his career was leaving Woody behind. In the spring of 1963 *Time* magazine had hailed him as the best thing since Woody. In the autumn of that year *Newsweek*, in an impossibly nasty way, had effectively told him to look beyond Woody.

In fact, if in his early years Bob Dylan was seeking to construct an identity for himself other than the global superstar that he would become, he did not have to look very far. He was not the first Jew to be cast in the mould of social justice, to have used his position and his talents in support of the civil rights movement. In the 1950s, rabbis in Arkansas, Alabama and Mississippi all used their ethical voices in support of the integrationist lobby, standing up to threats from segregationists, often in the face of appeals from their own flock that they not draw attention to themselves. Rabbi Ira Sanders of Little Rock, who helped found the town's birth-control clinic, tried in vain to persuade the Arkansas General Assembly not to circumvent a Supreme Court order declaring segregated schools unconstitutional. He so angered the 900-strong audience at the Assembly that when he finished speaking he was rushed from the scene to avoid a possible assassination. Rabbi Charles Mantinband entertained members of the National Association for the Advancement of Colored People (NAACP) in his home and sat on the porch in full view of the whole town with the activist Medgar Evers, whose assassination in June 1963 Dylan would sing about in 'Only a Pawn in Their Game'. Meanwhile Rabbi Perry Nussbaum was working with black and white clergy in Jackson, Mississippi, to rebuild churches that had been bombed by segregationists. He worked quietly, few of his congregation knew what he was doing. Until 1967, when the Ku Klux Klan bombed both his synagogue and his home. Most prominently of all, in March 1965 Rabbi Abraham Joshua Heschel marched arm-in-arm with Martin Luther King across Edmund Pettus Bridge in Selma, Alabama, where 400 unarmed black demonstrators were attacked, beaten and shot; Heschel also stood with Dr King in 1968 outside Arlington National Cemetery in Virginia, in protest at the Vietnam War.

Culturally and ethnically, Dylan's heritage was far closer to these religious activists than to Woody Guthrie. Yet it wouldn't have occurred to him even to treat them as role models, let alone to recast himself in their image. These men dedicated their lives to social justice, to ameliorating the lot of others, while Bob's protest phase only lasted a few years. Even though Woody had belonged to an earlier age, emulating him was far more appropriate for Dylan. It helped him to become the person he wanted to be, 'to set out to become what he is', as his brother David told Andrea Svedberg. It was music, the desire to innovate and push boundaries, that gave Dylan his authenticity, not politics. He would just have to put up with articles like the one that appeared in *Newsweek*.

MURDER MOST FOUL

A little more than two weeks after the *Newsweek* article appeared, on Friday 22 November, President Kennedy was assassinated in Dallas, Texas. Kennedy had embodied all the optimism that had ushered in the 1960s; a new decade of hope and transformation. Widely regarded as the man who would revitalise America, helping the nation to reach the potential its citizens always knew lay in store, Kennedy's murder shocked the world. For decades afterwards, anyone who was asked was able to instantly recall exactly where they were and what they were doing when they heard the news that the President had been killed. It was a defining moment in history – and a personal trauma for millions.

Two days after the murder, Kennedy's assassin, Lee Harvey Oswald, was himself murdered, at the Dallas Police Headquarters, by a local nightclub owner, Jack Ruby. Tragedy risked turning into farce.

Dylan was reportedly stunned by the assassination but musically he remained silent. It would take him more than half a century until he sang about it, in 'Murder Most Foul', a track on his 2020 album *Rough and Rowdy Ways*.

Perhaps he was still in a bad way because of the *Newsweek* article, or maybe, as has been suggested, he had just drunk too much. Either way, a month after the President's assassination Dylan was invited by the Emergency Civil Liberties Committee to receive the Tom Paine Award at their annual fundraising dinner. It was a prestigious invitation, the honouree the previous year had been the distinguished pacifist philosopher and Nobel Prize winner, Bertrand Russell. Dylan was embarrassed to accept the honour, saying all he had done was to write a few songs. Nevertheless he went along to the dinner, where there were around 1,500 dignitaries of the Old Left. By the time the award was about to be presented, and he was due to speak, he'd had quite a lot to drink. When he rose to speak, most of his speech was nonsense.

He told his audience that he was accepting the award on behalf of all those who had made an illegal visit to Cuba, 'because they're all young and it's took me a long time to get young and now I consider myself young and I'm proud of it. I'm proud that I'm young. And I only wish that all you people who are sitting out here today or tonight weren't here and I could see all kinds of faces with hair on their head.' He rambled on in a similar vein for a while, then said he needed to be honest: 'I got to admit that the man who shot President Kennedy, Lee Oswald, I don't know exactly what he thought he was doing, but I got to admit honestly that I too, I saw some of myself in him. I don't think it would have gone – I don't think it could go that far, but I got to stand up and say I saw things that he felt, in me – not to go that far and shoot.'[19]

It was not Bob Dylan's finest hour, but, notwithstanding his drunken rambling, he was putting across a valid point of view. Those who had gone to Havana, in whose name he reiterated he was accepting the award, had been associated with the left-wing, pro-communist Student Committee for Travel to Cuba. They had been invited by the Cuban Federation of Universities to travel on an all-expenses-paid trip, to see and evaluate Cuba for themselves. Their acceptance of the invitation was a direct challenge to President Kennedy's policy of non-tolerance towards Cuba, and contravened his ban on anyone travelling there. It had been rumoured that Oswald was a card-carrying member of the Fair Play for Cuba

Committee, a group associated with the Student Committee. The Warren Commission, which began to investigate President Kennedy's assassination in February 1964, would accuse Oswald of membership of the Fair Play Committee.[20]

There was therefore an implied connection between Kennedy's assassin and the students who had gone to Cuba, all of whom were purposely flaunting Kennedy's ban on travel to the country. In his speech, Dylan had told the audience that he did not see why people should not go to Cuba and had said that Phillip Luce, one of the leaders of the student trip, was a friend of his. The point that Dylan was trying to get across, in his convoluted, disjointed speech, was that he, Luce and Lee Harvey Oswald were all of the same mind, in opposing Kennedy's ban on travel to Cuba. That did not mean that he would have gone as far as Oswald; he would not have shot the President. But he shared Oswald's alleged point of view about the travel ban.

That is all he was trying to say. But of course, it did not come across like that. And a few days later, after he had sobered up, he sent a letter to the Emergency Civil Liberties Committee, together with a poem in which he offered to return the award and make up for any donations that may have been lost due to his speech.

Years later Dylan explained to the interviewer Nat Hentoff what was going through his mind that night:

> As soon as I got there, I felt up tight . . . I began to drink. I looked down from the platform and saw a bunch of people who had nothing to do with my kind of politics. I looked down and I got scared . . . I got up to leave, and they followed me and caught me. They told me I had to accept the award. When I got up to make my speech, I couldn't say anything by that time but what was passing through my mind. They'd been talking about Kennedy being killed, and Bill Moore and Medgar Evers and the Buddhist monks in Vietnam being killed. I had to say something about Lee Oswald. I told them I'd read a lot of his feelings in the papers,

and I knew he was up tight. Said I'd been up tight, too, so I'd got
a lot of his feelings. I saw a lot of myself in Oswald, I said, and I
saw in him a lot of the times we're all living in . . . They actually
thought I was saying it was a good thing Kennedy had been killed.
That's how far out they are.'[21]

SOUL BARIN'

The *Newsweek* piece and the criticism he received after his Emergency
Civil Liberties Committee speech weighed heavily on Dylan's spirit.
It wasn't helped by the general mood in the country; the President's
assassination had left many people feeling as if all their optimism, all
their hope for the future, had been drained away. The former Vice
President, Lyndon Baines Johnson, now walked in Kennedy's shoes.
Few knew who he was and none credited him with the motivation
or talent to maintain the dead President's agenda of radical change.
He knew this and sought to prove those who doubted him wrong,
vowing that he would make Kennedy's overriding priority, the Civil
Rights Bill, his own. 'We have taught long enough about equal rights
in this country. We have talked for 100 years or more. It is time now
to write the next chapter and to write it in the books of law.' His
words were designed to reassure, to calm fears, particularly among
the African American community and the activists who worked
among them, that the search for the shadowy, conspiratorial figures
believed to have been behind Oswald's deed might strengthen
the hands of the security and investigatory agencies; that it might
usher in a new era of repression and authoritarianism. The fear was
compounded every time Lyndon Johnson opened his mouth; he was
a Texan, speaking in a Southern drawl only too familiar to black
Americans. It was the drawl of the segregationist, the racist, the
oppressor. Johnson had to do more than say the right words. He
had to demonstrate he was sincere about equal rights and the fight
against poverty. The nation would take some convincing.

In late 1963 Dylan wrote a letter to Sis Cunningham, the editor of *Broadside* magazine, and her husband, Gordon Friesen. It was an open letter, intended for publication, running to six pages. The editors inserted it in their 20 January 1964 edition and announced it on the front cover as 'An article by Bob Dylan'. It was far more than an article, however. It was the most open and frank unveiling of Bob Dylan's heart that anyone, *Broadside* reader or not, had ever read. Coming from a young man who had worked so hard and for so long to shelter himself and his origins from the piercing gaze of reality. It was a revelation.

Dylan wrote the same way as he sang, a flurry of words, light on punctuation, devoid of final 'g's, a stream of consciousness worthy of anything written by Burroughs or Kerouac but lacking the niceties of regular spelling. It is clear from the start that he was feeling troubled; at the very beginning of the letter he declares how hard it is for him to be famous. He finds it hard, he said, to walk down the same streets as he did before because now he knows there will be someone waiting for his autograph, someone, he complains, who will treasure his handwriting more than their own. He doesn't like being asked for autographs, though sometimes he does; he feels he is living in a contradiction.

Much of the letter is taken up with complaints, about people who fail to understand why he writes the way he does, about his guilt at not being able to give enough of his new income to people who need it:

. . . how can I help not feel guilty
I walk down on the bowery and give money away
an still I feel guilty for I know I do not have enuff money t give
    away . . .
an people say 'think a yourself, dylan, you're
gonna need it someday' an I say yeah yeah
an I think maybe about it for a split second
but then the floods of vomit guilt swoop my

drunken head an I spread forth more gut torn
bloody money from the depths of my forsaken
pockets . . . an I whisper 'ah it's so useless'
man so many people need so many things
an what am I anyway? some kind a messiah walkin
around . . . ?

The state of his apartment comes in for particular abuse; the place is filthy and his clothes are strewn across the floor, though that doesn't seem to be his own fault. But the floor is tilting and rotting, plaster is falling off the walls, the heat goes off at ten, and he is woken up in the morning by 'gushes of warm, smelly heat . . . but somehow there is a beauty to it'. He knows he is getting screwed by the landlord, who is charging an exorbitant rent, but he doesn't have the time to go down to the rent-control board.

In his letter, he saves his most revealing anger for people in the folk world who are against the blacklist but refuse to speak out against it and are willing to appear on TV shows which refuse to accept blacklisted artists. Not just the singers, he insists, but their managers and agents too: 'they are the dishonest ones / for they are never seen / they play both sides against each other / an expect t be respected by everybody'.[22]

He had in mind ABC-TV's *Hootenanny* show, which in its heyday attracted an audience of up to 11 million viewers. In mid-twentieth-century folk-music parlance a hootenanny is a concert usually featuring a variety of performers, often turning up and playing impromptu. There was nothing impromptu about the eponymous TV show, it was little more than a musical variety show, cashing in on the folk boom, giving it a title that Pete Seeger had been using for years to describe the folk concerts he had been staging. But, contrary to the association of the name with Seeger, and in blatant violation of the democratic, inclusive spirit of a real hootenanny, the ABC-TV network refused to allow the blacklisted Pete Seeger or his group The Weavers to appear. The resulting uproar saw a host of folk

artists boycott the programme, the likes of Joan Baez, Peter, Paul
and Mary, Dave Van Ronk, The Kingston Trio, Ramblin' Jack Elliott
and of course Dylan. But these stars of the folk scene were not
the heroes of the *Hootenanny* boycott, wrote Dylan in his letter to
Broadside. They were successful, they could afford not to appear, and
if they had done so they risked being boycotted in turn at college
gigs, by students opposed to the blacklist. No, wrote Dylan, the real
heroes of the *Hootenanny* boycott were the people who would have
welcomed the fee that the show would pay them, but boycotted it
anyway. He listed Tom Paxton, Barbara Dane and Johnny Herald as
among those heroes, people who placed their consciences ahead of
possible material gain.

Without meaning to, in his letter Dylan had cast a light on the
damaging seepage of commercialism into the folk world. Folk artists
still saw themselves as a community of people whose music pushed
back against injustice and prejudice, who fought for civil rights and
equal opportunities. But the moneyed world of the record labels,
promoters and managers was splitting them in two. There were
the stars, Joan Baez, The Kingston Trio, Bob Dylan, Peter, Paul and
Mary, good people all. And then there were the less successful, or
never-to-be successful, folk singers; still playing on the small club
circuits, perhaps with a recording contract but not selling much,
or still hoping that a record producer would look their way. There
was no animosity between the two groups, far from it, but the folk
world was dividing. Reporting in the *Village Voice* on Pete Seeger's
exclusion from the programme, the journalist Nat Hentoff wrote,
'some of the singers who are going to appear have called fiercely
for the abolition of the House Un-American Activities Committee.
But by being part of *Hootenanny*, they have aligned themselves with
exactly the same vigilante "justice" which the HUAC represents.'

The split between those successful or principled enough to stand
up to commercial and political pressure, and those desperate for
recognition at any price, would ultimately contribute to the end of
the folk revival. Its decline was hastened by the arrival of the new

genre of 1960s pop, but the signs were in place even before The Beatles arrived. Folk music's day in the limelight had passed and protest songs, of which Dylan had been one of the most consistent exponents, were slipping out of vogue. The world of young people's music was a-changin', and so too was Bob Dylan.

Dylan's letter to Sis Cunningham and Gordon Friesen at *Broadside* can be read as his farewell to the folk world that had nurtured him since his arrival in New York. He didn't couch it in those terms and he continued to contribute to *Broadside* for many years, right up until 1978. But he was drifting away and he was cutting himself off from many of his early friends, not least from Suze Rotolo. He says in his letter that he still loved Suze, that he wished he could love everyone the way he loved her.

He ended his letter by telling Sis and Gordon they shouldn't think that he was no longer with them; when in fact he was with them more than ever, that theirs was the only paper whose side he was on. It was as good a way as any to say that he was moving on. With a final dig at *Newsweek* magazine, which he hoped to see burning in his dreams, and a signing off from the heart, he was gone.

5

A-CHANGIN'

RESPONDIN'

Dylan recorded his follow-up album to *Freewheelin'* during August and October 1963, though *The Times They Are A-Changin'* wasn't released until February 1964. Laid down over the course of six studio sessions, it was an album composed almost entirely of protest and topical songs, with his 'Boots of Spanish Leather' the only conventional love ballad. Ostensibly a tender exchange between a departing traveller and her lover who is left behind, the song may have been prompted by Suze's departure for Italy to study art. 'Boots of Spanish Leather' opens wistfully with the forsaken lover declaring he wants her to send no gifts or mementoes from her travels. As the song progresses he receives a letter saying she does not know when she will be back, it depends on how she's a-feelin'. In disappointment, or perhaps anger, he declares that he is certain her heart is no longer with him, that it is set on the place to which she is going.

If 'Boots of Spanish Leather' is a song of love for Suze and his disappointment, then 'One Too Many Mornings' is a darker reflection of their disintegrating relationship, perhaps written as the reality of his once again empty life sets in, as he turns his head back to the room where his love and he have lain. He has now realised that what lies between them cannot be reconciled. They are too far apart. Too much time has elapsed and the distance between them is insurmountable.

As far as his public was concerned, and more widely in the popular imagination, Dylan was still regarded as a folk singer. But, with the exception of 'Boots of Spanish Leather' and 'North Country Blues', *The Times They Are A-Changin'* was no longer an album of folk music, at least not of the conventional kind. Perhaps that is why it spoke to his generation, even more than *Freewheelin'* had done. Not because Dylan now had a better rapport with his peers; he had matured as an artist, composer and poet, but there is no substantive difference between his compositions on *Freewheelin'* and *The Times They Are A-Changin'*. Nor was it that Dylan had grown closer to his generation. Rather, they had grown closer to him. The album's title track, far and away the most outstanding piece in the collection, said it all. The times they were a-changing, and Bob Dylan was far-sighted enough to articulate it first. But he was only responding to what was going on in the world, to the growing awareness among the maturing baby-boomers of the scale and extent of the injustices taking place all around them, and the dangerous times in which they lived.

Three of the songs addressed the civil rights issue directly. He had sung 'Only a Pawn in Their Game' when he travelled with Pete Seeger and Theo Bikel to the cotton fields of Greenwood, Mississippi, to support the voter-registration campaign. He sang it again at Newport and at the March on Washington in 1963. The black civil rights leader Medgar Evers had been shot in the back in June that year as he walked from his car to his home in Jackson, Mississippi. His murderer was a deluded white supremacist, a small-time salesman named Byron De la Beckwith. It took 31 years and three trials for the courts to convict Beckwith. The first two trials, conducted in 1964, ended up with the all-white juries unable to reach a majority. He was finally brought to justice in 1994 after a lengthy campaign by Medgar Evers' widow Myrlie. Beckwith ended up with a life sentence, dying in jail seven years later at the age of 80. A 1996 movie, *Ghosts of Mississippi*, directed by Rob Reiner, chronicles the struggle to bring him to justice.

The murder of Medgar Evers caused a national outcry. *Life* magazine printed a picture of his funeral on the cover, with additional photos inside. They ran an angry editorial, headlined 'Martyr to an Immoral System', blaming the mayor of Evers' home town of Jackson for presiding over a racist culture, noting that 350 black demonstrators were arrested in the wake of the murder and that a procession leaving his funeral was broken up by police wielding guns and clubs. Like Dylan, Phil Ochs wrote a song about the murder, singing his 'Ballad of Medgar Evers' at the Newport Folk Festival in 1963.

The darkest song on *The Times They Are A-Changin'* is 'The Ballad of Hollis Brown', telling the story of a farmer and his family in South Dakota who live in abject poverty, starving, desperate and devoid of all hope. The farmer, Hollis Brown, can see no future, his well is empty of water, and the rats have eaten his flour. His empty-eyed children cannot smile and his wife is screaming in anguish. He has one dollar left. He spends it on shotgun shells and kills his family before turning the gun on himself. Dylan ends the song daring his listeners to find meaning in the family's death, to not turn a blind eye to their suffering. He sings of seven people dying on the farm, while far off in the distance an identical number is born. 'Do you imagine this is how I think?' he seems to be asking his audience. Cynicism is too easy, he implies.

The theme of starving farmers is one that Dylan would return to later in his career. He played at the Live Aid concert in July 1985, a global, multi-venue ensemble of rock artists put together by Bob Geldof and Midge Ure in response to a devastating famine in Ethiopia, one of the first famines to be graphically played out on our TV screens, in the days before the world became desensitised to hunger. Playing alongside The Rolling Stones' Keith Richards and Ron Wood, Dylan played 'The Ballad of Hollis Brown'. When he finished he said it was a fitting song for such an important occasion. 'I'd just like to say, I hope that some of the money that's raised for the people of Africa, maybe they could take just a little bit of it, maybe one or two million, and use it, say, to pay the mortgages on some of the farms that the farmers here owe to the banks.' His appeal led, two months later, to a benefit concert organised by the country singer Willie Nelson in aid of American farmers. Held in Champaign, Illinois, in front of an audience of 80,000 people, the event raised $9 million. Dylan played there also, and at Farm Aid II, held the next year at Manor Downs Racetrack in Texas. Farm Aid became an annual event; Dylan returned for the 37th Festival in 2023.

Perhaps even more disturbing than 'The Ballad of Hollis Brown' was Dylan's real-life account (cited earlier) of the murder, a year earlier, of the black waitress Hattie Carroll by an uber-privileged, 24-year-old tobacco farmer William Zantzinger. Drunk, abusive and obnoxious, the perpetrator had struck her with his cane because she was serving him too slowly. Zantzinger was given a six-month prison sentence. Each verse ends with a refrain telling those who philosophise and criticise to take their rags away from their face for this is not the time for their tears. When he reached the final verse, reporting on the six-month sentence that the perpetrator received, Dylan changed the refrain, telling his listeners that now was the time for their tears.

Despite, or perhaps because of, its topicality and Dylan's factual reportage, 'The Lonesome Death of Hattie Carroll' has never achieved the same prominence as many of his other songs. Certainly not to the same extent as 'With God on Our Side', a masterly, ironic polemic ridiculing the generals and politicians who claim divine sanction for their wars.

Like 'Masters of War' on the *Freewheelin'* album, 'With God on Our Side' is a no-holds-barred condemnation of the vanity and stupidity of warmongers and the utter futility of war, the most debased of all human endeavours. Ten years later, Leonard Cohen would tell an interviewer that 'war is wonderful' because of what it demands from its participants. 'Everybody is responsible for his brother. The sense of community and kinship and brotherhood, devotion. There are opportunities to feel things that you simply cannot feel in modern city life.'¹ Dylan was having none of that. The glorification of war is absurd, the triumphalist myths that poorly educated people are taught to swallow are an insult to their intelligence. Far from God being on the side of every belligerent who claims it to be so, Dylan concludes that if God were truly on our side he would stop the next war.

INVADIN'

The Times They Are A-Changin' was released on 10 February 1964. The previous evening, a world-record audience, an estimated 73 million viewers, had turned on their TV sets to watch *The Ed Sullivan Show*. Sullivan was hosting the first live appearance in America of The Beatles, the band whose name would become almost synonymous with pop music for the remainder of the 1960s.

Four young men from Liverpool, all roughly the same age as Dylan, give or take a year or two, The Beatles had already been a phenomenon in Britain for over a year. Their first single, 'Love Me Do', released in October 1962, had reached number 17 in the British charts – an encouraging but not an outstanding start – but three months later their follow-up, 'Please Please Me', reached number 1. So did all but two of their subsequent singles, for the rest of the decade. On Christmas Day in 1963 The Beatles were sitting in the top two places in both the British singles and album charts, with another three discs in the top 30. Singles always sold much faster than albums in those days, but their album *With The Beatles* was selling so quickly it even reached number 15 in the singles chart. Britain had never seen a music phenomenon like it.

But it wasn't just their record sales that made The Beatles such a sensation. What set them apart from every other performer in the history of music, even the biggest like Elvis and Sinatra, was the reception their fans gave them. It was impossible to attend a Beatles concert and hear what they were playing, the auditorium was thick with the sound of teenage girls screaming, often weeping, at their idols. Clamouring crowds would gather outside the Abbey Road Recording Studios in London – nothing more than a large but not particularly striking detached house in a residential street – whenever a rumour went around that The Beatles were recording there. The crowds would gather too, even if the band weren't recording there, as if the very sound of their screams and their teenage excitability might make The Beatles magically appear. The four young men from Liverpool were mobbed wherever they went.

The English media, which until now had been pretty snooty about young people's music, jumped on the bandwagon. They published profiles and interviews with The Beatles, and with everyone who had ever known them. Journalists remarked constantly on their 'zany' sense of humour, coined the world Beatlemania to describe their fans' behaviour, and rewarded the 'Fab Four' for their canny understanding of the power of image by devoting columns to their identical 'mop-head' haircuts and high-collared Nehru jackets. Then, when tired of eulogising them, or perhaps thinking that a different tack might sell even more newspapers, the media harrumphed about the damage that was being done to the morals and discipline of the younger generation and complained about stampedes when Beatles concert tickets went on sale. They ridiculed a judge for asking in court, 'Who are the Beatles?', and mocked the answer he received, 'a popular beat combo', even more.[2]

Teenage boys of course tried to assert themselves. They bought guitars, formed themselves into bands, became suddenly fashion-conscious and tried as hard as they could to become the 'next new thing'. One school banned its pupils from wearing their hair in Beatles fashion, with the headmaster saying 'This ridiculous style brings out the worst in boys physically. It makes them look like morons.'³

The Beatles were still to make it in America. They had released three singles in America during 1963 but only one of them, 'From Me to You', entered the charts; it peaked at number 116 in May. But the American media were on their case; by November the band had received enough breathless coverage in the USA for *Time* magazine to run a piece on them. Under the headline 'Singers: The New Madness', and describing them as a 'wild rhythm-and-blues quartet', the magazine sneered at their popularity in Britain, as if all they were doing was something that had been done in America for generations. The writer pontificated that 'Americans might find the Beatles achingly familiar (their songs consist mainly of "Yeh!" screamed to the accompaniment of three guitars and a thunderous drum).' *Time*'s coverage of The Beatles wasn't quite the hatchet job that *Newsweek* had meted out to Dylan a couple of weeks earlier, but it wasn't far off. Not that The Beatles would have minded. They were loving it all, whether snooty publicity or sycophantic praise. They had played in front of the Queen Mother a few weeks earlier, telling her she could rattle her jewellery instead of clapping. One could almost hear the apoplectic flames issuing from the nostrils of England's ageing colonels as they reeled from the disrespect shown to the nation's beloved former monarch. But the Queen Mum was not interested in stuffy English snobbery. 'Then the Beatles broke into 'From Me to You', and the Queen Mother beamed.'⁴

The Beatles landed in New York on 7 February 1964. Almost overnight they had become a sensation in the United States. 'I Want to Hold Your Hand' was number 1 in the charts. They were greeted at the airport by 200 reporters, 100 police officers and 3,000 fans cheering and screaming from the roof of the terminal building. Old newsreel clips show the four of them standing on the steps of the plane, overwhelmed but loving every moment. They stayed in America for two weeks, playing the Washington

Coliseum, performing twice at Carnegie Hall, and making an unprecedented three appearances in consecutive weeks on *The Ed Sullivan Show*.

The Beatles had flown home by the time Dylan's *The Times They Are A-Changin'* entered *Billboard*'s LP charts on 7 March, nearly four weeks after its release. The album came in at number 109, far below The Beatles, who occupied the top two places. Their record label had just announced that over the previous six months the Fab Four had grossed $17 million in album sales, and that figure did not include the value of their receipts in America. But The Beatles' record sales and dominance of the charts didn't tell the full story. Dylan's recordings, and those of the artists who sang his material, dominated the charts. *Freewheelin'* was still there at number 89, Joan Baez had five albums in the listings, and Peter, Paul and Mary three. Their most recent album *In the Wind* was in fourth place. Its title was a nod to 'Blowin' in the Wind', one of three Dylan compositions on their album, the others being 'Don't Think Twice, It's All Right' and the lesser-known 'Quit Your Low Down Ways'.

It was evident that the music business was going through rapid convulsions. The folk-music revival, which had never grossed big bucks anyway, was being overtaken by a more commercial and less politically contentious commodity. In Britain, the success of The Beatles had supercharged the industry; record sales were booming as never before, with dozens of new bands emerging. If America were to follow the same path, there was little doubt that teenage tastes, rather than more mature preferences, would continue to dominate the music industry for the foreseeable future.

Prescient as always, Dylan had seen much of it coming. He'd played Carnegie Hall at the end of the previous October, just as The Beatles were starting to have an impact in America. For the first time in his career there were teenyboppers in the audience. They weren't quite sure what they'd come to hear, but if Dylan was anything like The Beatles they knew they would be in for a good evening. Dylan rose to the occasion. He spoke to the audience more

Bob Dylan playing
guitar in Columbia
Recording Studio
for a session in
September 1961 in
New York.

Walking with
his girlfriend
Suze Rotolo in
September 1961
in New York.

(Clockwise from top) Dylan and his girlfriend Suze Rotolo pose for a portrait in New York, in September 1961; Performing on stage at Gerde's Folk City in 1961; An advertisement for Dylan's first New York concert, presented by the Folklore Center at Carnegie Chapter Hall on November 4, 1961.

THE FOLKLORE CENTER

Presents

BOB DYLAN

IN HIS FIRST NEW YORK CONCERT

SAT. NOV. 4, 1961   8:40pm

CARNEGIE CHAPTER HALL

154 WEST 57th STREET • NEW YORK CITY

All seats $2.00

Tickets available at: The Folklore Center
                          110 MacDougal Street
GR7- 5987   New York City 12, New York

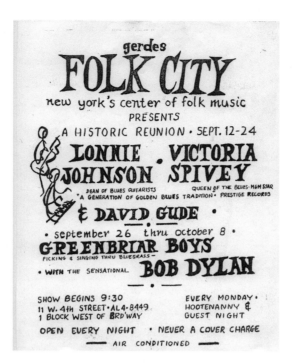

(Above) Poster advertising several performances at Gerde's Folk City, New York, in September 1961. (Below) Dylan performing live on stage at the Singers Club Christmas party on his first visit to Britain, December 22, 1962.

(Above) Lovebirds & Songbirds: Dylan and Joan Baez perform together on stage in 1963; (Right) Dylan performs 'Talkin' John Birch Paranoid Blues' during rehearsals for an appearance on *The Ed Sullivan Show,* New York, on May 12, 1963. After the rehearsal, Dylan was asked to perform a different song for the broadcast, a request he refused; he walked out of the studio and never appeared on the broadcast.

Dylan poses for a portrait to promote the release of his album *The Times they Are A-Changin'* in January 1965.

Dylan and Joan Baez seated together in London, England, April 1965.

(Right) Dylan on the grass of the tennis court at the Newport Casino (later the International Tennis Hall of Fame) during the Newport Folk Festival, July 1963; (Below) Joan Baez and Dylan sharing a stage during a duet at the Newport Folk Festival, Rhode Island, 1963. This was his first performance on the Newport stage.

The cover for the Bob Dylan album *The Freewheelin' Bob Dylan*,
released by Columbia Records in 1963. The cover features Dylan
and his girlfriend Suze Rotolo walking near their apartment in
Greenwich Village, New York.

(Above) Bob Dylan with Brian Jones of the Rolling Stones in 1965 in New York City.

(Below) Bob Dylan at a press conference after his arrival in Stockholm where he is to perform.

than usual, though he was as cryptic as ever. He introduced his final song, 'When the Ship Comes In', by telling them that:

> I wanna sing one song here recognizing that there are Goliaths nowadays. An' people don't realize just who the Goliaths are but in older days Goliath was slayed and everybody looks back nowadays and sees how Goliath was. Nowadays there are crueller Goliaths who do crueller things but one day they gonna be slain too. An' people 2,000 years from now can look back an' say 'remember when Goliath the second was slain'.[5]

It wasn't quite John Lennon telling the Queen Mother to rattle her jewellery. Much of what he said that evening would have gone way over the heads of his new teenage fans.

For a while it had looked as if the *Newsweek* article and his disastrous speech to the Emergency Civil Liberties Committee had buried Dylan's career before it really started. By the end of 1963 it was obvious that such fears were misplaced. Dylan was poised to break out as a global star. He'd written 34 new songs that year, had released one LP, with another on the way, his songs were scattered on albums and singles across the charts, he'd played dozens of concerts, appeared on radio and TV, been featured in *Time*, *Playboy* and yes, *Newsweek*. His rise had been stellar. Yet, within a few weeks, at least as far as the fickle media was concerned, he had been eclipsed: The Beatles was the name on everybody's lips. On his lips too. Bob Dylan thought they were great.

Early in his career some had accused Dylan of being opportunistic. He hinted at it himself, telling Nat Hentoff in an interview for *The New Yorker* that he had written some of his music 'because I didn't see anybody else doing that kind of thing'.[6] They would accuse him of opportunism once more when he went electric in 1965. But they misunderstood him. Dylan was a man who understood the inevitability of change. He had been changing all his life, even if sometimes it was more in his imagination than in reality. His Jewish psyche had been moulded by ancestors preternaturally sensitive to impending change, to disasters, persecutions, pogroms and upheavals that could permanently disrupt the course of their lives in a flash. He had set out to become a disciple of Woody Guthrie, largely because of the way that Woody had stood firm, maintaining his principles and values even in the face of destructive social and cultural change taking place at a degree never experienced before. It was no coincidence that Bob had written 'The Times They Are A-Changin' – or that the song had become a launchpad for his career.

Alert and sensitive to change, Dylan perceived from the appeal and success of The Beatles that the folk revival had run its course, that a new music was emerging and that its most ardent consumers would be teenagers. He was not an opportunist about to jump aboard The Beatles bandwagon just because they were the most popular band in the world. But he was a man whose thoughts ran deep, who had more to say than the topical messages of protest he had been declaiming since his arrival in Greenwich Village. He needed an audience, not for his ego but for his fulfilment. Like all artists, all creatives, all people of vision, his life had purpose. If he had to change the way in which he communicated, replace the tools he wielded to achieve his purpose, because the old way had gone and the former tools were damaged and rusty, so be it. That is what he would do.

So he paid attention to The Beatles. He would have done anyway, he liked their music and found it exhilarating. Yet he listened, not just with the ears of a fan, but with the scholarly attention of an analyst. He listened to The Beatles, and he learnt. And he realised that he could do so much more, achieve even greater things, if he only gave himself the freedom to evolve.

Not since the Zimmerman days of his youth in Hibbing, listening to Hank Williams, Little Richard and of course Woody, had Bobby listened so intensely to a musical style. He told Anthony Scaduto:

They were doing things nobody was doing. Their chords were outrageous . . . and the harmonies made it all valid. You could only do that with other musicians. Even if you're playing your own chords, you had to have other people playing with you. That was obvious. And it started me thinking about other people . . . You see, there was a lot of hypocrisy all around, people saying it has to be either folk or rock. But I knew it didn't have to be like that. I dug what The Beatles were doing, and I always kept it in mind from back then.[7]

The reason why Dylan's musical style evolved after he heard The Beatles was not because he was an opportunist, or because he wanted to copy them. His style changed because he realised there was so much more he could be doing.

Of course he wasn't alone in wanting to evolve, in wanting to do things differently, to try new things. In the early 1960s novelty was the hallmark of his generation. Whether it was experimentation with drugs or sexual liberation, with participation in political protest, with new models of communal living and family structures, with rejection of long-established social norms and values, this was a generation unafraid to push back the boundaries. And despite Bob Dylan having no intention or great desire to speak for them, to become their voice, in some ways that is what he already was. Because he was able to think faster and see further. Some called him a prophet for telling the world that the times were a-changin'. It wasn't prophecy, it was insight. It wasn't just the times that were a-changin'. He was a-changin' too. But unlike those who wanted to change the world, for Dylan the changes were in music, style and creativity: listening to The Beatles, realising the potential of playing with others rather than on his own; recognising the limitations inherent in folk music – limitations he was already being accused of breaking away from, in songs like 'With God on Our Side' and 'A Hard Rain's A-Gonna Fall'. Bob Dylan was ready for something new.

Nobody can say for certain which 1960s recording was the first to be categorised as folk-rock. Dylan suggested it was The Animals' version of 'House of the Rising Sun', an old blues number that they backed with an organ, bass and drums, and issued on a four-minute-long vinyl single, four minutes instead of the industry standard two and a half. Dylan had recorded it earlier, on his first album, 'borrowing' the chord changes from Dave Van Ronk. When he asked for permission to use his version, Van Ronk told him he'd rather he didn't, since he was about to record 'House of the Rising Sun' himself. But it was too late, Dylan had recorded the track before asking. Van Ronk, now unable to play or record the song lest he be accused of ripping it off from Dylan, got his revenge after The Animals had a hit with it. Dylan was accused of copying The Animals and he too stopped playing it.[8]

Irrespective of whether The Animals' version of 'House of the Rising Sun' was the progenitor of the genre, folk-rock was where Dylan was heading. It was the genre he would make his own. Not yet though. It was bound to take time until he got it right.

Anyway, there was another album he had to make first. It turned out not to be his best. He had spoken of the benefits of playing alongside others, but he wasn't doing it yet. On his new album, he was still a man with a harmonica and a guitar, even if he seemed to be on the way to becoming something else. Poetically, his lyrics were more sophisticated: playful, three-dimensional, introspective. Topically, there was a distinct lack of complaint and protest. Which was interesting, because his generation were just about to catch up with him, protest-wise.

TRANSITIONIN'

The week that The Beatles landed in New York, Dylan set off with three friends on a road trip. He'd been booked to play four concerts across America and, instead of flying as he would normally have done, they decided to make an odyssey of it. They set off in the Ford station wagon that Albert Grossman had bought with Dylan's fast-accumulating cash pile, with no plans other than to reach Atlanta, Denver, Los Angeles and San Francisco in time for the concerts

Dylan was due to play. They could have been any four young men in a car, off to see America, with their bags of grass, high spirits and sense of adventure. They were not quite travelling light, they carried clothes to donate to striking miners when they reached Kentucky, and Dylan had his typewriter with him; it may have been an adventure but it was to be a working adventure, he had songs to write and audiences to please.

It is hard not to draw a comparison between this journey – with its run-ins with cops, encounters with fans, and a visit to the elderly poet Carl Sandburg – and the one immortalised in Jack Kerouac's *On the Road*, the book that had exerted such a big influence on Dylan a few years earlier. Dylan had once said that the book had lost its appeal for him almost as soon as he had arrived in New York, that he came to consider the lead character, Neal Cassady's alter-ego Dean Moriarty, as purposeless, bumping and grinding his way through life. Dylan was far from purposelessly bumping and grinding, but with three albums behind him and stardom beckoning he was going through a transition. It seemed an appropriate distraction to set off on the road for a while, the first proper break he'd had since arriving in New York.

He had been through many changes since leaving Hibbing; it was only a little over four years since he had bid farewell to his Jewish identity in the frat house in Minneapolis, just three years since he had arrived in New York. Despite appearing to be a fixture on the Village folk scene, he was now on his way again, towards something that looked very much as if it might turn out to be life-changing. Who could blame him if he felt the need to step briefly out of the whirlwind, to reimagine the person he once thought he might be, take a leaf out of Jack Kerouac's book and set off on a road trip across America, as a writer wanting 'a new call and a new horizon' and things to come that were 'too fantastic not to tell'?[9] Maybe he was, after all, still looking for what he had read about in *On the Road*; maybe this trip was to be his last throw of the dice before his destiny kicked in.

Even if sitting in a car travelling across America mimicked to some extent the form of *On the Road*, it was never likely to imbue Dylan with Cassady's 'hungry for kicks' anarchic spirit. But maybe it was this trip that inspired him to reconnect with Kerouac's 'breathless dynamic bop poetry phrases'.[10] Something did, certainly. When he had lived in Minneapolis he had been enthusiastic about Kerouac's poetry, and arriving in Greenwich Village he heard Gregory Corso and Allen Ginsberg read their verse. Yet he had paid little creative attention to the Beats' surreal, linguistic imagery during his folk years. Dylan didn't incorporate their style into his early lyrics and, even when he moved away from singing traditional folk songs, his words remained more suggestive of Guthrie than Ginsberg. But if we listen to some of the lyrics in his next album, *Another Side of Bob Dylan*, released shortly after his road trip, we can hear echoes of Beat imagery gestating. The echoes emerged fully formed a year later, in songs like 'Gates of Eden', 'It's Alright, Ma (I'm Only Bleeding)' and 'Desolation Row' all released in 1965. The road trip across America must have contributed to his poetic evolution; his perhaps unconscious mimicking of *On the Road* being a step on the literary journey that took him away from folk and protest and led him to his own unique style, one which was undisputably Dylan but sprinkled with a handful of Beat seasoning.

Less speculatively, meeting Allen Ginsberg reignited Dylan's youthful interest in the Beats and inspired him to emulate their use of language. He had already heard Ginsberg read several times, but it wasn't until Boxing Day in 1963, shortly before the release of *The Times They Are A-Changin'*, that the two men met. They were introduced by the journalist Al Aronowitz, who invited Dylan to a party being given by the bookseller Ted Wilentz, to celebrate the return to New York of Allen Ginsberg and fellow Beat poet Peter Orlovsky, after two years overseas.

Ginsberg was fifteen years older than Dylan, a fellow Jew, and perhaps something of a father figure to him. A complex character, the son of a severely troubled mother who had spent her life in and out of hospital, Ginsberg opens his most famous poem 'Howl' with the words 'I saw the best minds of my generation destroyed by madness'.[11] He too had been incarcerated, at the age of 23 spending an involuntary eight months in the New York State Psychiatric Institute. Connected both by their Jewishness and an extraordinary capacity for creativity, Dylan and Ginsberg became good friends. They collaborated artistically, most notably when Dylan wrote the music and played keyboards and guitar to accompany Ginsberg's poem 'September on Jessore Road', written after his visit to Bangladesh in the wake of the 1971 war. Ginsberg in turn played the role of poet-in-residence on Dylan's 'Rolling Thunder Revue' tour in 1976.

All that of course was in the future. As he drove with his friends across America, Bob Dylan had more immediate, creative influences on his mind. Beatles songs were blasting out of the car radio, light, catchy cheerful music, and Dylan was listening intently. He enjoyed it. There was no agenda, no politics, no cerebral depth, just music to listen to, so different from anything that had gone before. Dylan was no copycat. Unlike dozens of bands in England and America, he had no aspiration to present himself as a Beatles wannabe.

But he must have wanted to see if he could compose in a similar style. A few weeks after returning from the road trip, in May 1964, he travelled to England, land of The Beatles. He was booked to play at London's Royal Festival Hall and it was there that he introduced the world to 'Mr Tambourine Man'. It is an undisputed Dylan classic yet one that displays all the jaunty hallmarks of Beatles influence. Dylan had once suggested that The Animals had inaugurated the new genre of folk-rock with their 'House of the Rising Sun'. But maybe it was The Byrds, when they released Dylan's 'Mr Tambourine Man' as a single in 1965. Whether this was the world's first folk-rock song or not, one thing was certain. Dylan's protest days were behind him.

Arriving in London in May 1964 Dylan found the British music scene aflame, revelling in the most remarkable period in its history. The astounding success of The Beatles had dispatched talent spotters, record producers and managers to the band's home town of Liverpool, all looking for the next great musical phenomenon. They in turn were inspiring every Liverpudlian youth who could strum a guitar, hammer out a rhythm on the drums, or project a half-decent voice, to go out and join a band. The Mersey Sound, named after Liverpool's river, was captivating the world and driving British music fans into a frenzy. The Searchers, The Swinging Blue Jeans, Cilla Black, Gerry and the Pacemakers, Billy J. Kramer, The Merseybeats, the list went on and on. And it wasn't just bands from Liverpool bedazzling British teenagers. Outfits like The Rolling Stones, The Kinks, Brian Poole and the Tremeloes and The Dave Clark Five, all from London, The Animals from Newcastle, Freddie and the Dreamers and The Hollies from Manchester – every town was joining the party. For the first time ever, British pop and rock fans were listening and dancing to local artists, new pretenders to The Beatles' crown emerging every day, bringing decades of American musical hegemony to an end. This was the furore that the American-born Bob Dylan, latterly of remote Midwestern Hibbing, was flying into. He could so easily have sunk like a stone.

He did not sink. Far from it. British fans, The Rolling Stones among them, swarmed to the 2,700-seat Royal Festival Hall; had the auditorium been twice the size they would still have filled it. Dylan, having forgotten his capo, the clamp used to shorten his guitar strings, had to call out from the stage, asking to borrow one. He played 18 numbers. Opening with 'The Times They Are A-Changin'', he treated the audience to the first-ever performance of 'Mr Tambourine Man' and delivered the last-ever outing of the obscure 'Eternal Circle' (reincarnated on the 'Rare and Unreleased' Bootleg album of 1991). His performance was loud, confident and assertive.

The audience loved him. Even the staid *Times* newspaper praised him, or at least his sincerity, though, they said, his enunciation was poor and his voice untamed and pinched. Anointing him a 'Minnesota Minstrel', the newspaper declared that musically, he inclined to monotony and questioned his right to be called a folk singer at all — a judgement Dylan would almost certainly have concurred with. But, the report graciously if somewhat obscurely concluded, 'this saint of the outsiders influences, probably benignly, a large and captive audience'.[12]

The Royal Festival Hall concert was not Dylan's first trip to the country. He had been to England twice before, but he'd never had a reception like this. No longer a Greenwich Village folk singer, this was Bob Dylan, a star in the making. He included several protest songs in his set, among them 'With God on Our Side', 'The Lonesome Death of Hattie Carroll' and the little-known 'Who Killed Davey Moore?'. But they came across as songs, rather than protests; the audience applauded each one politely, and even if some were outraged by the injustices he sang about, there was little indication that they thought him a campaigner for social justice.

FREEDOM SUMMER

Back home that summer of 1964, Dylan demonstrated even more conclusively that he had indeed moved on. It was a year since he had flown with Pete Seeger and Theo Bikel to Greenwood, Mississippi, to support the campaign for voter registration conducted by the Students' National Coordinating Committee. Now, 12 months later, the campaign was heating up. Students were arriving in Mississippi from across America, over 1,000 of them altogether, mainly white middle-class kids, including a disproportionate number of Jews. They volunteered alongside African American activists from Mississippi, instituting and running Freedom Schools in the churches, leading protests outside courthouses, organising meetings and knocking on doors, to encourage disenfranchised blacks to register their names in the voter registry.

The violence broke out just as soon as the campaign began. At first, it was the usual brutality by the Mississippi police and sheriff, bullying cops harassing volunteers, breaking up meetings, clubbing those who stood in their way and arresting activists. The 10,000-strong membership of the Ku Klux Klan enthusiastically joined in, intimidating and beating the local black population, attacking any white volunteers who they believed had pro-black sympathies, and pointlessly erecting wooden crosses just so they could set them on fire.

Then, on 21 June three young men disappeared. Two, Michael Schwerner and James Chaney, were employees of the Congress of Racial Equality, Andrew Goodman was a student volunteer. Chaney was a black activist from Mississippi, Schwerner and Goodman were both New York Jews. They had been to visit the burnt-out remains of Mount Zion church, one of 20 churches firebombed that summer by the Ku Klux Klan. Three weeks earlier Schwerner and Chaney had spoken at the church, urging its black congregation to register to vote. The three young men had visited the church again, three days after it was bombed, and had been arrested by a deputy sheriff on their way home. Briefly locked up in a police station, they were released at 10 p.m. the same evening and told to get out of the county. They were never seen again.

The search for them made the headlines nationally. Within 36 hours their disappearance had become a media-fuelled scandal. Over the course of the next six weeks President Johnson and Attorney General Robert Kennedy met their parents and ordered the director of the FBI, J. Edgar Hoover, to launch a major investigation and assist with the search. As they combed the area the searchers found eight bodies of African American men, all recently murdered. Only three were ever identified. After a tip-off, the bodies of Chaney, Goodman and Schwerner were discovered on a farm – 44 days later.

The search for the three young men uncovered a whole host of other, racially motivated crimes. By the end of the ten-week voter-registration campaign, four activists, including Schwerner, Chaney and Goodman had been murdered, four others were seriously wounded, 37 churches and 30 black homes had been set on fire or bombed. Over 1,000 volunteers and civil rights workers had been arrested. It was a civil rights catastrophe on a scale never before seen in the United States.

Even so, the campaign had some success. It didn't have a great impact on voter numbers in Mississippi but it helped keep the question of civil rights at the top of the national agenda. The Civil Rights Act had been passed in Washington just as the campaign was taking off, the events surrounding the voter-registration drive helped ease public acceptance of the new laws. The ten weeks of the campaign have been known as Freedom Summer ever since.

Dylan's near contemporaries Tom Paxton, Paul Simon and Art Garfunkel led the music fellowship's response to the murder of the civil rights activists and the lawlessness of the Mississippi summer. Tom Paxton's 1965 recording 'Goodman and Schwerner and Chaney' recalls the searchers' desperation as time ticked away with no sign of the men; the pain that the victims suffered and the smug cynicism of the murderers and their white-supremacist allies. Paul Simon rewrote the lyrics to 'He Was My Brother', a song he and Art Garfunkel had first recorded a few months before the events of summer 1964. He dedicated it to Andrew Goodman, who had been a classmate of his in New York and a friend to him and Garfunkel. But neither Paxton, Simon nor any other lament or eulogy from a white folk singer came anywhere close to the sorrow and rage of Nina Simone's 'Mississippi Goddam'. She had written the song the previous year, when four black girls were killed in a church bombing in Alabama, and was impelled to revisit and update it constantly, as one outrage followed another in the early 1960s. She sang the song at Carnegie Hall in 1964 and released it on her *Nina Simone in Concert* album of the same year. Responding to public demand, her record company brought it out as a single – with bleeps in place of the word 'Goddam'.

In yet another indication that his mind was no longer on politics or protest, Bob Dylan did not write anything to commemorate the events of Freedom Summer. Nor did he need to. His songs were already being sung in civil rights camps and on marches in the South, he had composed a heartfelt protest about the murder of Medgar Evers, 'Only a Pawn in Their Game', and had performed with Theo Bikel and Pete Seeger for the voter-registration campaign in Greenwood, Mississippi, a few months earlier. 'Blowin' in the Wind' was the closest thing that Freedom Summer had to an anthem. He didn't need to write anything more. He was already the prophet, or at least the oracle, of the civil rights movement, and no true visionary should ever need to say, 'I told you so.'

There is, though, perhaps another reason why Dylan remained silent during and after Freedom Summer. He had sung at the March on Washington and had attracted some criticism for being a white voice inappropriately intruding into an event devoted to black equality. After Washington, the African American comedian and activist Dick Gregory had asked, 'What was a white boy like Bob Dylan there for? Or – who else? Joan Baez? To support the cause? Wonderful – support the cause. March. Stand behind us – but not in front of us.' The black singer Harry Belafonte had risen to Dylan's defence, saying that, through their participation in the March, Joan Baez and Bob Dylan had demonstrated that freedom and justice were universal concerns to people of all colours. 'Were they taking advantage of the movement, he asked. Or was the movement taking advantage of them?'[13] It is possible that Dylan felt bruised by some of the responses to his appearance at the Washington event, and perhaps that influenced his decision to keep himself apart from Freedom Summer. Just as likely, though, he may have felt that he was in danger of being labelled, of becoming factionalised. And carrying a factional label, of being reduced to merely a member of an entity, whether civil rights movement, folk-music fraternity or Jewish descent, was something he had always steered clear of. A couple of years later he told Nat Hentoff:

> I agree with everything that's happening but I'm not part of no Movement. If I was, I wouldn't be able to do anything else but in 'the Movement'. I just can't have people sit around and make rules for me. I do a lot of things no Movement would allow. It's like politics. I just can't make it with any organization.[14]

6

MOVIN' ON

A-WARRIN'

The battle for civil rights was not the only concern in the summer of 1964. The military situation in Vietnam had been steadily worsening, the end appeared far out of sight. On 2 August, in the Gulf of Tonkin, just off the coast of Vietnam, the American destroyer USS *Maddox* was approached by three North Vietnamese torpedo boats. An exchange of fire took place and four Vietnamese sailors were killed. It was the first serious engagement between American and North Vietnamese forces, starting hostilities that would not conclude until 1975, the most devastating conflict since the end of World War II. The Vietnam catastrophe would destroy millions of lives, pit the communist and capitalist worlds against each other, send 2.5 million Americans to war, spawn a global protest movement on a scale and intensity never equalled before or since, exacerbate the generational divide in Western countries, and shape the politics of the baby-boomer generation.

Protests against the war had begun long before the skirmish in the Gulf of Tonkin. In May twelve students had burnt their draft cards during a rally in New York, chanting 'We Won't Go', a slogan that became a rallying cry for the anti-war resistance movement. Phil Ochs was early to the party; he had been singing about the senseless waste of lives in Southeast Asia since publishing his eponymous song 'Vietnam' in *Broadside* in 1962, in an edition headlined with James Meredith's battle to enrol at the University of Mississippi.[1]

Now Ochs penned and sang the satirical 'Draft Dodger Rag', a song about an 18-year-old making every excuse under the sun to avoid going to the war. It was a deeply personal tune; his younger brother Michael, who described himself as less political than Phil, had been one of the first to be expelled from the mandatory Reserve Officer Training Corps, for organising protests against the draft.[2]

Ochs never achieved the same fame as his better-known folk-singing colleagues. A tragic figure, his career came to an end after he fell into a deep depression, leading to his suicide in 1976, at the young age of 35. Unforgiving and graphic in his condemnation of the injustices he highlighted, his was the unrivalled voice of protest during the early days of the Vietnam War, with songs like 'What Are You Fighting For?', 'Talking Vietnam Blues' and 'One More Parade', all released in 1964. Yet for all his dogged opposition to the draft and the conflict, it was Buffy Sainte-Marie who was hailed as the doyenne of the anti-war malcontents with her hit 'Universal Soldier'. Like Dylan's 'With God on Our Side' and 'Masters of War', 'Universal Soldier' was a polemic against all war, not just Vietnam. It owes its popularity to the escalation in Vietnam and the war's status as the dominant topic of political protest. 'Universal Soldier' was first released in 1963 by the folk 'supergroup' The Highwaymen with limited success, not becoming a global hit until 1965, when it was covered by Glen Campbell in America and Donovan in Britain. The song's significance as an icon of protest was underlined by the release of a largely ignored riposte named 'The Universal Coward' by Jan Berry, one half of the duo Jan and Dean.

Dylan was as silent about the escalating Vietnam War as he had been about Freedom Summer. His silence was as clear an indication as any of the changes he was going through. It was as if he had passed the baton; he had made his contribution to the anti-war genre on his last two albums, and with 'Blowin' in the Wind' he had provided an anthem suitable for all protesters everywhere, whoever they might be, whatever the cause.

But to say that Dylan paid no attention to the Vietnam War is to misunderstand the changes he was going through in 1964, the year he accelerated his transition from folk singer to rock star. After his London triumph he spent a few days with his roadie Victor Maymudes, travelling first to Paris and then to Greece, before returning home to make another album. He recorded *Another Side of Bob Dylan* in just two nights; it was issued in August 1964, just as President Johnson was making preparations for America's further descent into the morass of Vietnam. The day the album was released New York police were breaking up an anti-war demonstration in New York's Times Square. One of the organisers was Phillip Luce, the man who Dylan had referred to as a friend in his rambling speech the previous year to the Emergency Civil Liberties Committee. Dylan had not abandoned his activist friends or changed his political orientation. But he had found a new way of dealing with topical issues. It was very much his own style, though reflecting something of the two influences he was now paying attention to: the poetry of the Beats and the music of the almost identically named Beatles. He expressed it most clearly in 'Chimes of Freedom'.

One of the tracks on *Another Side of Bob Dylan*, possibly the best, depending on your taste, certainly up there among the album's top three, 'Chimes of Freedom' does not on first hearing present itself as an anti-war song. It is far too complex and discursive to lend itself to simple categorisation. Here at the peak of his poetic powers, surrealistic and shot through with Beat undertones, Dylan blurs perceptions and confuses the senses, with chimes that flash and bolts that toll, singing of underdogs and the dispossessed, of refugees and outcasts stranded in their misery, while high in the skies strikes the mirage of freedom. It is not an anti-war song, it is a song for all those who dream of freedom, for the lost, the distraught and abused, the victims of disaster and tragedy. But there are no tragedies greater than those of war, and there are only so many times a man can merely protest against the fact of war. 'Chimes of Freedom' transcends the immorality and the injustice of war, taking us into its deeper recesses, the suffering, the pain and the undying vestiges of hope, the promise that freedom will chime, the striking of the bells that every victim strains so hard to hear. 'Chimes of Freedom' is not a protest against war as fought between nations. It is, rather, a protest against that war which comes from Thomas Hobbes's 'state of nature', when each one is pitted against the other, when life is 'solitary, poor, nasty, brutish, and short'.[3] A protest in which, unlike Hobbes's model, there hangs in the air a promise of freedom. And freedom, after all, is the ultimate goal of all anti-war protest.

ANOTHER SIDE

Most of them did not know it, even fewer appreciated it, but the baby-boomer generation was more fortunate than any other, before or since. It is true that they grew up 'under the shadow of the bomb', as the newspapers liked to describe the ubiquitous threat of nuclear weapons. But other than among the most committed anti-war campaigners there is nothing more than apocryphal evidence to suggest that the teenagers of the 1960s were kept awake at night, or were dejected during the day because they were worried about the proliferation of nuclear weapons. Theirs was a generation with more money than ever before, better education and the benefits of new technologies, particularly when it came to the playing of recorded music. Employment was plentiful, consumer spending at an all-time high, and leisure time in abundant supply. What was there to worry about? Life as a teenager in the 1960s, at least for those with families in the middle and higher economic tiers, was fun.

Most teenagers had grown up in families that considered the folk singers, at best, as a bunch of rebellious weirdos, obsessed with their music and their politics. At worst they were communist agitators who deserved to be locked up. As for the Beats, for those who had heard of them, they were nothing more than a gaggle of dissolute malcontents and irresponsible wastrels, not worth a moment's consideration. To the mass of 1960s teenagers, however, Beats, folk singers and parents were all an irrelevance, mostly old grey people who didn't dance and knew not how to have fun. Sex and drugs and rock 'n' roll had not yet quite become the slogan of their generation, but they were heading that way; until then they would have fun all summer long.

This generation shared a common language in music. Just as the civil rights activists had united around folk singers and their guitars, the teenagers of 1964 congregated around record players and jukeboxes, celebrating good times with The Beatles and The Beach Boys, falling in and out of love or breaking hearts to Roy Orbison and The Supremes. Bob Dylan, as far as the teenagers were concerned, was not even on the horizon.

Bob Dylan was never a teenager's icon. But, just as the boomers did not appreciate how lucky they had been, to have been born just when they had, neither did they appreciate how their horizons were gradually expanding, how their boundaries were being pushed back by the one-time folk singer whose lyrics soared above the formulaic predictability of pop music's Tin Pan Alley, challenging and influencing the bands whose discs were spinning on the jukeboxes and turntables.

Dylan's influence on mainstream pop and rock came largely through the medium of The Beatles. George Harrison was the first Beatle to pay attention to Dylan, encouraging John Lennon to listen to *Freewheelin'*. Paul McCartney had been given copies of Dylan's albums by someone he'd met while being interviewed in a Paris radio station and the band spent the next three weeks listening to them. And it was Dylan himself who urged Lennon not just to hear the sounds and rhythms of the early rhythm and blues tracks, the music they had both grown up listening to, but to pay attention to the words themselves.[4] For Dylan it was never just about the sound. Dylan's lyrical influence on The Beatles can be heard in songs like 'Rain' and 'Norwegian Wood', musically in their acoustic 'You've

Got to Hide Your Love Away' and 'Yesterday'. And the influence of The Beatles on the 1960s pop universe was all-embracing. John Lennon acknowledged that 'I'm a Loser' and 'In My Life' were among the songs he wrote in imitation of Dylan.

It is less easy to pinpoint direct influences the other way; with the exception of the alleged similarity of 'Fourth Time Around' to 'Norwegian Wood', there are no Dylan tracks that suggest he was trying to replicate the sound of The Beatles. But we only have to listen to the second album he brought out in 1964, *Another Side of Bob Dylan*, to appreciate how The Beatles helped mould his change of direction. If music was the common language for 1964's teenagers, it was The Beatles who articulated it most fluently. It must have been blindingly obvious to Dylan that the limits of the folk revival had long been breached, that while protest and topical songs were an effective means of pointing out what was wrong in the world, they had little impact when it came to engineering change. It was The Beatles who were changing things, inspiring a cultural upheaval by speaking in a language that the kids understood. And while Dylan had no aspiration to become a troubadour for the kids of his time, he had similar ambitions to The Beatles. Just like them he was hungry for success. He and Lennon both believed they had something important to say to the world, they both wanted to be recognised for the impact they made. The Beatles were showing Dylan the way to go; he would show them what to do when they got there. As he was recording *Another Side of Bob Dylan* he told Nat Hentoff that from now on he would be writing from inside himself, that rather than being a spokesman for causes, his writing would now be about his own experiences; he would write about what he knew and what he was feeling.[5]

Perhaps in illustration of this, since he had always been reluctant to talk about himself in public, he used his new album to reveal his disillusionment with the power of protest songs. In 'My Back Pages', one of the most personal songs on the album, he confessed to once having had a false sense of his own maturity when he parroted

slogans that he'd scarcely thought through. He had thought he was
mature, that he had all the answers. But it was an illusory maturity,
he was, he sang, younger now than he had been then. By casting off
his faux antiquity, he seems to be saying, he was about to become
true to himself in a way he hadn't been before.

Another Side of Bob Dylan is far from his best album. Recorded in
haste, over just two nights, and with Dylan undergoing a musical
and career transition, it was never likely to have become a classic.
He was going through another change too, his final break-up with
Suze Rotolo following a vicious argument with her and her sister
Carla. It ended with Dylan and Carla scuffling on the floor. In
another example of his sudden willingness to open up musically
about his emotions, he sang about the break-up, quite unkindly, in
'Ballad in Plain D'. Evoking the biblical Jacob in expressing his love
for the younger of two sisters, describing the older as a parasite,
and using words of regret over what happened, it is easy to imagine
that the changes he was going through were impacting his creativity.
There were no excuses, his 'Ballad' confesses, for his behaviour. It
had caused him to lose the love of his life.

Dylan's decision to change his musical style was, for those days,
profound and virtually unheard of. No major contemporary artist
had done anything like it before. The Beatles, Rolling Stones,
Moody Blues and a whole host of other bands would do so three
years later, in 1967, with their music either becoming psychedelic
or consciousness-elevating, depending on whether the band was
into acid, transcendental meditation, or frequently both. Other
artists, notably Elton John and David Bowie, would change styles
for strategic reasons, to get themselves in front of new audiences.
But all those changes were reactive; the artists changed their music
because of external events, things that had happened. Or that were
happening to them. Dylan's move from the lyrical and musical
constraints of the folk world towards a bardic, Beats-influenced,
narrative vein was prescient. The baby-boomers were approaching
their twenties, about to make their impact on the world. Like

Elijah of old, or the three wise kings, Bob Dylan was to be their herald. Not because he had the gift of prophecy; there was nothing supernatural about the changes he was going through. He was just a bit smarter and possessed of greater foresight; he got there before anyone else. He could see that the folk revival had run its course. He wasn't about to hang around to pick over the remains.

STAGGERIN'

Another Side of Bob Dylan did not go down well with the folk purists or with those who preferred listening to songs that were melodic, meaningful and easy to understand. Nor had they appreciated Dylan's performance a couple of weeks earlier at the 1964 Newport Folk Festival.

That was the year when the Newport Folk Festival found itself more popular than it possibly wanted to be. An audience of 70,000 turned up, but the ethos of folk aficionados gathering for their annual celebration could no longer be discerned. Most of the audience seemed to be there to watch celebrities perform, rather than to listen to folk music. It wasn't so much that folk music had suddenly become hugely popular; it was rather that many of the performers – Joan Baez, Peter, Paul and Mary, Judy Collins, Johnny Cash, Peter Seeger and of course Bob Dylan – were now household names. George Wein summed it up after the event: 'Never was there so clear a contrast between the "authentic" folk audience – a small, devoted band of aficionados – and the wider public. We were learning first-hand the so-called national "folk boom" had more to do with celebrity than with any deep grassroots interest.'[6]

Newport in 1964 was bigger and ran for longer. It expanded from two to three days, from three evening concerts to four, and, at 228, the number of performers were over three times as many as the previous year. Dylan played three sets. He sang 'It Ain't Me Babe' and 'Mr Tambourine Man' on the Friday morning, then that evening came on at the end of Joan Baez's set to sing 'It Ain't Me Babe' again, in a duet with her. His main solo appearance was on Sunday evening when he played in front of 15,000 people, the largest crowd for a single set that Newport had ever seen. He seemed to be out of sorts even before he went on, telling a friend that he didn't care, that he would just go on and do his music. He opened the set with 'All I Really Want to Do', following it with 'To Ramona', 'Mr Tambourine Man' and 'Chimes of Freedom', before calling Joan Baez onto the stage for a duet of 'With God on Our Side'.

Most of the press gave his performance good reviews but his presentation rankled with the cognoscenti. He was accused of being desultory, of failing to connect with his audience, of being sloppy, and even of staggering onstage. He wasn't even dressed in the casual, couldn't-care-less style that a folk singer was supposed to wear; he was looking smarter than usual and better groomed. He even wore a black turtleneck jumper, like those the Fab Four were seen wearing on the cover of *With The Beatles*.

Even his long-term ally, the reporter Robert Shelton, was disappointed. He didn't even mention Dylan's performance in his *New York Times* review of the festival. When Dylan sang his powerfully political 'Chimes of Freedom' the misalliance between his lyrics and demeanour led one critic to write, 'It is noticeable that the higher the moral stakes in the song the more Dylan's composure appears to crumble . . . as if struck by moralistic requirements that he strike the attitudes of preacher, saviour, prophet or leader, Dylan is unable to stop grinning incongruously over and over again.'[7]

After Newport, Irwin Silber, the founder and editor of the country's most important folk magazine *Sing Out!*, wrote an open letter to Bob Dylan. A long-term left-wing activist, Silber, like many people, had grown used to regarding Dylan as the folk movement's most prominent voice, and he was saddened by Bob's abandonment of the role into which he had been projected.

It was not a nice letter. Silber started off politely, praising Bob for his success and for the 'new ideas, new images, and new sounds' that he was creating. But he was troubled. And, he wrote, it wasn't just him, but 'many other good friends of yours as well'. (It is always an advantage, when going on the attack, to conjure up anonymous allies.) He told Bob that, after seeing his performance at Newport he was concerned for him, for 'that awful potential for self-destruction which lies hidden in all of us and which can emerge so easily and so uninvited'.[8]

Having established his credentials as a concerned friend, at least to his own satisfaction, Silber attacked. He asked how it could be that Bob did not consider himself a writer of protest songs; surely, he intimated, any songwriter who tried to deal with the world honestly 'is bound to write protests. How can he help himself?' He criticised Bob for surrounding himself with sycophantic cronies (rather, presumably, than with people like himself), then threw his own lyrics back at him, telling him that the old Bob Dylan 'never wasted our precious time'. Of course, he concluded, it wasn't Bob's fault that such things had happened to him. 'I think, in a sense, that we are all responsible for what's been happening to you'. They had all, he intimated, failed to protect him. It was obvious to Silber that Bob had become a victim of the American Success Machine and the Establishment, which make it impossible for artists to function and grow. He urged Bob to give his letter some thought; he was of course writing out of 'deep love and concern'.[9]

Silber's letter was just the tip of the iceberg. The following month *Broadside* published a further attack on Dylan, this time by the 'songwriter and college student' Paul Wolfe. He acclaimed Phil Ochs as having emerged at Newport as 'the most important voice in the [folk] movement', comparing him with Dylan, who had left the 'majority of the audience annoyed, some even disgusted and, in general, scratching its collective head in disbelief'. The audience's disappointment with Dylan's new songs, wrote Wolfe, was heightened by their juxtaposition with 'the eloquent musical force of Phil Ochs'.[10]

The *Broadside* editors waded in below Wolfe's three-page article with an attempt to put the issue into perspective. They said they had received many letters expressing views across the spectrum, from those at one extreme hailing Dylan as a superb poet who was ascending new heights, to others who now regarded him as burnt out and at the end of his career. For his part, Dylan had previously offered Wolfe a rare instance of unsolicited praise, writing in response to a song Wolfe had published in *Broadside*: 'I've never met Paul Wolfe but I'd like to. He has an uncanny sense of touch.'[11]

Silber's letter to Dylan has been both applauded and criticised. Dylan's own response was to tell his manager Albert Grossman not to send *Sing Out!* any more songs. There is another way of looking at it though. Yes, the letter was preachy and its tone superior, that of an older folk enthusiast writing to a younger member of the club who had gone off the rails. But Dylan and Silber both belonged to another club. Like many in the American folk and music scenes, they were both Jews, as indeed was Paul Wolfe. Jews can be direct in their speech, speaking plainly to each other, almost as if they are members of the same family. It's not necessarily intentional; rapport between members of any ethnic group or minority is sometimes guided by unconscious cultural signals, a turn of phrase or body language. And, just as Wolfe and Silber had no qualms in speaking their minds about Dylan, even at the risk of causing some offence, it fell to a fourth Jew to take up the cudgels on Bob's behalf. Appropriately, in the light of Paul Wolfe's article, it was Phil Ochs, who published a sarcastic open response to Silber in the January 1965 issue of *Broadside*.

Phil Ochs was bemused by what Dylan could have done at Newport to cause such offence. 'Was Dylan raped by success? Did Dylan rape his fans? . . . Nobody seems to know for sure.' He pointed out that, having changed the subject of his songs, Dylan had to remain true to himself and not simply pander to the audience's expectations. 'As for Bob's writing, I believe it is as brilliant as ever and is clearly improving all the time. On his last record, "*Ballad in Plain D*" and "*It Ain't Me Babe*" are masterpieces of personal statement that have as great a significance as any of his protest material. How can anyone be so pretentious as to set guidelines for an artist to follow?'[12]

DEMONSTRATIN'

Freedom Summer was over and the student volunteers were now back at college. They had only spent a few weeks in the South but as a formative experience it had been life-changing. The hatred they had witnessed, the casual violence regularly meted out to black men, women and children by the white authorities, their almost pathological refusal to register black voters, these things by themselves would have been enough to radicalise the student volunteers. Add in the senseless and brutal murder of Schwerner, Chaney and Goodman and it was little wonder that when the volunteers returned to their homes and campuses, they were angry, impassioned and militant.

Mario Savio was one of the returning volunteers. He had been deeply moved by the courage of those determined to inscribe their names on the register of voters, who refused to be turned away from the registration booths by snarling dogs and club-wielding Ku Klux Klansmen, who stood firm in the face of obstruction and the humiliation hurled at them by those whose job it was to enter them onto the electoral roll. He returned to his university at Berkeley, determined to carry on the struggle for civil rights on the green lawns of its Californian campus.

The university, however, had different ideas. There had already been demonstrations at Berkeley, against the death penalty, racial discrimination, and the continued blacklisting of alleged communists. Now the university authorities were faced with several dozen returning Freedom Summer volunteers of whom Mario Savio was the most articulate, the student most steeped in political ideology. It seemed to the university that there was too much politics on campus, that protests and political meetings were distracting students from their studies. On 1 October 1964 the university announced that it was forbidden for students to hand out political leaflets.

The university authorities did not understand the impact on the Freedom Summer returnees of the events they had witnessed in the

South. They had seen the determination and courage of hundreds of oppressed black people, prepared to stand up to their oppressors, refusing to back down in their demand to be enfranchised. By volunteering for the voter-registration drive, by standing up to the bigots and the supremacists, sometimes even to their own parents who tried to dissuade them from volunteering, the students too had shown their mettle. It only required a fraction of that mettle to oppose the ban on campus leafleting, and that is exactly what they did. Calling themselves the Free Speech Movement, the students massed in protest on the main square of Berkeley's campus. Over the coming weeks they held strikes and demonstrations, widening their sphere of protest to encompass the entire system of education at the university, characterising it as 'dehumanizing'. The Berkeley protests spread like wildfire across the country. Images of 10,000 students surrounding a police car for 36 hours, to stop them taking the arrested protester Jack Weinberg to jail, or of nearly 1,000 occupying Sproul Hall, the university's main administration building, were catnip to aspiring protesters in other institutions who shared the Berkeley grievances but had no Mario Savio on campus to help them turn their dissatisfaction into action.

As the students surrounded the police car containing Jack Weinberg, Mario Savio climbed onto its roof. In an iconic performance, Savio removed his shoes so as not to damage the car's paintwork, then turned to the crowd, stirring them up with a fiery address. Emerging as the leader of the newly formed Free Speech Movement, Savio gave a speech on 2 December that has gone down in history as defining the drive behind the 1960s protest movements:

There's a time when the operation of the machine becomes so odious, makes you so sick at heart that you can't take part! You can't even passively take part! And you've got to put your bodies upon the gears and upon the wheels, upon the levers, upon all the apparatus – and you've got to make it stop! And you've got to indicate to the people who run it, to the people who own it – that unless you're free the machine will be prevented from working at all![13]

Thus began the first of many student protests that would come to characterise the 1960s. Protests that rapidly escalated into coordinated opposition to the Vietnam War, and would culminate in May 1968 in the killing by National Guardsmen of four unarmed students at Kent State University, Ohio.

Joan Baez was at the rally on 2 December when Mario Savio gave his speech. Bob Dylan was not. When Savio finished speaking, Baez led the students in a rendition of Dylan's 'The Times They Are A-Changin''. As he had indicated in his letter to *Broadside* and reinforced in the lyrics of 'My Back Pages', Dylan had moved on, he had left topical protest behind. Nevertheless, it was he who had supplied the anthems and the vocabulary. He just wasn't on the front line.

He wasn't far from the front line though. He turned up at Berkeley Community Theater a year later, on 3 December 1965, for a celebration of the first anniversary of the Free Speech Movement. He was with his band The Hawks, later to be known as The Band. In Greil Marcus's recollection of the event, it was quite apparent to everyone in the audience, to all the supporters of the Free Speech Movement, that even in their radical, left-wing, supposedly folk-oriented eyes, Dylan had made the right decision in putting his folk-music days behind him:

> That was a time when there was a tremendous dispute raging around the country, a dispute that now seems utterly quaint, over whether or not Bob Dylan had sold out by abandoning folk music and acoustic guitar to play commercial, corrupt rock-and-roll and make a loud noise. It was very refreshing, it was very interesting, that at Berkeley Community Theater that night, nobody cared. People sat fidgeting while Bob Dylan went through the acoustic/folk music part of his set, like 'Get on with it, get on with it, we want to see the band.'[14]

HALLOWEEN

'Stay in line. stay in step. People are afraid of someone who is not in step with them. it makes them look foolish t' themselves for being in step.' It is obvious, from these opening words to Bob's lengthy poem, 'Advice for Geraldine on her Miscellaneous Birthday', that he was rattled by the criticism he had received. Irwin Silber and Paul Wolfe had made their opinions known in print. No doubt countless numbers of other fans, who weren't magazine contributors and had no public medium in which to express their feelings, held similar views. Dylan's poem appeared in the programme notes for his Halloween concert at New York Philharmonic Hall in October 1964, and it was apparent that Dylan was not prepared to be cowed. He made it clear that he was not prepared to stand in line, to conform to someone else's assessment of how he should behave, because, he asserted, such assessments were made from fear, from a terror of being confronted by something they could not understand. He used the concert to drive this message home.

New York Philharmonic Hall was the most prestigious venue Dylan had performed at. Indeed, it was among most the prestigious auditoriums in Manhattan, a sparkling new building opened only two years earlier, the home of the New York Philharmonic Orchestra under its conductor Leonard Bernstein. Purpose-built for the orchestra, who relocated there from their previous home at Carnegie Hall, the hall had been plagued by acoustic problems since its opening night. The bad acoustics meant that certain orchestras refused to play there and ultimately the hall was remodelled, but they didn't seem to bother Dylan or his audience. The concert, which was sold out 10 days in advance and grossed $11,500, has gone down in Dylan lore as one of his most important, his rapport with the audience merry – so good that he could even ask them, with a titter, to prompt him for an opening line he had forgotten. 'Then the giggling stops and this unbelievable voice bursts from his larynx and New York's Philharmonic Hall vibrates like an over-filled balloon. Listen closely and you can hear people's minds opening.

Every person in the room wishes they were even a fraction as cool.'[15] The pundits agree that it was one of his best performances ever.

There was no doubt in the minds of his fans that this concert marked another step in his transition away from politics and protest. The transition was far from complete: he played 'Talkin' John Birch Blues' and 'The Lonesome Death of Hattie Carroll'. But when it came to 'The Ballad of Hollis Brown' he changed his mind after the first few chords, muttered 'Nah . . . I can't . . .; I'll do this instead', and played 'A Hard Rain's A-Gonna Fall'. Was the personal tragedy of the starving, unemployed, broken-down Hollis Brown, so desperate that he killed himself, his wife and five children, a heartbreak too far for Bob? Or did he just think it didn't fit into his set at that particular moment?

There were still social ills he felt the need to oppose, such as the needless death of the boxer Davey Moore, whose neck was broken when he fell against the ropes while fighting for the featherweight championship of the world. Bob detached himself from the song's content when he played 'Who Killed Davey Moore?' at New York Philharmonic Hall, telling the audience that 'This is a song about a boxer . . . it's not about boxing. It's not even about a boxer . . . It's got nothing to do with nothing! I just shoved all these words together, that's all.'[16] Notwithstanding his introduction to the song that night, 'Who Killed Davey Moore?', which Dylan never recorded in the studio but Pete Seeger did, is a denunciation of the sport of boxing and everybody involved in it – from the referees and the managers all the way down to the crowd and the punters who bet on fights. It has a political edge; the fighter who knocked down Davey Moore was a refugee from Cuba where, as Dylan notes in the song, Fidel Castro's regime had banned boxing.

Whatever Dylan's thoughts about poverty, social justice and boxing at the Philharmonic Hall, there was another statement he seemed to be making that night. His album *Another Side of Bob Dylan* had only been out for a few months, yet he played fewer than half of its tracks, ignoring 'Chimes of Freedom' and 'My Back Pages', two of the four most recognisable songs on the album. And he didn't sing the most recognisable of all, 'It Ain't Me Babe', until Joan Baez joined him onstage towards the end of his act. Instead he introduced three numbers from his next album, *Bringing It All Back Home*, among them his new classic, 'Mr Tambourine Man', that he had first played when he visited London the previous May and had twice introduced to his home fans at the Newport Folk Festival three months earlier. All in all, it felt as if Bob Dylan was celebrating his past, looking forward to his future, and was not particularly focused on where he had just been, putting behind him the poorly received *Another Side of Bob Dylan*.

Meanwhile, the outside world had also been going through changes. Earlier that month the Soviet leader Nikita Khrushchev had been deposed by the leadership of the Russian Communist Party, ushering in a fresh round of geopolitical uncertainty. Khrushchev's belligerence had worried the West during the Cuban Missile Crisis but overall he had been seen as a moderating force in Russian foreign policy, choosing to pursue a path of détente rather than an escalation of the Cold War. Nobody could predict how his removal from power might affect the fragile peace between the Soviet bloc and the West, but the prognosis was not good. Little was known about his successor, Leonid Brezhnev, a man generally assumed to be a hardliner. A toughening of leadership in the communist world, just as America was increasing its efforts to prevent the spread of communism in Vietnam, did not bode well. Coming hard on the heels of President Kennedy's assassination, Khrushchev's removal did not seem likely to cheer anyone up.

That wasn't all. Two days after Khrushchev was overthrown, China conducted its first test of an atomic bomb. They accompanied their entry into the coven of nuclear-armed states with a statement of menacing sophistry. After reminding the world that Mao Tse-Tung had declared the atomic bomb a paper tiger, and that this remained their view, they said China was not developing nuclear weapons because it believed in their omnipotence, nor because it planned to use them. 'On the contrary,' they declared, 'in developing nuclear weapons, China's aim is to break the nuclear monopoly of the nuclear powers and to eliminate nuclear weapons.' Believe that, if you like. Cheerfully, they concluded their statement by saying, 'We are convinced that man, who creates nuclear weapons, will certainly be able to eliminate them.'[17]

The tensions at home, in American society, were as palpable as those on the global stage. Freedom Summer had shown just how deep the political divide was in the country and how difficult it would be to heal the rift. A conservative backlash to the civil rights movement had surfaced in the Primaries for the forthcoming presidential election, even before Freedom Summer began. George Wallace, the Southern states' poster boy for racism, had campaigned strongly in the Primaries for the Democratic nomination, briefly looking as if it would be he rather than President Johnson who would be the party's candidate in November's elections. Eventually though he withdrew from the race, allowing the bellicose Republican candidate Barry Goldwater a free shot at deposing the President, who both he and Wallace considered too liberal. Goldwater was an ideological Republican. He had the qualified support of the conservative icon Ayn Rand, was the candidate of choice for Young Americans for Freedom, and was seen as a beacon of hope by those who felt that their traditional values were threatened by the left-leaning radicals of the civil rights and anti-war movements.

The 1964 presidential election had all the makings of a watershed moment in American politics. Goldwater had made it clear in his acceptance speech to the Republican convention that he regarded communism as the chief enemy of peace in the world and that 'only the strong can remain free, that only the strong can keep the peace . . . we do no man a service by hiding freedom's light under a bushel of mistaken humility . . . I would remind you that extremism in the defence of liberty is no vice. And let me remind you also that moderation in the pursuit of justice is no virtue.'[18] While Goldwater was delivering his speech, outside the convention hall African American and White demonstrators sang 'We Shall Overcome'.

And overcome they did. Three days after Bob Dylan's Halloween concert the incumbent, President Lyndon Johnson, defeated Barry Goldwater in the presidential election, winning 61 per cent of the votes, the largest share in American history. For liberal-minded Americans, for the baby-boomer generation who were just coming of age, for those who did not confuse 'Chimes of Freedom' with a specious, political rant for liberty, it was a moment of relief in what was otherwise a very troubling time.

7

BACK HOME

SARA

On 12 November 1964, Bob Dylan was a guest at Albert Grossman's wedding to Sally Ann Buehler. Also there was Sally's friend, Sara Lownds, a 25-year-old model who had recently divorced from a brief marriage to fashion photographer Hans Lownds. Sara, who was a couple of years older than Bob, had been born Shirley Noznisky in Wilmington, Delaware, where her father owned a scrap-metal business and her mother ran a dry-goods store. Her father had been murdered in a shooting five years earlier and her mother had suffered a stroke when Shirley was nine, leaving her to be brought up by her great-aunt. It was her former husband Hans who had encouraged Shirley to change her name to Sara; apparently so that he wouldn't be reminded of his first wife, also called Shirley.

Sara was the first Jewish woman with whom Bob had a serious relationship. It is important to many Jewish parents that their children marry somebody Jewish and they often go to great lengths to discourage their kids from even seeing someone from a different background. Bob's previous romances, his teenage fling with Echo Helstrom, his first serious love affair with Suze Rotolo, and the celebrity relationship with Joan Baez, had been with women who were not Jewish. Whatever pressure Abe and Beatty Zimmerman may or may not have put on young Robert to persuade him to marry someone from the faith, all the evidence suggested that it hadn't worked. At this point in his life Bob seemed to pay little attention to his Jewishness. It was purely coincidental that he knew many Jews in New York among the civil rights activists and in the music business. His connection with them was a consequence of the lifestyle he had chosen, not because he overtly displayed any particular affinity with those who shared his ethnic background.

Yet within a very short while, Bob gave up his small apartment in Greenwich Village and moved uptown with Sara and her three-year-old daughter Maria, taking a suite in the Chelsea Hotel, the iconic lodging house for New York's peripatetic community of up-and-coming musicians, actors, artists and radicals. She and Bob married a year after they met, in November 1965, when Sara was pregnant with their oldest child Jesse.

That Bob Dylan chose to marry a Jewish woman might be of no significance whatsoever; their wedding was an extremely quiet affair, just the two of them, with no friends or family. Bob's parents weren't even there, which must have hurt them considerably. Dylan may not have intended to remain unmarried until he found a Jewish wife, though it would not be surprising, given his background, if he had. In any event, for the man who had changed his name from Zimmerman to Dylan, and his upbringing from the middle classes to the circus, marrying a Jewish woman was the closest yet that he had come to publicly acknowledging his roots.

SALLY

The cover of *Bringing It All Back Home*, the album that Bob spent just two days recording in January 1965, features a dark-haired woman in a red dress, languidly lounging on a chaise longue, holding a cigarette and staring impassively at the camera. It wasn't Sara, she and Bob were doing a good job of keeping their relationship out of the public eye; it wasn't until December 1965, a month after the wedding, that the British paper *Melody Maker* revealed that they were married.

Some people, bizarrely, thought the reclining lady was Bob Dylan in drag, representing the feminine side of his psyche.[1] In a passage that now strikes us as incredibly dated, Dylan's earliest biographer Anthony Scaduto wrote, 'there is much that is androgynous in Dylan. One result of being an inner-directed man whose life is based on feeling and not intellect, is to break down the distinctions between the strong, unemotional rational male, and the emotional, sensual, unstable female. Friends have recognized a good deal of each in Dylan.'[2]

In fact, the woman on the chaise longue was Sally Grossman, Albert's new wife, who had brought Sara and Bob together. She had introduced them, allegedly to help stop him moping about his loss of Suze and because he was so uncertain about his relationship with Joan Baez.[3]

Sally Grossman's picture was not the only intriguing image on the cover of *Bringing It All Back Home*. Fans spent hours, and pundits filled column inches, trying to decipher the meaning and significance of the many objects portrayed on the cover. There was no surprise that Dylan's image features in the foreground, his face had appeared on all his albums so far and would continue to do so until 1973. But it was noticeable that the striking bright red of Sally's dress drew the eye away from the almost monochrome Dylan, and it was a little odd that he was holding a cat. Yet it was the semiotics of the assorted paraphernalia that captured most interest. Behind the woman in red was a fireplace, on the mantelpiece was an old photograph, the cover of the cult comedian and monologuist Lord Buckley's '*Best of*' album, a poetry magazine, a couple of candlesticks, some artwork and a figurine. Dylan seems to be reading a magazine article about the actress Jean Harlow, alongside him is the current issue of *Time* magazine, there is a Fallout Shelter sign, various album covers are scattered about and behind the chaise longue, on the hearth, is the cover of *Another Side of Bob Dylan*. Almost as much attention has been concentrated over the years on trying to decode the meaning of all these objects as has been directed to understanding the essential meaning of any of Bob Dylan's most surreal lyrics.

In fact, it seems there is very little that is cryptic about the cover. Years later Daniel Kramer, who took the shot, explained that it was set in the original kitchen of Albert and Sally Grossman's house in Woodstock. The chaise longue that Sally was sitting on was a gift from Mary Travers, of Peter, Paul and Mary, to the Grossmans for their wedding. The items that had caused so much head-scratching among the fans were those which always adorned the room. The only items that were not in the room when Kramer first entered it were the magazines Dylan was reading and the albums he was currently listening to. Apart from his last album, *Another Side of Bob Dylan*, poking out of the fireplace, almost as if that aspect of his oeuvre had been discarded. As for why Kramer chose that particular shot out of the many he took that day, he told *Rolling Stone* magazine it was the only one in which the cat was looking at the camera.[4]

Sally was on the cover almost by chance. The art director at Dylan's record company, who had originally objected to the young and inexperienced Kramer shooting the artwork for the cover, was harangued by Grossman until he relented, subject to one condition. He insisted that, in return for allowing Kramer to do the shoot, there had to be a woman on the cover, preferably Dylan's girlfriend, just as Suze had been on *Freewheelin'*. But Bob had no steady girlfriend at the time; he was still going through his lengthy break-up with Suze and was in a complicated relationship with Joan Baez, who wouldn't have been suitable anyway as she was a star in her own right. He and Sara had begun to see each other but Bob was already protective of their privacy, there was no way he would allow her to appear on the album cover. Sally Grossman happened to be in the room when they were discussing who to ask, and Dylan suggested she do it.

MAGGIE

The times that Bob Dylan had already warned were a-changin' were now undergoing a tumultuous upheaval. Those who had grown up before World War II found it hard to comprehend. Of course there had been tremendous difficulties then too, not least the horrors of war, but overall life had seemed a lot simpler, black and white, with not too many shades of grey. By and large people knew what they believed in and whose side they were on. The 1960s were far harder to fathom. The scope of technological change was baffling, with rockets flying to the moon, phone calls bouncing off satellites, a pill to prevent pregnancy, sick people receiving new hearts, a colour TV in the living room, the first computers, portable record players. People were even talking seriously about robots that would perform all the mundane tasks, taking care of all the drudgery and freeing people up for a life of unfettered leisure.

Values were fluctuating too. Religion, which was thought to have kept society on the straight and narrow for the whole of human history – although actually causing more conflict than anything else – seemed to be losing its grip. Secularists were claiming that organised faith had outlived its purpose, that science could explain all mysteries, that there were no such places as heaven and hell. But then the TV would announce that, far from God being dead, Billy Graham or some other superstar evangelical preacher would be bringing him to a stadium somewhere near you. People didn't know what to think.

Social attitudes were in a state of flux too; age-old taboos were being broken, homosexuality, free love, women's liberation, everything was up for grabs. Psychedelic drugs were making an appearance; few people yet knew what they were but they sounded both exciting and terrifying at the same time. To be old in the 1960s was confusing. But to be young was exhilarating, dynamic, it felt like standing on the threshold of a new world. And yet, despite all this, or perhaps because it was all so overwhelming, young people were angry. Better educated than ever before, they

could see what they thought was wrong with the world and they
had no hesitation in speaking their minds. Rejecting the values of
their parents' generation, they refused to toe the line sartorially,
socially, sexually, culturally. Often it seemed as if they opposed
their parents' opinions simply because those were the opinions
their parents held. Little wonder that the new music, the language
in which the young communicated, became a symbol of division;
energetic, enthusiastic, vibrant and compelling; the kids loved it.
No wonder then that parents shouted 'Turn it down!', that the
newspapers spoke of a 'generation gap'.

Anyone who thinks that Bob Dylan stopped being a protest singer
with the release of *Bringing It All Back Home* hasn't paid enough
attention to his words. Yes, the album was controversial because for
the first time it no longer exclusively featured Dylan alone with
his harmonica and guitar. *Bringing It All Back Home* contained both
electric and acoustic tracks, and many of his fans were displeased.
And while it is true that the album contains no topical protests,
that he highlights no specific injustices and issues no grim warnings
against war or the threat of nuclear holocaust, the album does contain
some protests, written in the spirit of the age. Beat-inspired, surreal,
challenging, humorous, they are capable of multiple interpretations
or none, but they remain protests nevertheless. 'Maggie's Farm' is
a song about someone who hates their workplace, who is abused
in turn by every member of the family that employs him, who
just doesn't want to work there anymore, and who tells us in the
final stanza, faithful to the zeitgeist, that he doesn't want to be like
everyone else, that he is not prepared to conform. He tries his best
to be himself, but everyone around him wants him to be the same
as them.

'Maggie's Farm' is a chaotic, funny song, it has none of the pathos
of Dylan's earlier tales of oppressed people, like 'North Country
Blues', and none of the rage of 'The Ballad of Hollis Brown'. We
don't feel sorry for the abused worker, he is by no means the only
person treated badly at work, rather the song is an exaggerated

parody on the thoughts that went through the minds of myriad baby-boomers during the 1960s. Refusing to submit to the conventions of their parents' world, they were not prepared to do as they were told. Even if the best argument they could come up with was 'I don't like it, so why should I?'

The most surreal song on the album, 'Subterranean Homesick Blues', defies analysis, as indeed it should. As Leonard Cohen would do a few years later, Bob Dylan always refused to discuss the meaning of his lyrics. If he was asked what a song meant he would dismiss the question with a joke or a nonsense answer. When 'Subterranean Homesick Blues' was released as a single a few weeks later and the *Melody Maker* journalist asked him what it was about, Dylan replied, 'It's just a little story, really. It's not about anything.'[5] It's not an inaccurate answer, though we can find themes in the song that seem to support the idea that Dylan still had plenty to say about the state of the world. The many characters in the song include Dylan himself, who is thinking about the government, someone apparently scoring from a man in a skin hat, bail jumpers, losers, dropouts and an unneeded weatherman. We get the impression that he is writing for his own pleasure, playing a rhyming game, manholes and candles, vandals and handles. There are tapped telephones, drug busts, No-Doz energy pills, snippets of life advice, echoes of Woody Guthrie. 'Subterranean Homesick Blues' may not be a song about anything, but there are an awful lot of different things in it.

However, it is the penultimate track on the album, 'It's Alright, Ma (I'm Only Bleeding)', which truly shatters the myth that Dylan's days of topical commentary were over. Perhaps the darkest song he had ever written, echoing pessimism and anguish, the song is a succession of surreal images, each one of which reinforces the idea of a broken and decaying society. Addressed to his ma, who he is trying to alert to his predicament while also attempting to reassure her, the song is a litany of despair. Expressed, as in 'Subterranean Homesick Blues', through brief snippets, though this time mournful rather than exuberant couplets, we hear of the darkness of the world, the shallowness and futility of modern life, the struggle to find meaning and purpose, our overpowering vulnerability. Among the most powerful songs he has written, straddling a line between mockery and rage, 'It's Alright, Ma' repudiates those who believed that Dylan's days as a protest singer were done. The scope of the song is wider than in his earlier protest songs, taking in almost every aspect of the social cosmos, replacing the sense of injustice with one of resigned acceptance. While his greater personal maturity permits the ludicrous, like the thought that the President of America is also sometimes naked, to occasionally puncture the cloud of despair.

For Bob Dylan, the song's most powerful feature was not the sentiment, it was the poetry. Years later, he told the *New York Times*, 'I've written some songs that I look at, and they just give me a sense of awe. Stuff like "It's Alright, Ma", just the alliteration in that blows me away.'[6]

Bringing It All Back Home was a landmark album, confirming that, even if some of his songs were, on close listening, clearly still topical, Bob Dylan was moving on, into another stage of his career. Even the romantic songs, of which there were several, had a descriptive, literary quality to them, a tenderness that had been lacking in his earlier albums. Tracks like 'Girl from the North Country', probably the most sensitive number on *Freewheelin'* and a classic in its own right, is left in the shadows by the tranquil beauty of 'Love Minus Zero/No Limit'. When he introduced the album at the Royal Albert Hall in 1965, he said, 'The name of this song is a fraction. Love minus zero is on the top and underneath no limit. I made the title before I made the song.'

Despite the album's power, many of Dylan's fans were unhappy with *Bringing It All Back Home*. To be backed by musicians playing electric instruments was a display of heresy that flew in the face of everything that folk purists held sacred. A cardinal endeavour for folk musicians and enthusiasts is to recover and preserve traditional tunes and their mode of performance. Even when composing new songs, authentic folk artists do not deviate from established musical styles or instruments. No serious folk artist would consider using electrical instruments, because the musical tradition they are preserving dates from a period long before the discovery of electricity. That, in the eyes of his traditionally oriented followers, applied to Bob Dylan as much as it did to any other folk singer.

Disappointment for the folk aficionados was mitigated only somewhat by side two of the album, a series of acoustic tracks including 'Mr Tambourine Man' and 'It's All Over Now, Baby Blue'. The lyrics on side two were just as alienating, they weren't what a traditional folk singer was supposed to sing. But at least the acoustic performance gave them hope that Dylan hadn't abandoned his folk roots completely.

Some of his fans were assuaged by side two. But not all. The British folk singer Ewan MacColl was scathing. Dylan had watched him with admiration years earlier, when he was still known as Robert Zimmerman and MacColl was playing together with his wife Peggy Seeger in Minneapolis. MacColl did not reciprocate. He already had form with Dylan. In 1963, as Bob was just beginning to make an impact, MacColl had said, 'I am still unable to see in him anything other than a youth of mediocre talent. Only a completely non-critical audience, nourished on the watery pap of pop music, could have fallen for such drivel.'[7]

Nor did Dylan's one-time admirer and now critic, Irwin Silber, like *Bringing It All Back Home*. He dipped his nib in resentment once more, *kvetching* in *Sing Out!* that 'it's a pity and a frustration, for if ever the world was in need of the clear and uncompromising anger and love of the poet, it is now'.[8]

The problem of course was that Bob Dylan no longer thought of himself as a folk singer, indeed he no longer had any desire to be one. Those fans who objected to him playing or being backed by electric instruments were trying to keep him trapped in a box that he no longer wanted to be contained in. Such attitudes are not a problem restricted to folk music; he would have received similar criticism had he been a blues, jazz or classical votary. Folk music had made him famous, indeed it was his love of folk music that had launched him on his career. But he had become famous and popular, and it was this that exacerbated his offence in the eyes of his critics, which caused them to exhibit such an extreme reaction. They could not regard him merely as a former folk singer who had set off on a wayward path. Rather, they considered him to be a traitor to their cause.

However, those who criticised Dylan for playing an electric guitar were missing the main point. It is true that he was no longer just a folk singer but the change that he was going through was far more significant than his journey away from a particular musical genre. It was a change that could be recognised to a far greater extent in the lyrics he wrote than in the musical instrument he chose to play. Maybe he was just growing older and maturing, perhaps he was just going through a natural change. Dylan is a poet, far more than he is a musician. Just as *Bringing It All Back Home* came out he was asked by an interviewer whether he thought his songs contained sufficient poetry to be able to stand by themselves, without music. His reply was 'If they can't do that, then they're not what I want them to be. Basically, I guess I'm more interested in writing than in performing.'[9] So, to understand the changes that he was going through when he went electric, it makes far more sense to look at what he was writing, the images and ideas he was trying to get across, rather than the more technical matter of the instrument he was playing. If he believed that his choice of instrument enhanced what he was trying to say, that was his prerogative.

DOLLY

His fans don't pay too much attention to it – perhaps they take it for granted, perhaps it has never occurred to them – but in the corporate world Bob Dylan is sometimes held up as a model for thought leadership. Often he is regarded in this way simply because he was the first to articulate the self-evident fact that the times they were a-changin', or because there are phrases in his lyrics that possibly offer practical advice, like those in 'Subterranean Homesick Blues' about not following leaders, or not needing a weatherman to find out which way the wind blows. The need for experts is a question under scrutiny in a world driven by populist sentiment.

It is undoubtedly true that business people might be able to benefit from listening to some of Dylan's lyrics. But it is not because of soundbites or maxims that they might find in the words he uses; his influence is far more extensive than that. If Dylan can be considered to be a thought leader it is not because he encourages different behaviours in the workplace, or tries to change the mindset of business executives. Dylan's thought leadership is not about how or what to think, rather it is about the far more fundamental act of changing one's way of thinking. It is about breaking out of constraints and boxes. Not just as he had done with folk music, but even breaking out of the very expectation of what a song could be about.

The first two slots in *Billboard*'s Hot 100 Songs of 1964 were occupied by The Beatles, with 'I Want to Hold Your Hand' and 'She Loves You'. Both songs, in fact well over 80 of the Hot 100, were simple, catchy ditties about the love of a man for a woman, of a girl for a boy. Even the third song in the *Billboard* Hot 100, 'Hello, Dolly!' the theme song from a musical comedy about marriage, is sung by a man, Louis Armstrong, to a woman. There is no surprise in that, music is the food of love, and the vast majority of popular songs have always been romantic. Every Dylan album, including *Bringing It All Back Home*, had love songs on it. But *Bringing It All Back Home* raised the intellectual bar for rock and pop music.

Audiences had long grown used to songs with little or no meaning, tunes projecting cloying sentiments through banal words, written merely for the sake of a catchy and memorable melody. Dylan changed all that. He had been doing so ever since *Freewheelin'*, but in *Bringing It All Back Home* the challenge he presented to his audience was unprecedented. No performer had ever produced an album that encouraged its listeners not only to pay attention to the words, but to try to understand what they meant. It was one thing to listen to 'With God on Our Side' or 'The Lonesome Death of Hattie Carroll' and be affected in some way by the lyrical narrative. Trying to decipher 'Subterranean Homesick Blues' or 'It's Alright, Ma (I'm Only Bleeding)' was a wholly different experience. This was Beat poetry set to music, as defiant as anything that Ginsberg or Burroughs had ever written, and with a far greater reach.

Dylan has been called the voice of his generation because he articulated their concerns about injustice, race, power and war. He has been called a prophet because he was far-sighted enough to anticipate the issues that would become the subject of popular protest. And he was accused of betrayal when he stopped protesting about topical issues, when he picked up an electric guitar and sang obscure and puzzling words. But Dylan's far-sightedness did not come to an end when he picked up an electric guitar, and he did not stop articulating the imaginings of his generation simply because his lyrics were no longer topical. This was a generation which expressed itself through its music, which was living through times of such baffling change that, while they might enjoy listening or dancing to catchy, cheerful, sing-along pop songs devoid of content or meaning, such music was never going to satisfy their questing spirits. Even rock 'n' roll wasn't enough for them. They needed ideas as well as rhythm and melody.

Within the next couple of years nearly every major rock and pop band would abandon their signature style, the music that had made them famous, and become purveyors of 'head' music. Dreamy, mystical, hallucinatory, inspired by the psychedelic drugs they were either experimenting with or the meditations they were practising, their fans couldn't help but listen to the words. When the musicians weren't reliving their trips or transcendence, or even if they were among those few bands who eschewed heightened awareness, they were telling stories, delivering social commentaries, professing revolution, attacking the 'system', or simply shattering consciousness through the sheer volume and aggression of their playing.

There was a backlash of course, not everyone wanted to hear experiential music. In the world the cool kids derisively labelled as 'straight', soppy songs became soppier, crooners doubled down on sentimentality, one or two artists got into the charts simply by spoofing what everyone else was doing. But overall, the music that the boomer generation was listening to during the mid-to-late Sixties was more thoughtful, more intelligent, more complex than the music their parents had danced to when they were young. The age of record companies competing to produce the catchiest melodies was over; mid-Sixties pop music needed to have something to say. Hallucinogens and oriental mysticism played their part, but it was Bob Dylan who kicked off the idea of music to get you thinking, two years before everyone else, with *Bringing It All Back Home*.

None of this meant that Dylan was a prophet and nor did his generation think of him as their voice. It was the media who called him that, not the young people. Nor was he the only one who could see that the world was changing and that his peers were becoming increasingly concerned about the great issues of the day. The Beats, the folk singers, the student activists all saw it just as clearly. They just didn't have Dylan's magic, his skill at capturing the ear of the world. But for all those who were disturbed or felt let down by the electric tracks on *Bringing It All Back Home*, there were many, far more in fact, who were ready for them, who had been waiting, even though they hadn't known what they had been waiting for. Dylan was no prophet. He just arrived at the right time.

JOAN

Bringing It All Back Home was released in March 1965. Its release coincided with the end of an East Coast tour Dylan had been playing, joining Joan Baez as a guest at some of her performances and playing a few gigs on his own. He was due to be heading off for a tour of Britain in April. Joan would be going with him and she expected Bob to invite her to join him onstage midway through his act, just as she had been doing for him during most of the past year.

It didn't work out like that. They arrived in England on 26 April, to be received at London Airport by a crowd of journalists and hundreds of fans; it was the sort of reception that The Beatles were by now used to, but which was way beyond Dylan's expectations or desire. He had agreed that the American cameraman Donn (D.A.) Pennebaker could accompany him on the tour as a roving eye, with the intention of making a film of the tour. The footage he took, using a hand-held camera, was released in 1967 as the documentary *Don't Look Back*. Pennebaker's footage shows Dylan and his entourage calmly entering the arrivals lounge, only to instantly find themselves swamped by screaming fans and surrounded by bobbies in old-fashioned helmets helping them to make their way through. The camera cuts to an unremarkable press conference, where Dylan is asked why he is carrying an oversized light bulb ('I always carry a light bulb – someone gave it to me.') and Albert Grossman loses his rag with the inane questions, telling one of the journalists that Dylan wasn't in England to perform for newspapermen, that he was one of the most important figures in American life. Then the entourage was off to the Savoy, London's pukka hotel by the River Thames because, as Dylan said, 'I can't live in a shack.'

Britain was the acknowledged global centre of pop music in 1965, due to The Beatles and The Rolling Stones, and the very many other bands that found popularity in their wake. The teenage fans, born to parents traumatised by everything they had lived through during World War II, had grown up in an austere, repressive, post-war Britain. The older ones remembered food rationing and had grown up playing in rubble-strewn gaps on the streets where bombs had fallen among terraces of houses.

They had offered pennies to the war-wounded begging on the streets, and at school had been lectured by disillusioned teachers, variously knocked back by their own war experiences or regretting the lives of friends that had been sacrificed, mourning the decline of Empire and the nation's diminishing global influence, or lamenting that, after all the years of suffering and 'pulling together', the country was still no closer to a socialist utopia. That went on until the second half of the 1950s. Then it all changed. As the first of the baby-boomers, those born in the first months of peace, were approaching their teenage years, an economic miracle wiped away their tears. Prime Minister Harold Macmillan told them that they had never had it so good, and indeed they hadn't. The end of rationing, ramped-up government investment in nationalised industries, and a boosting of the workforce through increased immigration precipitated a rise in per-capita income and a boom in consumer spending. People were buying cars, cookers, washing machines, sitting in the new coffee bars, eating out, going abroad, many of them for the first time in their lives (unless they had fought in the war). The deprived boomer children were suddenly affluent teenagers and now able to buy records and clothes. It was a liberation. Economic freedom made the world so much more exciting. And few things were quite as exciting as going to see your favourite stars perform. Or better still, getting to see them in the flesh.

The exuberance of the fans was one thing. The behaviour of the British pop establishment visiting Bob Dylan as he held court in the Savoy was wholly another. The Beatles and The Rolling Stones came, also new-on-the-scene Donovan — the wannabe touted as Britain's answer to Dylan. So did The Animals, Marianne Faithfull and a whole host of lesser-known figures, up and coming, down and fading, or just hangers-on. They queued up to pay homage to him in his hotel room. At least, that is what they should have done. Instead, they burst in, en masse, treating his hotel suite as they treated those that they stayed in themselves on tour, drinking, abusing the hotel staff, throwing stuff out of the window, including glass shelves. Much to the anger of Bob Dylan, who had limited experience of loutish British behaviour and who owned up later to an old-fashioned belief that if you threw glass out of the window into the street, somebody might get hurt.

Journalists came and went. One asked him if he was Jewish. 'No, I'm not,' Dylan replied, 'but some of my best friends are. You'd better interview Tito Burns, the agent for the tour, because I know he is Jewish.'[10] The Savoy experience was all too much.

If being mobbed by excitable fans is a measure of stardom then in April 1965 Bob Dylan was more popular in Britain than he was in the States. The charts seemed to bear that out too: *Bringing It All Back Home* reached number 1 in the British album rankings, whereas in America it peaked only at number 6. Tickets sales too suggested that something called Dylanmania – a word coined by John Lennon in a conversation with the *Melody Maker* journalist Ray Coleman – was about to break out in Britain. 'I'm not saying the kids in this country won't grow to like his stuff, but there can't really be Dylanmania,' Lennon had said.[11] Why that was, he didn't say.

Of Joan Baez, little was seen and even less heard. She may have expected that Dylan would invite her to join him onstage, but it didn't happen. She was deeply hurt. Not simply because he didn't invite her onstage, though that would have been bad enough. Because Joan taking him under her wing and having him perform publicly with her had been one of the catalysts for the sudden uplift in his career. The real hurt was that Dylan was clearly no longer interested in her, that their relationship had come to an end. He just didn't have the grace to say anything to her, he just kept her hanging around. It is said that Joan didn't know about Sara, that she only found out about her when they were back in the States, when Joan rang the bell and Sara answered the door.

Dylan's rejection of Joan in favour of Sara mirrored the way he had treated Suze when he first became involved with Joan. He was now 24 years old, still young enough to be precocious in his attitudes to women, famous enough to be arrogant and, increasingly, stoned enough to not think too deeply about the way he treated people.

MARY JANE

Rock-music legend has it that the first time The Beatles smoked a joint was when Bob Dylan visited them at the Hotel Delmonico in New York, in August 1964. Some dispute this, saying that The Beatles had first come across marijuana, Mary Jane or pot as it was then known, when they played in Hamburg in 1960. Maybe they had come across it then, but Paul McCartney confirmed the Hotel Delmonico account:

> And Bob had disappeared in the backroom; we thought maybe he'd gone to the toilet, but then Ringo came out of that backroom looking a bit strange. He said, 'I've just been with Bob and he's got some pot!', or whatever you called it then. And we said, 'Oh, what is it like?' And he said, 'Well, the ceiling is sort of moving, coming down.' And that was enough. After Ringo said that, the other three of us leapt into the backroom where Dylan was, and he gave us a puff on a joint.[12]

By the time he met The Beatles, Dylan was a regular smoker of weed. There was nothing unusual about that, bohemians of all stripes and creativities had been smoking marijuana for decades. In his 1956 poem 'America', Allen Ginsberg wrote, 'I smoke marijuana every chance I get.' When, a few months earlier, Dylan had set off with his pals, driving across the country to his gigs in Denver and California, they had reportedly arranged for friends to post bags of grass to post offices ahead of them along the route, so they wouldn't be caught carrying too much if they were stopped.

Dylan had been an early adopter of marijuana, but the rest of his generation were not far behind. Marijuana was illegal in nearly all western countries but its popularity was growing. In America it was most commonly smoked as 'grass', rolling the dried leaves of the cannabis plant into a 'joint', a fat cigarette, either with or without tobacco, or smoking it neat through a pipe or hookah. The cognoscenti removed the seeds before smoking; they tended to go pop when hot, often landing onto the smokers' clothes and burning a hole. Those who weren't so particular kept the seeds in; grass was not cheap, so why throw away any part of it? In Europe, where marijuana tended to be imported from Pakistan, Nepal, Afghanistan, Morocco or Lebanon, it arrived compacted into blocks of cannabis resin. They didn't call it grass in Europe, they called it hash, short for hashish, or dope. It was smoked in the same way though, and burning embers could, and did, frequently burn holes in the smoker's clothes. It was easy enough to spot a doper: you just took a look at their shirt.

The high-profile celebrities who smoked grass in the States tended to be discreet about it. Not only was it illegal, attracting a two- to ten-year sentence and a $20,000 fine, it wouldn't have been good for their public image in 1964 or 1965 to be outed as a drug user. Discretion notwithstanding, marijuana use grew prolifically, in black communities and on the jazz scene where smoking was cool and nobody made too much fuss about it, and as a badge of honour among the young, white middle classes: students, anti-war protesters, civil rights activists, anyone seeking to distance themselves from the norms of a society they were growing increasingly disillusioned with. Dope smoking was part of their rebellion, they enjoyed the mild, hallucinogenic high that marijuana gave them, an intoxication more pleasant and dream-like than alcohol. And they took to it precisely because it was illegal, knowing that their parents' generation would disapprove. Smoking grass was both a pleasure and a proclamation of personal independence. In the tumultuous 1960s, where it was clear to all that the world was a-changin', smoking marijuana marked out the young, white, middle class as pioneers of the new age, proud

to be different, unafraid to take risks (as long as they were mild),
doing what they could to ensure that the changes the world was
going through would be for the better and not for the worse.
Over the next couple of years they, and the tens of thousands
who would join them, would identify themselves as hippies, a
label that was soon to become popularised. They had listened to
Dylan, they shared his views on war and injustice; when he sang
that the times were a-changin', telling parents that their sons and
daughters were no longer within their command, they knew he
was singing about them. He could have been their leader, if he
hadn't stopped singing about politics and protest. They admired
him but increasingly they were unsure about where his lyrics
were taking them. He didn't seem to be leading them towards
the mysterious springs of enlightenment, where some were now
heading, to the raised levels of consciousness that could only be
reached through the use of hallucinogens, like mescaline or LSD.
Granted, some of the stuff on *Bringing It All Back Home*, like 'Bob
Dylan's 115th Dream', seemed to deliver hidden messages to
them when they were tripping – but so did William Blake's poetry
and they knew for certain that he'd never done acid, he'd lived
too long ago. There was no reason to believe that Bob Dylan did
acid too; his protest songs were powerful but they were pretty
certain he wasn't on the same transcendental plane as them. They
couldn't have been more wrong about that.

LSD was legal in America until 1966. In 1960 Timothy Leary,
a professor of psychology at Harvard, had begun researching
the hallucinogenic effects of psilocybin, the active ingredient
of magic mushrooms, and soon extended his research to LSD,
a mind-altering drug that had been used in medical treatments
since the 1950s. Leary and his assistant Richard Alpert gave both
drugs to volunteers as part of a research programme known
as the Harvard Psilocybin Project. His colleagues at Harvard
grew concerned about the methodology of his experiments, in
particular that he and Alpert were ingesting the drugs themselves

while carrying out their research. When Alpert was discovered to have given psilocybin to a student gratuitously, and not as part of their research, the university brought the project to an end. Leary and Alpert were ejected from Harvard. Alpert reinvented himself as a guru and spiritual guide (he was not the first nor the only Jew to have done so), and changed his name to Ram Dass. Timothy Leary became an evangelist for LSD, dispensing it liberally, conducting group sessions, writing acid-promoting books and articles until he was eventually sent to prison for possession of marijuana.

Dylan was not an apostle of Timothy Leary, but he took acid all the same, even before he smoked grass with The Beatles. His first 'trip' was in April 1964 but it wasn't until 1989 that anyone knew, and only then because the journalist Bob Spitz reported a conversation he'd had with the influential record producer Paul Rothchild. Rothchild had worked with The Doors, Janis Joplin, Neil Young, Joni Mitchell and Tim Buckley among many others, producing some of the most important rock albums of the 1960s. He had been in a car, driving from Massachusetts to Woodstock with Dylan and his road manager Victor Maymudes, ending up at Albert Grossman's new house where Dylan was living at the time. They'd smoked a lot of grass on the journey, carried on smoking once they arrived, and were all suffering from the munchies. Maimudes went into the kitchen to find food. In the fridge were two sugar cubes wrapped in foil. It was obviously acid. In those days the most common way to dispense LSD was to impregnate a sugar cube with the liquid chemical. From the way Rothchild told the story, he and Maimudes were already familiar with the effects of acid, but Dylan was not. '[Victor] shuffled over to me with a twinkle in his eye, nodded in Bob's direction and said "Let's do it! If there's two people in the world who can make him comfortable it's us. After all, someone's gonna do it to him." I looked at the sugar cubes and thought, "Why not?" . . . . And if you ask me, that was the beginning of the mystical Sixties right there.'[13]

Whether Dylan's acid trip was the catalyst for the surreal imagery of *Bringing It All Back Home* is debatable. Bob Spitz certainly thought so. 'Subterranean Homesick Blues', 'On the Road Again' and 'Bob Dylan's 115th Dream' could certainly have been written under the influence of acid, but the memory of one trip is unlikely to have produced an album of such sustained quality. He would either have needed to be tripping when he wrote those songs, or have taken so much acid that his life was one long hallucinogenic journey. The same goes for 'Mr Tambourine Man', it could have been written in the mellow, coming-down stage of a trip, while conceivably Dylan could have composed 'Maggie's Farm' during a vivid, post-trip flashback. But this all presupposes an intense ongoing engagement with LSD, of which Dylan's life story shows no evidence and which most likely would have had long-term effects that would severely impede his prospects. Plenty of former rock musicians can testify to the damaging effects of too much LSD on their careers.

Indeed, in an interview he gave to Nat Hentoff for *Playboy*, with his tongue almost certainly not in his cheek, he came out firmly against hard drugs and LSD:

> I wouldn't advise anybody to use drugs – certainly not the hard drugs; drugs are medicine. But opium and hash and pot – now, those things aren't drugs; they just bend your mind a little. I think everybody's mind should be bent once in a while. Not by LSD, though. LSD is medicine – a different kind of medicine. It makes you aware of the universe, so to speak; you realize how foolish objects are. But LSD is not for groovy people; it's for mad, hateful people who want revenge. It's for people who usually have heart attacks.

Such a speech doesn't sound like the opinion of a man using acid to help him compose his lyrics.

Equally debatable is Rothchild's assertion that Dylan's 1964 trip was the beginning of the mystical Sixties. Mysticism, whether as a result of drugs or Eastern meditation, did not surface properly until 1967, the hippie Summer of Love, when The Beatles, The Doors, Jefferson Airplane and The Rolling Stones led the psychedelic revolution. Dylan had moved on, no longer surreal, his 1967 *John Wesley Harding* album marking a transition to a style something closer to country than psychedelia.

Bob Dylan used drugs, like many other popular musicians and a significant proportion of his peers. As we know, he exerted a profound influence on the social upheavals of the 1960s. But even if we believe, perhaps without foundation, that acid-rock music and tripping musicians were responsible for the proliferation of mind-expanding drug use in the 1960s, we would be hard pushed to number Dylan among them.

8

ELECTRIC SHOCK

SWINGIN'

Dylan stayed in England for a little over a fortnight, playing his final two gigs at London's Royal Albert Hall on 9 and 10 May 1965. Built in 1871 and named after the German husband of Queen Victoria, the Royal Albert Hall is a large, circular building constructed in the style of Rome's Colosseum, with a glazed-iron domed roof and a faux classical frieze running around the top of the building in celebration of Victorian England's global dominance. Sited in the fashionable Kensington district, the Albert Hall was the city's most prestigious venue. With an audience capacity in those days of over 7,000 and containing an organ with 10,000 pipes, the hall had hosted the world's most celebrated orchestras and performers, and had staged everything from political meetings to boxing matches. Playing the Albert Hall was the sort of gig that might make or break a lesser artist's career. Winston Churchill had spoken there over a dozen times, Albert Einstein addressed a rally in support of Jewish academic refugees from Nazi Germany, and one month after Dylan's gig, Allen Ginsberg, William Burroughs and Lawrence Ferlinghetti would join a couple of dozen other poets onstage for the International Poetry Incarnation, an anarchic, exuberant celebration, the forerunner of the many counter-culture, or underground, happenings that would spring up in the city over the next few years.

The 7,000 tickets for Dylan's first concert sold out in just two hours – and this was in the days before the internet, when you either had to queue up to buy tickets in person, or vainly hope that you might manage to get through on the phone. The two concerts were flagship events for a city that was fast becoming the coolest in the world, with expectations riding high. Particularly among those who were late to the party, who didn't even know Dylan had played the Royal Festival Hall the year before, who hadn't even heard of him back then.

Before he went onstage Dylan heard that both The Beatles and The Rolling Stones were in the audience. So was Eric Burdon of The Animals, who the previous year had released a version of 'The House of the Rising Sun', a track Dylan had recorded on his first album, *Bob Dylan*. Dylan had sung it as a folk song, his adenoidal voice tempered by an acoustic guitar. Burdon sang it for The Animals as a rock number, backed by Alan Price on the organ, along with guitar, bass and drums. When Dylan heard The Animals' version he raved, telling a friend that it had blown his mind.

Those turning up at Dylan's gigs during his English tour may have been offered a copy of a red booklet with his name and picture on the cover. Straplined 'This is Not a Programme' and declaring him the 'The Folk Genius of his Generation', with the word 'Folk' in quotation marks, today we would call the 12-page booklet a fanzine. Consisting mainly of photos of Dylan alongside laudatory snippets of biography, the booklet preserved the fantasy story of his origins, telling readers that between the ages of ten and eighteen he had run away from home no fewer than seven times, and had been returned on six occasions. By the time he was 19 he was said to have gained wide experience of life, having travelled around such places as Gallup, New Mexico; Cheyenne Sioux; Burbank, California; and Phillipsburg, Kansas. Published by the Blackpool-based photographer Jack Vale, known for his postcards of pop stars he'd photographed when they played his home town, the fantasy biography said more about the authors of the booklet than about Dylan. They hadn't even bothered to research his life story properly. More interestingly though, they reported that he was 'said to have had some influence on The Beatles, The Rolling Stones, Sonny and Cher, Donovan for example'. The booklet didn't spell out what sort of influence he may have had, but most Dylan fans would have agreed about Donovan, at the very least. Donovan was the new kid on the block, the Scottish solo folk singer who'd just had his first hit and was being touted in the British press as the nation's answer to Bob Dylan.

Dylan must have heard a lot about Donovan during the tour, his name kept cropping up in *Don't Look Back*, the documentary that Donn Pennebaker was making as his camera followed Bob around Britain. At one point in the film, Dylan is seen reading about Donovan in a music paper and laughing, as if he was aware of the comparison and didn't think much of it. But he listened attentively when Donovan, two days before his 20th birthday, picked up a guitar in Dylan's Savoy suite and played 'To Sing for You'. Released the previous year on his first album *What's Bin Did and What's Bin Hid*, 'To Sing for You' is not Donovan's best song – he'd just had a hit with his far more memorable 'Catch the Wind' – but the young wannabe's chutzpah in playing anything at all in the presence of the master (all of four years older) won him plaudits from those sitting around Dylan's room. When he had finished, Dylan smilingly offered a few words of encouragement, took the guitar back, and launched into a confident rendition of 'It's All Over Now, Baby Blue' that made Donovan look like the warm-up act. Was Dylan competing? It certainly looks like that.

In fact the comparisons in the press between Dylan and Donovan were more about national self-interest than musical ability. Over the past two or three years the London that Bob Dylan and his entourage had flown into had become the hip capital of the world, famous for its fashion, music, art, discos and sexually permissive outlook. It would soon be called 'Swinging London', an epithet supposedly coined by *Time* magazine in 1966, quite some time after the city had actually begun to swing. The British press, *kvelling* in

London's transition from post-war austerity to being a player on the global stage once again (albeit culturally this time rather than imperially), could not brook any area in which the nation was not dominant. Particularly in music, the essential component of Britain's new cultural hegemony. Music was even more culturally important than fashion, earning more money and garnering more attention than the designs and sartorial concepts that seemed to be renewed almost daily, displayed to the world in London's Carnaby Street. Fashion was important but music was what Swinging London was all about.

British bands, even the most obscure, were being booked to play in the United States, their winged odysseys over the Atlantic described by the press as an 'invasion'. Leading the invasion, of course, were The Beatles, with The Rolling Stones coming something of a distant second. Behind them, Gerry and the Pacemakers, The Kinks, The Dave Clark Five, Herman's Hermits, The Hollies and The Yardbirds, all flying into the States in the spring and summer of 1965. The Moody Blues should have been on the list too, but their work permits didn't arrive in time.

The only other popular musician on the planet to rival The Beatles in creativity, innovation and cultural impact was Bob Dylan. That a star of such statute was not British, at a time when Britain dominated the world musically, was anathema to the partisan British press. Fortunately, Donovan had just arrived on the scene. And although he seemed to be far more of a Dylan copycat than a rival, even wearing a similar trademark cap, since the country needed a challenger to Bob's hegemony, Donovan was to be the man. Whether he liked it or not.

Bob Dylan probably didn't think twice about Donovan's putative challenge. But he did think quite a bit about England, and about Swinging London. He always had a soft spot for Britain, he toured the country many times, and in the 1980s and 1990s reports would occasionally circulate that he had been seen hanging out in a London club, or was about to play a gig in a small, obscure venue, but only for those of the cognoscenti who got to hear about it in time (there was no social media back then). In 2006 he and his brother David bought an estate in Scotland, keeping it for 17 years. And in 2012 a letter appeared in *The Times*, referring to a 1985 visit Dylan had made to the home of the British musician Dave Stewart in London's Crouch End:

> In 1985 Stewart had been working in Los Angeles with Bob Dylan and invited him to stop by his recording studio any time he was in London. Some months later Dylan decided to visit him and asked a taxi driver to take him to the address in Crouch End. There's a Crouch Hill, a Crouch End Hill, and a Crouch Hall to name but three. Dylan knocked at the front door of a house where he had been dropped off and asked the lady who answered if Dave was in. The woman said he was out but would be back in 20 minutes and invited Dylan to come in and wait. 20 minutes later, Dave – a plumber rather than a rock star – returned and asked if there were any messages, to which his wife said: 'No, but Bob Dylan's in the living room having a cup of tea.'[1]

Dylan had visited London several times before the 1965 tour, but his trip that year was seminal in the development of his career as an international star. In 1964, when he played at the Royal Festival Hall, he was still a star in the making, an up-and-coming singer of folk and protest songs. The fans who swarmed to see him on that occasion were those who typically frequented folk clubs, not the teenagers who favoured The Beatles, Gerry and the Pacemakers, and the rest. Now a year later, riding the crest of two waves simultaneously – his own career and the burgeoning British music scene – Dylan was mainstream. His record company issued three singles in Britain that spring and summer: 'The Times They Are A-Changin'' backed with 'Honey, Just Allow Me One More Chance' in March 1965, just before he arrived in London; 'Subterranean Homesick Blues' and 'She Belongs to Me' in late April, during the tour; and 'Maggie's Farm' with 'On the Road Again' in June, after he had returned home. All three singles did well, although, unlike the first two, 'Maggie's Farm' did not get into the British Top 10, peaking only at number 22. Nevertheless, three singles in four months, all entering the Top 30, was a big deal in those days; it was the quantity of singles one sold, rather than LPs or live appearances, that came to define a star. As far as Britain was concerned, Bob Dylan was now up there with The Beatles and The Rolling Stones. The Brits had adopted him as one of their own and when he went home it was as a sort of honorary member of the British music invasion of the States. The distinction could only propel him to greater heights in his native country.

Back home, *Billboard* took exception to the idea that Dylan's success in Britain somehow enhanced his reputation in the States. Far from it, they implied. 'In a successful tour of the British Isles, Bob turned the tide and reversed the English wave which has captivated the US. Bob's new album and his single, *Subterranean Homesick Blues*, are riding high on the British bestseller charts.'[2]

Bob Dylan's 1965 London tour was another rung on the ladder of his career. Both in terms of his popularity among the music-loving public, as well as the influence he exerted on those British musicians who listened to his music and came to hear his gigs. Or if they were lucky, visited him in his room in the Savoy Hotel.

Like every other musician, Dylan's trajectory to stardom in Britain was boosted immeasurably by a quirk of the country's archaic broadcasting laws. It was forbidden to operate a radio station in Britain without a licence, and broadcasting licences were about as difficult to get as an invitation to tea with the Queen. Kids could only hear their music on the wireless by tuning into Radio Luxembourg, based in the European country of the same name, its transmissions only arriving at night, fading in and out and accompanied by a cacophony of hisses, crackles and whistles. In 1964 a young entrepreneur, Ronan O'Rahilly, circumvented the law by broadcasting non-stop pop music from a boat in the North Sea outside British coastal waters. Others soon followed and within a few months a rash of 'pirate' radio stations were operating in the sea, beaming singles, 24 hours a day, to the nation's music-hungry fans.

In part it was listening to pirate radio, the thrill of being an accessory to transgression, that turned British youth into a tribe of music lovers. Pirate radio was cool. Broadcasting wasn't quite illegal, though the authorities did their best to shut the pirate stations down. But no crime was committed by listening.

PORTUGAL

After London, Dylan went to Portugal for a brief holiday, before returning to London to record a couple of shows for the BBC. Sara went with him. Dylan mentions their time together in Portugal in the eponymous song 'Sara' that he wrote after they broke up. Joan Baez, rejected and unhappy, remained in London. She was unaware of who he was with; she and Sara had not yet met.

When he got back to London and resumed his sojourn at the Savoy, Bob was feeling groggy. He paid it little attention, thinking it was just the after-effects of his Portuguese excursion. But when he woke up the next morning he was decidedly ill. The Savoy called the hotel doctor, who gave him an antibiotic, but that only made things worse. So Albert Grossman brought in a Harley Street physician, who diagnosed a stomach virus, probably something he had picked up in Portugal. Dylan was due to be at the BBC studios that afternoon and by the time that the producer heard he was not fit enough to appear, an 800-strong audience were already on their way to see the show. Rather than cancelling, the BBC cast around for a stand-in, eventually settling on the singer-songwriter Oscar Brown Jr to deputise. No record has survived of what the audience felt about the substitution.

Meanwhile, Bob's condition did not improve. Two days later he had a temperature of 104 and was admitted to the Lindo Wing, the private-patient unit of St Mary's Hospital in Paddington. Sara sat by his bed. By the time he had recovered and was ready to fly home, Sara was part of his life and Joan Baez was no longer to be seen. Once again he was a-changin'.

OUTRAGE

Back home the boomer generation was divided. Not so much divided among themselves as divided in their own minds. The oldest were now approaching their twenties, still young enough to hang on to their teenage dreams but now old enough to begin to comprehend the compounding fears of their parents' generation.

Music fed their dreams. The invading British bands dominated the singles charts, but their American counterparts were far from out of the picture. As Dylan's tour of England was winding down, British bands had nine records in the Top 10 in the USA, but American groups dominated *Billboard*'s recently revived Rhythm & Blues charts. Berry Gordy's stable in Detroit was churning out its distinctive Motown sound, producing hits for The Supremes, The Four Tops, The Temptations, Marvin Gaye, Martha and the Vandellas, and a good few lesser-known names. The Righteous Brothers topped the charts on both sides of the Atlantic with 'You've Lost That Lovin' Feelin''. Otis Redding, Sam Cooke and Ben E. King plumbed soulful depths that the lesser of the British mayflies could only aspire to. Popular music and youth walked hand in hand in 1965. But you only had to pick up a copy of *Broadside* – if you could find one – to be immediately reminded that music had a higher purpose, that it was more than just a vehicle for dancing and a love potion for the lonely of heart.

The cover of *Broadside*'s issue on 10 March featured the drawing of a barefoot young girl seated on the floor, her elbows on her knees, head in her hands. Hers was a picture of utter dejection.

Three weeks earlier the civil rights activist Malcolm X had been murdered, shot by a gunman while delivering a speech, with his daughters and wife sitting among the audience. A radical voice and former leader of the militantly religious, supremacist organisation, Nation of Islam, Malcolm X had been a controversial figure in his youth but had somewhat mellowed after his conversion to Islam. He had split from the Nation of Islam a few months earlier, after denouncing its leader for fathering several illegitimate children and 'religious fakery'.

A week before he was assassinated his family home had been firebombed, presumably as a reprisal for his secession from the Nation of Islam. The firebombing and his assassination were almost certainly connected. Three members of the Nation of Islam were arrested and convicted of his murder. Nearly half a century later, in 2021, after allegations of witness intimidation and suppression of evidence by law-enforcement agencies were deemed to be true, two of the convicted men were exonerated.

Broadside was not overtly concerned with the identity of Malcolm X's killers, it was his death they mourned, and the racial injustice that he had spent his short life fighting, notwithstanding the violent statements he had made in his youth. Steven Strake's eulogy in the March 1965 issue summed up *Broadside*'s position: 'Perhaps with his thinking you did not agree / But if you were scarred by the scars that had marred him / You may have reasoned the same way as he.'[3]

Now proclaiming itself to be the National Topical Song Magazine, the March issue of *Broadside* included the words and music of Tom Paxton's lament over the Freedom Summer deaths of Andrew Goodman, Michael Schwerner and James Chaney, and his condemnation of the Mississippi police, who were seen shaking hands with the rednecks, laughing and joking as they swore to find the murderers.[4]

As if to confute Paxton's elegy, a few pages further on *Broadside* printed a letter from Moses Asch, the founder of Folkways records.

In much the same way as Irwin Silber had railed against Dylan for no longer protesting, Asch was bewailing the magazine's apparent relinquishing of the fight against injustice. He had noticed that in the latest editions of *Broadside*:

> . . . the expression of the day seems to be 'Love', 'Moon', 'Spoon', etc., although an effort is made to bring this up to date in topical form by expressing it in anger, or the twist, or in cries of loneliness. Neither 'Broadside' nor [its sister paper] 'Sing Out' seems to understand that the true folk song or ballad deals usually with an injustice to man, and through this incorporation into song it attains a universality in which all people can share.[5]

Asch attached press clippings highlighting two incidents that he believed should have attracted the attention of the folk community, one from New York where police had framed an innocent man, George Whitmore Jr, for murder, the other an international outcry about the plight of Abram Fischer, a Jewish lawyer in South Africa who had been forced to go into hiding because of his opposition to the country's 'monstrous policy of apartheid'.[6] If Asch was right then Bob Dylan was far from being the only troubadour to have abandoned topical protest. Indeed, since his repertoire was somewhat wider than songs about moons and spoons, Dylan's offences against Asch's ideal of folk purity were less egregious than the sins of some of *Broadside*'s other contributors.

Dylan had nothing to say in public about the murder of Malcolm X. The two men had never met, the closest they would come was after the activist's murder, when segments of their faces appeared on the cover of the September 1965 edition of *Esquire* magazine, combined into a composite image together with those of Fidel Castro and John F. Kennedy. They were, according to the headline, '4 of the 28 who count most with the college rebels'.[7] But even if he had known Malcolm X, and even if he was still singing topical protests, Dylan would probably have said nothing explicitly about his assassination. It had never been his style to write eulogies to public figures, or to lament deaths that, unlike Medgar Evers or Hattie Carroll, were not those of ordinary people slain through oppression or injustice. Nevertheless, with the release of *Bringing It All Back Home* that month, it was time for *Broadside* to reproduce another Dylan song. The lyrics that he sent them were those of his tirade against the futility and absurdity of broken, latter-day society: 'It's Alright, Ma (I'm Only Bleeding)'.[8] With its images of guns and bullets, killers, death, and a dystopian world of darkness and confusion, if there is any track on the album that brought Malcolm X's murder to mind, it can only be 'It's Alright, Ma'. Whether Dylan deliberately sent that song to *Broadside* in response to the assassination, or whether it was just a random choice, can only be a matter for speculation. Nevertheless, we keep returning to the same conclusion: Dylan had given up topical protest but he was still fully engaged with the struggle against injustice and inequality. No other song from *Bringing It All Back Home* could have been quite so appropriate, given the darkening state of the world at that moment.

Confuting Moses Asch's accusation that *Broadside* was weakening its political stance, there seemed to be no limit to the number of injustices highlighted in that March 1965 issue of *Broadside*. Alongside the eulogies to Malcolm X and the three murdered Freedom Summer activists, directly above Dylan's 'It's Alright, Ma', the paper reproduced a biting, satirical criticism of American policy in Vietnam, written by a 26-year-old African-American, civil rights activist, Julius Lester. 'Everybody knows we're a peace-loving nation. The more peace the better – peace for every man – Piece of an arm – Piece of a leg – Six feet apiece – for everybody.'[9]

The son of a Methodist minister, Lester would go on to write dozens of books, teach Afro-American studies at the University of Massachusetts, convert to Judaism in the 1980s, and end his career as a Professor of Judaic and Near Eastern Studies while serving as a lay religious leader at a synagogue in Vermont. He died in 2018. In his obituary the *New York Times* called him the 'Chronicler of Black America'.

In the minds of the radical baby-boomers, the ratcheting up of the war in Vietnam was replacing the struggle for civil rights as the issue of most concern. By February 1965 America was conducting a sustained campaign of bombing against communist-backed North Vietnam and the following month the first servicemen specifically designated as combat troops arrived in the country. The University of Michigan was the first to stage a response. At first, a group of professors decided to organise a one-day strike, during which all lessons would be cancelled and replaced instead by lectures and discussions about the war. Then, after encountering objections from some of their own colleagues and the university administration, they modified their plans and held an all-night teach-in instead. The idea spread rapidly to other campuses and within a few weeks, tens of thousands of protesters were marching through the streets of Washington DC. At the Washington Monument, Joan Baez, Phil Ochs and The Freedom Singers all sang. If Bob Dylan was missed, nobody remarked upon it.

The morality of the war that America was conducting; the ethics of intervening in an internal struggle in a far-off land when America itself was under no military threat, were augmented by a concern that lay far closer to home. The draft was now beginning to touch those who had previously thought that it would pass them by. In July 1965 President Johnson announced that the numbers of those drafted each month would rise from 17,500 to 35,000. Although those drafted were selected by lottery, the increase in numbers raised the probability for every young man that he might be drafted. College students were exempted from the draft but it was only a short-term exemption – it would lapse once they had graduated. The previous year, 12 students had burnt their draft cards at a rally in New York. It was only a symbolic gesture; draft cards could easily be replaced. But as a symbol it rapidly caught on. In May 1965, 40 protesters burnt their cards at the Berkeley campus of the University of California and a further 19 followed suit a fortnight later. Draft-card burning was to become the most theatrical and widely copied gesture of the anti-war protests; it was easy to do and, even though President Johnson amended the law so that burning one's card became treated as a criminal act, for many people the threat of imprisonment or a fine was preferable to the alternative of risking their lives, and those of others, in Vietnam. Draft-card burning did nothing to directly impede the progress of the war, but it drew attention to the futility of the conflict. America was fighting to prevent the communists from seizing power in Vietnam, the Masters of War sending the nation's children to be slaughtered alongside the invisible foreigner, all to try to prevent the world from turning Red.

As horrific as it was, war was not the only matter on young people's minds. On 11 August, in the Los Angeles suburb of Watts, white traffic police pulled over a black driver they believed was drunk. The driver failed a sobriety test and panicked, believing he was about to be arrested. There was a scuffle, the police called for backup, bystanders gathered, and with minutes a fight had broken out. The driver of the car was arrested, as was his brother who had been in the car with him, and so too was their mother, who'd turned up when she heard of the trouble. Meanwhile the crowd was growing larger and angrier, and the police were wielding batons and guns to try to keep them at bay. An event that had begun as a possible traffic infraction was escalating out of control. Still the crowds came, still police reinforcements arrived. It seemed as if it would never end. Six days later, after non-stop rioting, looting and violence, 34 people were dead, over 1,000 were injured, and 4,000 arrests had been made. America had never experienced a race riot on such a scale.

The underlying causes of the disorder were not hard to discern. The underprivileged Watts suburb was overcrowded and grimy, and that particular week it was sweltering in temperatures of over 90

degrees. The buildings were derelict and crumbling, many stores
were empty, and unemployment was ubiquitous. Some 98 per cent
of the inhabitants of Watts were African American, yet the area
was policed by a force of whom only 5 out of 205 officers were
black. Civil rights workers had described the local police force as an
occupying power. Destitution and homelessness were rife, a former
policeman spoke of seeing a black woman give birth to a baby on
a sidewalk in the rain, after giving up in her attempt to walk to a
charity hospital.[10]

The author Thomas Pynchon visited Watts some months after
the riot. He wrote of the poverty, the despair, the oppression, the
violence, the abnormal realism of its residents: 'Man's got his foot on
your neck,' said one guy who was there, 'sooner or later you going
to stop asking him to take it off.' Pynchon compared Watts with
the white culture outside it, 'that creepy world full of pre-cardiac
Mustang drivers who scream insults at one another only when the
windows are up . . . of an enormous priest caste of shrinks who
counsel moderation and compromise . . . it is next to impossible to
understand how Watts may truly feel about violence.'[11]

This was the America that the baby-boomers were growing up
in. A nation of two tribes distinguished only by the colour of their
skin, the dominant ruling by force, insensible to the suffering of
the oppressed, the cowed too forsaken, erupting only in sporadic
outbursts of violence. A land in which extremists would murder
a political ally for not being extreme enough, and firebomb his
family's home. A country conducting a war thousands of miles
distant, irrationally fearing the spread of a political ideology that
time would prove posed no threat at all.

If that was all that 1960s America had to offer, a young person's
life would have been miserable in the extreme. But that wasn't
all. Far from it. In place of the chaos and suffering, the horrors
and the futilities that their parents and grandparents seemed likely
to bequeath to them, the baby-boomers were creating a culture
of their own. Granted, it was not a culture they had created

themselves, it had been passed down to them by folk singers, jazz bands and blues musicians, refined by rock 'n' roll, and spiced with the exotic plants and chemical potions that were becoming ever easier to obtain. It was positive and optimistic with an outlook that at this stage leaned more towards rejecting than rebuilding. They knew they did not want to live in the authoritarian, discriminatory, competitive world their parents and grandparents were bequeathing them; they weren't yet sure what the world they would construct might look like. (It turned out not to be very different, but that was far in the future.) The more politically aware were listening to Joan Baez, Pete Seeger and Phil Ochs, attending rallies and marching against the war. The intellectuals were reading Burroughs, Ginsberg, some had even discovered Rumi, Hesse and Rimbaud. Those with no interest in literature or politics were into their music, listening to The Beatles, The Beach Boys, Elvis, The Supremes, and those many bands with the funny accents known collectively as 'the British invasion'.

Music was the glue that bound young people to their peers and distanced them from their elders. Music was the only thing that made sense. There were songs for every mood. Love songs obviously, as ever there were plenty of those. Songs of rebellion – The Animals' 'We Gotta Get Out of This Place' – as big a hit with the draftees in Vietnam as among gate-fevered teenagers. Nonsense rags: 'Wooly Bully' was the number 1 single of 1965. The Rolling Stones' '(I Can't Get No) Satisfaction' expressed frustration and humour, while The Beatles offered light, catchy, memorable numbers, as did anyone else from the north of England who could play a guitar.

Dylan may not have been singing topical protest songs but there was still a place for politics and despair; few painted as dystopian a picture as Barry McGuire's 'Eve of Destruction', written by P. F. Sloan, a man who never received as much recognition as he deserved. Sloan was 19 when he wrote it, a boomer articulating the feelings of his peers. Castigated by pop-music snobs and intellectuals as puerile, simplistic, and a poor imitation of Dylan in his protest years, the song reached number 1 in the *Billboard* Hot 100 in September 1965. Castigated it may have been, but Dylan did not seem to consider it a poor imitation. Confirming the significance of music in a world that was a-changin' he was quoted as saying, 'If you want to find out anything that's happening now, you have to listen to the music. I don't mean the words. Though Eve of Destruction will tell you something about it.'[12]

There was music for every mood, but Bob Dylan was still outpacing them all. 'Work this out', he seemed to be saying to those whose outlook wasn't obscured by his shift of musical technology, as his surreal lyrics barrelled through their ears, distorted images flashed before their eyes. Maybe he did make sense after all. And even if he didn't, did it matter? Nothing else in the world their parents were bequeathing them made sense, what did they expect from him? Buy *Bringing It All Back Home*, listen to it, don't try too hard to work out what he is saying. Just enjoy it.

Dylan was the only artist with a universal appeal within the generation. Topical enough to appeal to the politically minded among the boomers yet sufficiently commercial to feature on the radar of those turned off by current affairs, Bob Dylan was coming to terms with his new-found fame. It was changing him, as fame changes everyone who finds themselves snared in its web, but Dylan was smart enough to manage the transition. His musical development had taken place almost in lockstep with his growing popularity. *Bringing It All Back Home* was a far more adventurous and mature album than *Another Side of Bob Dylan*, recorded just a few months earlier, and the interval between the two albums coincided with the explosion in his popularity. In changing he had upset many of his original followers, not just Irwin Silber and Paul Wolfe but the many others who didn't bother to complain publicly about his perceived loss of folk purity and radical integrity. The reason they were so upset was because they still saw Bob Dylan as one of their own and believed he was abandoning them. They were wrong. It's just that he chose to be an enigma, because being enigmatic was one of the principal drivers of his stardom. To understand Bob Dylan at that time meant looking at what he was actually doing, not what he was presumed to be doing.

For example, if Bob Dylan did not see himself as, in some ways, still wedded to the world of folk music, why did he continue to send songs to *Broadside* until 1978? Equally, why did he return in the summer of 1965 to perform again at the Newport Folk Festival. After all that had happened the previous year, after all the criticism levelled at him, the bad reviews, Irwin Silber's tirade, it would have been quite understandable if Dylan had decided that he had indeed moved on, that he really had left the world of folk behind. But he went to Newport in 1965, and there are two possible reasons why he decided to go. The first is that he still felt connected to that world, to the people he had known in Greenwich Village, to the enthusiasts who had given him a leg up as he started his career, to the memory of Woody and the inspiration he had drawn from him. The other possibility is that he had something to show them. Maybe it was educational; he wanted to show them that folk music could, and needed to, evolve and this was how to do it. Or maybe it was to make a point; that he was playing at Newport because he refused to be alienated; whatever they might think of him, Bob Dylan was not prepared to be written off as a performer who had sold out. Either way, Newport 1965 marked probably the single most dramatic turning point in Bob Dylan's career.

NEWPORT AGAIN

On 20 July 1965 Columbia Records released 'Like a Rolling Stone', Bob's second single of the year. One second short of six minutes long, in an age when singles rarely exceeded half that duration; the length of the song proved to other young artists that they need not feel bound by the recording industry's conventions; that change was as much in the air of the recording studio as it was on the university campus or in the overheating, protest-ridden, summer streets. More importantly though for Dylan, he had recorded 'Like a Rolling Stone' with an electric backing band. It wasn't his first electric single; he'd made one called 'Mixed-Up Confusion' in 1962, while he was recording the tracks for *Freewheelin'*, but the record failed to make an impact. Columbia had also released a single edition of 'Subterranean Homesick Blues', to coincide with the release of *Bringing It All Back Home* earlier in 1965, with Dylan backed by two electric guitars, a bass and a piano. His long-term producer Tom Wilson had encouraged Dylan to put his acoustic guitar to one side and play with an electric band; the venture was one Dylan was more than happy to undertake. He had been overawed by the way The Animals had taken the blues classic 'The House of the Rising Sun' and turned it into a rock number and, now that he was in the front line of the biggest revolution in popular music the world had ever known, he had no qualms about going out on a limb and doing the unexpected. In terms of his own artistic progression he was on fire. The folk purists might have thought him a traitor, but the change he was going through was honest; he was being himself, rather than the person Greenwich Village wanted him to be.

He said as much, when interviewed a few months later by Nat Hentoff for *Playboy*. Hentoff asked if, given the widespread negative reaction to his new style, he thought he'd made a mistake? Dylan replied: 'A mistake is to commit a misunderstanding. There could be no such thing, anyway, as this action. Either people understand or they pretend to understand – or else they really don't understand.'[13]

There had been no time for the market to react to 'Like a Rolling Stone' before the Newport Festival opened on 24 July 1965. He played that afternoon, just him and his acoustic guitar, singing 'All I Really Want to Do'. The same afternoon The Paul Butterfield Blues Band played at a workshop, with

Dylan's friend Mike Bloomfield on guitar, and nobody batted an eyelid at the amplified music. John Lee Hooker and Dave Cash had each played electric guitars at Newport in previous years; nobody cared then either. A scuffle broke out though, between Dylan's manager Albert Grossman and the folk musicologist Alan Lomax. Grossman had taken exception to the way in which Lomax had introduced the Butterfield Band, sneering at them and implying that, as white musicians, they had no business playing the blues, and anyway they had no idea how to do it. Grossman, who was about to sign up the Butterfield Band as his clients, was outraged and told Lomax so. Their argument became physical and they ended up wrestling on the ground.

It may have been Lomax's disdain for white musicians playing music that didn't belong to them which influenced Dylan that afternoon; perhaps he was reminded of the criticisms he'd received from Irwin Silber and others about his own musical transition. For that reason or another, Dylan made up his mind there and then that he would play an electric set. It hadn't been his intention when he arrived at Newport, but Mike Bloomfield and Al Kooper, both of whom had backed him on 'Like a Rolling Stone', were at the festival, electric was the direction Dylan was heading in, and he saw no reason to conceal his evolving musical trajectory from the Newport crowd. He had a word with Bloomfield, they assembled some musicians, and they all went that evening to the large nearby home of Newport founder George Wein, where they rehearsed.

Dylan's set the next afternoon did not turn out quite as the audience expected. The first shock was that Dylan appeared onstage dressed like a rock star, in London's latest Carnaby Street fashions. The unwritten code among the folk crowd was to dress in simple, conventional clothes, dark or grey jackets and trousers, perhaps a colour in the shirt, but nothing too bright. Folk wasn't about the clothes, it was about the music, and the closer its ambassadors came to wearing a uniform, the less opportunity for individual performers to project their egos or for the audience to judge an artist on their looks rather than their music. Folk artists just didn't wear narrow trousers, boots, leather jackets and orange shirts with high, extravagant collars; the very idea was anathema. So when Bob Dylan walked onto the stage, dressed in the selfsame outfit, it took a moment for the audience to take in the incongruity of his appearance. By the time they did, they realised that he wasn't on the stage alone. There were other musicians with him, guitars, a keyboard, drums. And the sound they were making was dreadful. The amplifiers and speakers were too loud, the instruments all out of balance with each other. In the audience Dylan's voice could hardly be heard.

Dylan opened with 'Maggie's Farm'. The jeering and booing began as the first note was struck. Mike Bloomfield was having the time of his life on lead guitar, but all anyone could hear in the crowd was the feedback from his amplifier. Not that they wanted to hear Bloomfield's rocking riffs; it was Bob they were booing, not Mike.

Clearly taken aback by the audience's reaction, Dylan launched straight into 'Like a Rolling Stone'. The audience's response was the same. Backstage, the normally mellow Pete Seeger was reportedly having a meltdown, threatening to cut the electric cable. He'd never heard anything like it. He claimed later that it wasn't the electric music that distressed him but the distorted sound coming off the stage; his elderly father was in pain at the noise.

Bob led the band off the stage after the third number, a song called 'Phantom Engineer' that he would reincarnate on his next album as 'It Takes a Lot to Laugh, It Takes a Train to Cry'. The audience thought they had jeered him off. In fact, having assembled the band just the night before, they'd only had a chance to rehearse three numbers, and they had come to the end of their repertoire. But they might as well have been jeered off; Dylan was plainly numbed by the reception he had received. He hadn't done anything wrong, he genuinely didn't understand the audience's hostility.

Once they realised that Dylan wasn't about to return after just three songs, the audience grew even more restless. Still thinking it was their booing that had driven him off stage, they now wanted him to come back. Many of them had only bought tickets and travelled to Newport so that they could hear Bob Dylan, they expected more than three barely recognisable cacophonies. It took Peter Yarrow of Peter, Paul and Mary to restore some equanimity. He came onstage and suggested that Bob might come back if the audience called for it. Then he turned around to call out to Dylan, asking him politely if he might return for one more number. He did. He strapped an acoustic guitar around his neck, borrowed an E harmonica from the audience, and played 'Mr Tambourine Man'. It was the right song to play, it soothed his jangled nerves and calmed the audience. He ended with 'It's All Over Now, Baby Blue', appropriately, and bade farewell to Newport. He would not return until 2002 – 37 years later.

It would be too simple to imagine that the audience was unhappy with Dylan at Newport because he played an electric set. As we have seen, he wasn't the first to do so in the festival's history, and it would have been hard to be a Dylan fan, to have listened to 'Subterranean Homesick Blues' or the recently issued single of 'Like a Rolling Stone', and to have convinced oneself that he only played acoustic. All true Dylan fans knew that he had been recording electric music long before he went onstage at Newport. The audience reaction was clearly based on something more than Dylan wielding an electric guitar or having a band behind him. Many fans were simply upset at the poor sound quality, as Pete Seeger claimed he had been. Some just didn't like it; it wasn't what they had come to Newport to hear. And tellingly, not everyone in the audience was unhappy with his set; some applauded, some were dancing.

Of course there were those with a passion for authentic, unadulterated folk songs, whose politics leaned to the left, who felt betrayed, who considered Dylan to have sold out to capitalist interests, peddling a commercial product to undiscerning consumers. For such fans, rock music of any description was an ethically suspect genre, devoid of values and principles, a musical genre with no more purity than that of the crooners and family entertainers, for whom the word 'blacklist' never held any meaning. Phil Ochs condemned their booing of Dylan saying they were 'in reality booing themselves in a most vulgar display of unthinking mob censorship'.[14]

But for a good proportion of the audience, it wasn't about the music at all. It was about Bob Dylan. About the man they had grown accustomed to thinking of as a spokesperson, a leader who called out injustice, who had the ability to articulate so well what many of them thought but could not put succinctly into words, let alone set to music. An artist who, just by singing forcefully about it, had shown them that it was safe and legitimate to shine a light into the dark corners of the world. A young man whose fame and popularity had shown them that they were far from alone in the way they thought, an icon around whom a movement had seemed to be coalescing. Yet a man who now appeared to have turned his back on it all, to have walked away from the pressing issues of society and politics. Who was heading off in another direction. To a place they knew nothing of, who was leaving them behind.

For most of them the disillusionment didn't last long. Newport was a shock, but they got over it. By the time Dylan's new album came out at the end of August, they were ready to buy it, play it, talk about it, attempt to decode the meaning of his words. They were beginning to understand now. It was true that Dylan had become much more complicated. But so too had the world. Everything was going topsy-turvy. Fear and hatred in the streets, the old certainties disappearing. Like apple pie and ice cream the features of American life they had thought were permanent were now memories of a vanished innocence. Dylan hadn't abandoned them, he was going through changes just as they were, and he was giving them the confidence to recognise that about themselves. To appreciate that they could and should respond to their misgivings and uncertainties about the world they were growing up in. Just as he could change, throwing off the limiting shackles of the narrow folk world, so too they had the power and means to discard the fetters keeping them tethered to the old order.

HIGHWAY 61

Even those who were convinced that Dylan was wrong to abandon the folk tradition must surely have reconsidered when they heard *Highway 61 Revisited*. Widely acknowledged as his best album to date, the whole of *Highway 61* was recorded with an electric backing band. Although when it was released, the electric take of the final track, 'Desolation Row', had been replaced by an acoustic version.

'Desolation Row', high up on the list of contenders for Dylan's greatest song, is an 11-minute-long commentary on the fractures of a society that in his telling seems to be fictional, but in actuality reflects the left-behind parts of America in the mid-1960s. Decaying and underprivileged, down and out, filled with bizarre characters – a tightrope walker, Einstein in the garb of Robin Hood, Cinderella, Dr Filth, whose comic-book personas conceal the desperation of their masks. A string of loosely connected images, one could easily dismiss 'Desolation Row' as a preposterous fantasy. Until we remember that it was penned by the poet still most noted for highlighting the injustice and inequality rife in society. Its opening line about selling postcards of a hanging refers, in the author Aaron J. Leonard's opinion, to 'the monstrous practise in the US of picture postcards of lynchings'.[15] In the same vein as 'It's Alright, Ma (I'm Only Bleeding)', 'Desolation Row' marks Dylan's transition away from condemning the terrible things that have happened to individuals and towards the dreadful state of the world we live in.

The opening line of the track that gives the album its name, *Highway 61 Revisited* is sometimes, oddly, cited as evidence of

Dylan's erudition in Jewish textual studies and the depth of his immersion in Judaism's literary tradition. Spoofing on the story in Genesis 22, where Abraham is commanded to sacrifice his son Isaac, the song has been described as 'Dylan's most obvious attempt at Midrash'[16] (the ancient Jewish technique of bible interpretation). It is inevitably quoted in compendia of biblical references in Dylan's work.[17] Yet, while it is certainly the case that Dylan regularly inserts biblical references and allusions into his work, all this proves is that he is familiar with the Bible, just as he is with many great works of literature. Unlike, for example, Leonard Cohen, whose writings reveal a deep familiarity with Jewish scholarship,[18] there is nothing in Dylan's early oeuvre to lead to the conclusion that he had studied Judaism in greater depth than anyone else who grew up in a middle-of-the-road, traditional Jewish home.

Among the musicians who backed Dylan on *Highway 61 Revisited* were Mike Bloomfield and Al Kooper, both of whom had appeared with Dylan at Newport in 1965. Both Jewish and a couple of years younger than him, they would go on to become successful rock artists in their own rights, although like so many young musicians Bloomfield died before he even reached the age of 40. They had backed Dylan a few weeks before Newport when he recorded 'Like a Rolling Stone', the opening track on *Highway 61 Revisited* and another contender for the best Dylan number of all time.

Dylan initially recorded 'Like a Rolling Stone' as a single. He had returned from England exhausted from the tour and even more so from the virus that had seen him end up in hospital. Seriously considering giving up music and just concentrating on writing, he sat down to try his hand at a literary composition, ending up, he told the interviewer Martin Bronstein, with 'this story, this long piece of vomit, twenty pages long and out of it I took *Like a Rolling Stone* and made it as a single'.[19] It was the catharsis he was hoping for. It made him realise that writing songs was his vocation, releasing him from the uncertainty of what he was supposed to be doing. '*Like a Rolling Stone* changed it all: I didn't care anymore after that about writing books or poems or whatever. I mean it was something that I myself could dig. It's very tiring having other people tell you how much they dig you if you yourself don't dig you.'[20]

The record-buying public dug it too, turning 'Like a Rolling Stone' into his most successful single, keeping it in the charts for 12 weeks. Though it only reached number 2, kept off the top by The Beatles' song 'Help', one of their less memorable successes.

That Dylan was now a star was in no doubt. But that wasn't all. Everybody sensed it but *Billboard* spelled it out most clearly. Bob Dylan was responsible for a new genre of music. 'With Bob Dylan as the stimulus and the Byrds as disciples, a wave of folk-rock is developing in contemporary pop music.'[21] Explaining that acts like Billy J. Kramer, Jackie DeShannon and Sonny and Cher were now using 'folk-oriented material on singles', and misnaming The Lovin' Spoonful as 'The Living Spoonfull', the paper declared a 'folkswinging wave on' and opined that 'a song's lyrical content could become as respected as the dominating beat'. One wonders where *Billboard* had been for the past few years.

Not all those who had jeered at Newport had moved on from the disillusionment and learnt to love Dylan again. To the hardcore folk fans the betrayal was real. It was not so much the electrification of his music, that was merely the consequence of what he had changed, not the cause. Change can be threatening, and when one fears it is about to destroy things that are close to one's heart, the fears can quickly become irrational. If the crown prince of the folk world could so easily spurn the music that launched him to stardom, might that threaten the future of the entire genre? Dylan's old adversary Ewan MacColl thought so. After Newport, he sharpened the attack he had launched a couple of years earlier. He told *Melody Maker*, 'We're going to get lots of copies of Dylan – one foot in folk and one foot in pop . . . Dylan is to me the perfect symbol of the anti-artist in our society. He is against everything – the last resort of someone who doesn't really want to change the world . . . I think his poetry is punk. It's derivative and terribly old hat.'[22]

The surprise is that attitudes like that of MacColl persisted for so long. A year had passed since Dylan had sung 'It Ain't Me Babe' and 'Mr Tambourine Man' at the 1964 Newport Folk Festival, prompting Irwin Silber facetiously to praise his 'new ideas, new images, and new sounds'. Surely that was long enough for fans and critics to appreciate that he was undergoing a transition. Yet the resentment among those who felt betrayed by Dylan's new style showed no sign of abating. It would carry on for quite some while. As the world tour he was about to begin would show him.

ABUSIN'
Indeed if there is one feature of the tour that Dylan embarked on after Newport that stands out in nearly every gig, it is the hostility of some members of his audiences. Over the course of the next nine months, from the end of August 1965 when he played at Forest Hills, New York, until almost the final days of May 1966, when his peregrinations came to a close with two more gigs at London's Royal Albert Hall, he played to nearly 100 audiences in North America, Australia, continental Europe and Britain. He was given a hard time in nearly every venue, boos and jeers whenever he launched into an electric number, interspersed with a sort of quiet, smug triumph from his so-called fans when he played acoustic. Not every audience was hostile of course, by and large the Californians were more respectful, but the overriding impression that an impartial observer of the tour would have come away with, was that he was playing to people who were happy to pay money for their tickets, as long as they didn't have to listen to him.

He wasn't the only performer to play to audiences who didn't listen. In the early years of Beatlemania, when the Fab Four were playing to crowds made up mainly of teenage girls, the screaming was so loud that nobody, not even the performers themselves, could hear what was being played. It was different, though, to Dylan's experience. The Beatles-obsessed screamers were teenagers carried away by the excitement of seeing their idols. Those who booed Dylan were not excited, they were angry. And they were young adults, not teenagers.

There was one area of overlap, though, between the girls who screamed at seeing The Beatles and the tribe of Dylan abusers. Looking back at those days after they had grown up, girls who had screamed their hearts out at The Beatles and wept tears of joy described themselves as having been caught up in an infectious, mass frenzy. Years later, the author Linda Grant told an English reporter, 'I didn't understand why you had to scream and I didn't have an impulse to scream but it was what you did. It was mandatory. There was this cult-like element to it.'[23] Those who jeered during Dylan's sets would rarely own up to it, they were mostly too self-conscious, but they too had allowed their emotions to be whipped up into turmoil by the behaviour of those around them. Few rational individuals allow themselves to carry out a sustained campaign of abuse on their own, in a crowd, when those around them disapprove. The jeers and boos hurled at Dylan were driven as much by emotional contagion as by any deeply felt rage at Dylan's electric music.

Yet there was rage, and it was a far more existential rage than disappointment at a favourite musician. The boomer generation was growing angry. War was on everybody's mind and the protests against it were becoming more frequent and divisive. October 15th and 16th, days when Dylan was playing Baltimore and Princeton, were designated as International Days of Protest by the Berkeley Vietnam Day Committee and the newly created (but short-lived) National Coordinating Committee to End the War in Vietnam. Protests and vigils were held in 80 American cities and several European capitals. In Berkeley 15,000 protesters trying to get to the Oakland Army Terminal to hand anti-war leaflets to the soldiers found themselves twice turned back by the police, assisted by local Hells Angels. The leaflets they had wanted to hand out read, 'You may soon be sent to Vietnam. You have heard about the war in the news; your officers will give you pep talks about it. But you probably feel as confused and uncertain as most Americans do. Many people will tell you to just follow orders and leave the thinking to others. But you have the right to know as much about this war as anyone. After all, it's you – not your congressmen – who might get killed.'[24]

One protester, David Miller, burnt his draft card in New York, despite the new law imposing a five-year sentence and a $10,000 fine on anyone who engaged in such 'wilful destruction'. By the standards of the anti-war protests that would erupt over the next few years, the number of people who participated in the International Days of Protest was still small, but the underlying currents of public opinion show just how rapidly anger was building up. There was even outrage among the clergy. When Attorney General Nicholas Katzenbach responded to the International Days of Protest by declaring, 'There were some communists involved in it. We may very well have to prosecute', a group of Protestant, Catholic and Jewish clergymen angrily responded that 'to characterise every act of protest as communist-inspired or traitorous is to subvert the very democracy which loyal Americans seek to protect'.[25] Rabbi Abraham Joshua Heschel, the Jesuit priest Daniel Berrigan, and Lutheran pastor Richard Neuhaus instituted a programme of rallies, vigils, fasts and demonstrations protesting against the war. Those who expected Bob Dylan to be leading the protests, rather than apparently ignoring them, were not alone in feeling let down; a growing number of young Americans felt that betrayal was exactly what their government was doing. The target of one's rage hardly mattered, whether it was the government, or the man you believed was twice letting you down, once over electric music and again over his dereliction of the obligation to protest.

And so it went on. A combination of generational anger, a sense of having been let down, intensified by the herd instinct of crowds, found its outlet in abuse of the man on the stage – abuse which, it has to be said, after the first few occasions didn't seem to bother him too much. In his memoir, Al Kooper reminisced about the Forest Hills gig, the first of the tour. Having been subjected to a full five minutes of booing during which Dylan had told his band to 'keep playing the intro over and over until they shut up . . . We then segued into *Like a Rolling Stone* which was number one in the charts that week. Everyone sang along and then booed when it was over!'

A couple of hours later, when he and the bass player Harvey Brooks (formerly Goldstein, who in Zimmermanesque fashion had adopted a new surname) walked into the post-concert party at Albert Grossman's New York apartment, according to Al Kooper, 'Dylan bounded across the room and hugged both of us. "It was fantastic," he said, "a real carnival and fantastic." He'd loved it!'[26]

In fact the abuse that Dylan put up with during his nine-month tour wasn't just about generational anger, his style of music, or his abdication from his presumed role of generational spokesman. Sometimes it was just down to the technology: amplifiers and systems that were too powerful, badly balanced, and turned up too high for venues he was playing in, letting both Dylan and his audiences down. Time and again, musical journalists reporting on his concerts during the tour complained about the quality of the amplification. Either because it was a muffled, hazy wall of sound that made it impossible to distinguish between instruments, obliterating the skills of the musicians and drowning out Dylan's voice. Or it was thunderous, shaking the floor and hammering the air. The problem was that Dylan's entry into the world of amplified music had been poorly engineered; he had been lumbered with equipment that was far too powerful for the sound he wanted to create. On many occasions the booing was as much a response to the cacophony of sound as it was a reaction to Dylan's new musical style.

Close to 100 gigs in nine months is a huge burden for any artist to undertake. Being on the road for extended periods of time involves interminable journeys, in buses and on planes. Living out of suitcases, every night in a new hotel, always surrounded by the same people, never seeing one's home, family, lovers or friends. Each day punctuated by the stress and adrenaline rush of another gig, a new venue to scope out, a different audience to try to get the measure of. Journalists, autograph seekers, groupies and chancers hoping to piggyback on your success. Dealing with uncooperative venue managers, more used to working with classical orchestras and crooners than rock superstars, who had rarely, if ever, been asked to cope with a precocious, stoned entourage of young prima donnas or had been expected to accommodate a technical set-up on such a scale. Constant pressure, constant change, it's little wonder that little by little Dylan's backing musicians, once known as The Hawks and now as The Band, peeled off and went home. Al Kooper and Harvey Brooks were the first to go. They'd had enough. The drummer Levon Helm left, saying of the abuse they received, 'It wasn't that much fun ridin' around havin' people starin' at ya, booin' . . . it wasn't like people were comin' up and puttin' money in my pockets and makin' me rich . . . It was a drag.'[27]

Dylan, by contrast, had not had anything like enough. The tour was all-consuming but he did not let it take over his life. He found time to marry Sara, on 22 November, quietly, under an oak tree on Long Island, and ten days later to go into the studio with The Band to record a song first known as 'Seems Like a Freeze Out' and eventually as 'Visions of Johanna'. Then on 6 January, Sara gave birth to their first child, Jesse. Trying as hard as they could to retain some degree of privacy, they kept his arrival as quiet as their marriage.

'Visions of Johanna' was the first track to be recorded for Dylan's next album, *Blonde on Blonde*. The early sessions were held intermittently during January in New York, and then, because he and his producer Bob Johnston were not satisfied with what they had done, they went to Nashville to finish the album off. The only members of Dylan's backing group who played on the Nashville recordings were Robbie Robertson and Al Kooper, all the other musicians were local session artists.

Maybe it was the manic pace at which everything was happening that led Bob to place too much faith in Albert Grossman's handling of his affairs. The same month as he was recording *Blonde on Blonde*, a few days after Jesse was born, he and Grossman set up a new company, Dwarf Music, that would own the rights to all Bob's new songs. Bob signed the agreement without reading it; he had always trusted Grossman to act in his best interests and so when he was told that it was OK to sign the papers, that is what Bob did. He did not realise that under the agreement he and Grossman had equal shares in the new company; that they were each entitled to 50 per cent of the profits despite Dylan having done the greater bulk of the work. Dylan's lawyer later complained that while he was trying to explain the terms of the contract to him, Grossman had burst into the room and brought their discussion to an end, telling the lawyer there was no need for him to explain the contract to Bob, that he had done so already. Astonishingly, the lawyer obeyed.

The incident became one of the factors that would lead Bob eventually to part ways with Grossman. It's hard to know who was most at fault; Bob for signing a contract without reading it, Grossman for his manipulation, or the lawyer for his pusillanimity. It wasn't the first time Bob had been taken advantage of commercially – he was still only 23 years old – and it wouldn't be the last. Still, he was learning.

The pressure of his life at this time was unrelenting but, apart perhaps from his lethargic approach to the Dwarf Music contract, there is no suggestion that the stress was wearing him down. Some of those around him have indicated that he was a heavy user of

amphetamines, 'speed' as it was already called in those days, but
if the pressure was truly getting to him then drugs would have
been likely to make things worse, not better. He wasn't the only
rock star to be working at such a rate, the music business was on
fire in the mid-1960s, but unlike The Rolling Stones, The Beatles,
The Beach Boys and nearly all the other headline acts, there was
only one of him. Bands could, to some degree, share the burden
between them, allocate different tasks to different members.
Dylan couldn't do that, he had musicians behind him onstage,
but his career was his own, he had no partners or colleagues on
an equal footing. Everybody he worked with was paid, in one way
or another, because of him. When it came to pressure he was on
his own.

This is exactly how he liked it. A lesser solo artist would not have
coped. But, as we have seen, Dylan was not just a hugely talented
poet and musician at the peak of his powers, as popular as any artist
had ever been. Much more than that, he was also consumed by a
desire for success, a drive almost entrepreneurial in character that
encouraged risk-taking and extremes of behaviour. Risk-taking
by gambling with the loyalty of his fans, as he evolved musically
and poetically, refusing to remain in the same furrow despite
knowing it would guarantee his popularity. Extremes of behaviour
in subjecting himself to ever more stressful activities, paying no
attention to the need for, or conventions of, leisure or relaxation.
Stemming in part from his cultural and ethnic heritage. The quality
that most distinguished the hugely ambitious Bob Dylan from other
young Jewish visionaries, each with their own utopian dream, was
that the motivating factor in his case was not money (though that
came of its own accord) but fame, popularity and recognition.
Even when he was operating at maximum intensity he would push
himself further. Not enough to tour virtually non-stop, marry,
start a family, and record yet another album, his second of the year.
Pushing just that little bit harder, he would make it a double album.
Twice the amount of work.

BLONDE ON BLONDE

More ambitious than any of his other albums, for its length, the vast number of musicians involved, and its recording in two centres, Nashville and New York, *Blonde on Blonde* was released in May 1966. Acknowledged as the first double album in rock history, the seventh album in Dylan's career, *Blonde on Blonde* weighed in at 72 minutes, almost half as long again as *Highway 61 Revisited*. Columbia might have managed to squeeze it all onto a single LP had it not been for 'Sad-Eyed Lady of the Lowlands', the track that takes up the whole of side 4, playing for over 11 minutes.

The album opens with 'Rainy Day Women #12 & 35', Dylan's most provocative song since 'With God on Our Side' or 'The Times They Are A-Changin''. But now the provocation was not about injustice or war, it was considerably more facetious than that. The provocation was in the refrain, that everybody had to get stoned, together with the cheering and giggles in the background, Dylan's voice cracking with laughter, and the overall sense that the track was recorded at a party. In 1960s youth parlance getting stoned had already shifted its meaning from being drunk to smoking dope, and as soon as it came out the song was roundly condemned as advocating drug-taking. Particularly as it reached number 2 in the singles chart. Even more particularly because, according to some reports, most of the musicians were pretty stoned when they recorded it, though others frankly refute the charge.[28] As soon as they realised what they thought the song was about some radio stations banned it. Dylan was outraged, or claimed to be at the insinuation. On 27 May 1966, at his concert at the Albert Hall, and at the end of his seemingly interminable tour, he declared, 'I never have and never will write a drug song. I just don't know how to. It's not a "drug song". It's just vulgar.' However, he did preface his assertion that 'Rainy Day Women' was not a drug song by saying he would never play a gig in England again, a vow he has been breaking throughout his career.

Blonde on Blonde was the first of Dylan's albums not to contain anything that could be considered topical or a comment on the state of the world. There is nothing to compare with the social commentary of 'Desolation Row' or 'It's Alright, Ma (I'm Only Bleeding)' on his previous album and certainly no return to the protests on *Freewheelin'* and *The Times They Are A-Changin'* that anointed him with the unwanted accolade of spokesman for his generation. 'Stuck Inside of Mobile with the Memphis Blues Again' reverts to the jabberwocky image of 'Subterranean Homesick Blues' but feels more like an opportunity for Dylan to write and play a country-flavoured blues number, rather than make any meaningful contribution to the resolution of boomer-generation angst. 'Fourth Time Around' is said to have upset John Lennon because of its obvious melodic similarity to The Beatles' 'Norwegian Wood' and Dylan's apparent spoof of its lyrics. But Dylan had felt that in writing 'Norwegian Wood', Lennon had poached his style. Which just goes to show how beneficial cross-influences and creative rivalry can be.

'Leopard-Skin Pill-Box Hat' has sometimes been described as a satire on fashion or contemporary cultural trends, but it does not need to be taken so seriously. He may well have had somebody's sartorial extravagance in mind, perhaps Jackie Kennedy who was famous for her pill-box hats. But mockery is not social commentary, and like so much of Dylan's output he is laughing, not complaining, asking if he can jump on the pretty hat to see if it really is the expensive sort.

If there is any one lyrical theme to *Blonde on Blonde* it is love. We hear the wistful, haunting 'Visions of Johanna', the unattainable woman who transcends the mysteries of the Mona Lisa, the yearning for whom puts the lover he is with in the shade. 'I Want You' bears its subject in the title, even if the images and characters are typically Dylanesque surreal. As in the slow blues number, 'Pledging My Time', we are not told the identity of the woman he is addressing – allowing Dylan's many analysts and interpreters unlimited free punts at speculation. Similarly, 'One of Us Must Know (Sooner or Later)' invites suggestions as to who the subject is. Ostensibly about a woman who, despite his trying, was too young for him to get close to (the fault lying with her apparently, not with him), he may be harking back to his relationship with Suze Rotolo. More likely though, like most rock and pop love songs, it is not about anyone in particular.

Dylan continued his metamorphosis from generational hero to putative villain by offending the emerging new wave of feminists with 'Just Like a Woman'. The *New York Times* asserted 'There's no more complete catalogue of sexist slurs than Dylan's "Just Like a Woman", in which he defines woman's natural traits as greed, hypocrisy, whining and hysteria.'[29] But, as is often the case, controversy did nothing to dent the song's popularity. The single version that Columbia released in August 1966 reached 33 in the *Billboard* charts and 'Just Like a Woman' has been covered dozens of times. Frequently by women artists who have put their own gloss on the lyrics, turning the song into a celebration of womanhood rather than restating its original smug male egoism, in which women's emotions are dismissed as if they were those of little girls.

Of all the unnamed women who Dylan pays homage to, mocks or condemns on *Blonde on Blonde*, the standout one is the 'Sad-Eyed Lady of the Lowlands', who occupies the entire fourth side of the album. Dylan told Robert Shelton it was 'the best song I ever wrote'. (Shelton copied down those words in 1977; by now Dylan may have other songs at the top of his best-ever list.) Poignant and wistful, it is one the greatest romance songs of the contemporary era, the verbal imagery dazzling, the folkish balladry tantalising. The 'Sad-Eyed Lady' herself is often considered to be Sara, at least in the eyes of various commentators who have discovered potential allusions to her in the song. If so, the Lowlands from whence the sad-eyed lady hails may be a play on Sara's previous married name, Lownds.

TRANSCENDIN'

At the end of January 1966 Sergeant Barry Sadler guested on *The Ed Sullivan Show*, singing a song he had written himself and recorded a few weeks earlier. He was undoubtedly swimming against the tide. The Beatles were topping the *Billboard* Hot 100 that week with 'We Can Work It Out', closely followed by The Beach Boys' 'Barbara Ann'. The two biggest bands of the 1960s were occupying the top two places, followed by a generous sprinkling of British bands, Elvis Presley, Roy Orbison, Stevie Wonder and James Brown. It is hard to imagine a line-up of artists that better represented the musical culture in which the baby-boomers were immersed. All the big names of the mid-1960s were there. Dylan too, at number 58 with 'Can You Please Crawl Out Your Window?', a single he had recorded while making *Blonde on Blonde*. One of his least remarkable songs, its position in the chart that week was as high as it would go.

None of the discs in that week's *Billboard* Hot 100 were particularly political. Nevertheless, the worldview of the hit-record-buying public of 1966 was undoubtedly heavily weighted towards the anti-war lobby. But not Sergeant Barry Sadler. Born in 1940 he, like Bob Dylan, was a few years too old to be a boomer; unlike Dylan he most certainly did not share that generation's culture. His record 'The Ballad of the Green Berets' was as far removed as one could get from an anti-war song. A paean to the Special Forces, it was a patriotic tub-thumping song about brave fearless men who fight by night and day, who mean what they say, with silver wings on their chests they were among America's best. Unashamedly patriotic, the song served as a beacon of hope to the beleaguered silent majority who supported the Vietnam War, who felt as if their beliefs and values were under constant siege from the rowdy, vitriolic anti-war campaigners, who yearned for nothing more than a return to the calm certainties of former times. 'The Ballad of the Green Berets' spent five weeks at the top of the *Billboard* charts in March and April 1966, selling nine million copies and earning Sadler a 15-month tour of the country, commissioned by the Pentagon, to promote both the song and the Special Forces. The success of his song at a time when the anti-war protests and draft-card burnings were reaching their peak demonstrates just how wide the gap was between the different wings of American politics, and between the generations.

Among those with very different views to Sergeant Sadler, opposition to the war was growing. The nation had been shocked the previous November when Norman Morrison, a 31-year-old anti-war protester, paid homage to the Buddhist monks in Vietnam, who were self-immolating in protest at their persecution by the South Vietnamese government, by setting fire to himself in front of the Pentagon. A week later, 22-year-old Roger Allen LaPorte did the same, outside the United Nations building in New York, declaring 'I'm against wars, all wars. I did this as a religious act.' Much as LaPorte and Morrison might have hoped that their actions would change public opinion about the war, they had no impact. A Gallup poll conducted at the end of August 1965 had found that 24 per cent of Americans thought that the United States had 'made a mistake sending troops to fight in Vietnam'. By March 1966 the figure had only risen marginally, to 25 per cent. But two months later it had shot up to 36 per cent. The long arm of the draft was now reaching into homes whose occupants had given little or no thought to the far-off conflict, whose support for the war had just been a patriotic knee-jerk reaction to a crisis they little understood or cared about. But by the spring of 1966 they were lifting their heads out of the sand.

The news coming out of Vietnam was not good. Casualties were escalating and even the pictures that were allowed to be shown on TV were horrific. Important figures at home were voicing their opposition. Martin Luther King, who had always tried not to become distracted from the struggle for civil rights, was now sensing that he could not, in good faith, ignore the war and the suffering of both sides in Vietnam. In February he told his associates that he wanted to take a more active role in opposing the war. Speaking at a rally in Los

Angeles he complained about America's 'declining moral status in the world', castigating the nation for being 'engaged in a war that seeks to turn the clock of history back and perpetuate white colonialism'. He called for a halt to the bombing of North Vietnam. Linking the campaigns to which he had dedicated his life, he was 'disappointed with our failure to deal positively and forthrightly with the triple evils of racism, extreme materialism and militarism'.[30]

Robert Kennedy was also upping his criticism of the war. A younger brother of the murdered President John Kennedy, he had begun his political career supporting President Johnson's conduct of the war, but as the battles raged he grew increasingly concerned that the policy of belligerence was wrong. In January 1966 he returned from a European trip where nearly every major politician he met had criticised America's conduct of the war, where several had indicated that the opposing side was ready to negotiate, should the bombing stop. In February, at the same time as Dr King began speaking out against the war, Kennedy enraged President Johnson by calling for peace talks, telling the Senate that 'if we regard bombing as the answer in Vietnam, we are headed straight for disaster'.

Of all those who spoke out against the war, perhaps the most influential voice was that of the world heavyweight boxing champion, Muhammad Ali. He was in Miami, training for a forthcoming fight, when he was told that the draft board in his home town had changed his status and that he was now eligible to be called up to serve in Vietnam. Ali had recently converted to Islam and was adamant that, because of his religion, he could not fight in Vietnam. Anyway, he did not agree with the war. He submitted an unsuccessful application to be treated as a conscientious objector and spent the next two years fighting outside the ring, against the military, the legal establishment and the boxing authorities.

The first boxer of superstar status, never shy to remind the world that he was the greatest, that his boxing prowess was due to his ability to 'float like a butterfly, sting like a bee', he was treated by the authorities as a recalcitrant adolescent. Muhammad Ali parried by making increasingly outspoken criticisms of the war. Pointing out that he had never been racially abused by the Vietcong his comments were rarely out of the headlines. In April 1967 he was stripped of his title of World Heavyweight Champion and lost his boxing licence, on the grounds that his refusal to serve brought the sport of boxing into disrepute. Two months later he was sentenced to five years' imprisonment for refusing the draft and fined $10,000, the maximum penalty the court was empowered to impose. He was released on bail, pending appeal, but it took another four years, until 1971, when the Supreme Court reversed the lower court's decision, quashing his conviction. Martin Luther King gave him his blessing, although in a somewhat equivocal fashion, telling his parishioners, 'No matter what you think of Mr. Muhammad Ali's religion, you certainly have to admire his courage.'

Invariably eloquent, whatever he was speaking about, Muhammad Ali was a celebrity whose words carried weight with the politically disengaged. Unashamedly 'the greatest', he was as effective a spokesman for the anti-war movement as any politician or activist. Perhaps even more so. He was a powerful spokesman for civil rights too, telling an audience at Howard University in Washington, 'See, we have been brainwashed. Everything good and of authority was made white. We look at Jesus, we see a white with blond hair and blue eyes. We look at all the angels, we see white with blond hair and blue eyes. Now, I'm sure if there's a heaven in the sky and the colored folks die and go to heaven, where are the colored angels? They must be in the kitchen preparing the milk and honey . . . Even Tarzan, the king of the jungle in black Africa, he's white!'

Denied his boxing hegemony, for a couple of years Muhammad Ali was a contender for the crown that Dylan had not wanted, as spokesman for his generation. After Ali's death in 2016, Dylan posted a tribute on his website. 'If the measure of greatness is to gladden the heart of every human being on the face of the earth, then he truly was the greatest. In every way he was the bravest, the kindest and the most excellent of men.' Few have been graced with such effusive praise from Bob Dylan.

The International Day of Protests held the previous October had galvanised the anti-war movement. The numbers involved were small but the draft-card burnings, the vigils across the country, and the attempts to persuade soldiers of the injustice of the Vietnam War, had all helped to keep the movement in the public eye. However, the National Coordinating Committee to End the War in Vietnam was plagued by internal conflict. Made up of an uneasy alliance of over 30 left-wing and pacifist groups, it had never managed to project a unified image. It disbanded in January 1966. Before disappearing, though, the Committee called for a second International Day, or more accurately Days, of Protest, to be held on 25 and 26 March.

The protests were twice as large as those held the previous October, with an estimated 200,000 people taking part in 100 cities worldwide. Some 50,000 marched in New York and although only 5,000 demonstrated in Chicago, it was a sevenfold increase over the previous October. Military veterans marched in Philadelphia while, in a sign of things to come, Jefferson Airplane played at the University of California's Berkeley campus, site of the 1964 civil rights sit-in, where 40 protesters had burnt their draft cards the year before. The Jefferson Airplane 'rock and roll benefit' for the peace movement sparked controversy, with complaints of participants high on marijuana, a light show projecting nude figures, and allegations that the event was communist-inspired. Ronald Reagan, campaigning at the time to become Governor of California, condemned the event, speaking about the morality gap at Berkeley, with 'beatniks, radicals and filthy speech advocates' who were more interested in rioting and anarchy than academic freedom.[31] Jefferson Airplane, pioneers of the cerebral, LSD-inspired, psychedelic sound that would become the bedrock of the hippie phenomenon, would hear their performances described in similar terms and worse for the rest of their career.

In California the baby-boomer generation was subsuming its rage at the politics of its nation and the state of the world beneath a psychedelic haze, transcending the quotidian, trucking towards a higher state of being. Young people across the globe would soon follow. When psychedelia, tempered by Eastern meditation, finally enraptured The Beatles, they summed up the new philosophy in five words: all you need is love. Bob Dylan didn't bother. He was no more a disciple of the counter-culture than he was an anti-war activist. His place was among those who had spawned the new movements; he shared their beliefs and values but he was no longer among their leaders, he was at the age of nearly 25 already an éminence grise. And it was that, his refusal to protest, his apparent aloofness from the cultural evolution of his peers, which so enraged his fans. But if he thought he was above it all, beyond protest, more interested in allegorising his own acid trips than turning the world on to the new ideology, his audiences were there to tell him differently.

9

JUDAS

DOWN UNDER

Dylan resumed touring at the beginning of February. *Blonde on Blonde* wasn't finished, the recording sessions had now moved to Nashville, juggled between gigs that took him from New York south to Memphis then north again, to Ontario, seven performances in 14 days. The next month was more relaxed; he only played 12 gigs and travelled the length and breadth of the country just twice. On 9 April, Dylan flew to Hawaii. He played one gig, at the International Center in Honolulu, then got back on the plane for a flight to Australia where he was booked to play seven concerts, two in Sydney and Melbourne, one each in Brisbane, Adelaide and Perth. The Australian media, having never met anyone like Dylan before, asked him the same sort of inane questions he'd been asked when he first performed in England. 'You've been described as the king of the protest groups throughout the world. I'd like you to interpret what, perhaps, the public mean when they give you this accolade.' Dylan gave him short shrift. 'Well, the public never said that. *Time* magazine, *Newsweek* magazine, *Look* magazine, *Life* magazine . . . All described me a protest singer. But people have never described me as a protest singer.' Piling foolishness upon idiocy the interviewer then asked, 'How do you describe yourself?' Bob's answer: 'I wouldn't describe myself. How do you describe yourself?'

Australia is not America or England. A nation prone to colourful language, their journalists were happy to give back as much bounty as they received. The *Sydney Morning Herald* trashed him as 'the latest and strangest of the new breed of mop-haired anti-socialite, non-conformist, pseudo-beatnik comedians to invade Sydney'.¹ Not to be outdone, the *Sydney Sun* wheedled, 'He bore the expression of a man being wheeled out of the operating theatre still under anaesthetic. Throughout the 45 minutes of nonsensical spluttering, ho-hum mumbling, and vague gabbling, I received the distinct impression he was trying to say something, but didn't know what.'²

Melbourne was where the heckling began again, reprising the churlishness that had failed to manifest seriously at the last few venues he had played. It was nothing new, the usual slow handclaps, boos, and a few placards accusing him of selling out. Bad enough though for *Variety* magazine to pin the blame on him, running an article under the headline, 'Bob Dylan Destroys His Legend in Melbourne'. 'His manner towards his audience bordered on insolence. More than once he had a fit of spluttering and coughing, which he seemed to delight in doing right into the mike . . . The performance caught was on the second night. It's understood that at the opening performance there was considerable booing from the audience.'³

'Considerable booing' was bad enough, but it was nothing compared to the reception Dylan received when he played in Dublin on 5 May. He had flown from Australia to Sweden and Denmark, playing one night each in Stockholm and Copenhagen before heading to Ireland for two gigs, one in Dublin and the next night across the border in Belfast. Dublin was where things really kicked off.

The sound wasn't great. It hadn't been good all tour but it was particularly bad in Dublin. Dylan's voice could hardly be heard. Writing in *Melody Maker*, Vincent Doyle gave a flavour of the show:

After an hour of the opening Dublin concert on Thursday, Bob Dylan, the folk-poet genius credited with re-routing the entire course of contemporary folk music, suffered the humiliation of a slow hand-clap. It was the climax of a growing mutual contempt – Dylan for the audience and the audience for Dylan's new big sound . . . It was unbelievable to see a hip, swinging Dylan trying to look and sound like Mick Jagger and to realise after the first few minutes that it wasn't a take-off. Someone shouted 'traitor'. Someone else, 'Leave it to the Rolling Stones.' Dozens walked out.[4]

Mostly, Dylan didn't seem to mind the abuse. There were times on the tour when he almost seemed to be enjoying it. But Dublin soured his mood. Fifty years after it was shot, a clip of Bob Dylan refusing to sign an autograph for two young Irish fans went viral. It was taken from Martin Scorsese's film of Dylan, *No Direction Home*. The clip begins with Dylan in the back of a car, a young man and woman at the window, autograph books in hand. They are pleading with him to sign their books:

'Come on, it won't take long.'
Dylan's response, pointing at a couple of others in the street:
    'They don't ask me; those other two people don't ask me,
    why do you?'
'Why shouldn't you give it?' asks the man politely, with a smile
    on his face.
'What do we come to see you for,' adds the woman, looking upset.
'You called me a bum,' accuses Dylan, an insult that doesn't
    appear on the video.
'That's all you are!' she retorts.
'May I have your autograph please,' asks the man again, politely.
'I'll call you a bum,' shouts the woman.
'Oh come on,' begs the man.
'You don't need my autograph. If you needed my autograph, I'd
    give it to you.'
'What's wrong with him today?'

Perhaps they hadn't been at the concert.

ROCK BOTTOM

After playing Belfast the following evening, Dylan left Ireland for England. He may have wished he'd stayed. If Dublin was bad, Leicester sounds as if it were no better. The *Leicester Mercury* asked whether he had sold his soul to 'pop'. The audience, it reported, 'booed, slow hand-clapped, chanted "Off" "Off" and "We Want Dylan."' Many, said the paper, walked out in disgust.[5] The city's other paper, the *Leicester Chronicle*, however, enjoyed the concert. Its reviewer, David Sandison, who was clearly more of a poetry aficionado than the *Mercury*'s 'D.H.S.' (what do we make of their shared initials?), asserted that Dylan was producing poetry, equated him with Corso and Ginsberg, confessed to being a bit bored with the acoustic first set Dylan invariably played on the tour, and the 'church-like reverence afforded the poet'. But when he came out for the second set, when 'the shouting electric poet with his all-steam rave band jumped on the stage . . . he was alive again!'[6]

Even when Dylan was being booed, the vast majority of fans shared David Sandison's views. The dissenters were always a vocal but small minority.

Dylan's lengthy, exhausting world tour was due to climax at the Royal Albert Hall in London, where he would play for two evenings, just as he had done in May the previous year. But, despite its age and prestige, the Albert Hall is not the first venue that comes to mind when his fans talk about Dylan's 1966 performances in Britain, any more than the concerts in front of a 14,000-strong audience at Forest Hills or 17,000 at the Hollywood Bowl were spoken of as stand-out events of the previous summer. That summer of 1965, both for Dylan's fans and the folk-rock revolution, was defined by his performance at the Newport Folk Festival, when his electric set upset and freaked out almost the entire folk music establishment. And his 1966 visit to Britain stands out, not for his second-half electric sets or the booing that accompanied them, nor indeed for anything he said or did, but for his concert on 17 May at the Free Trade Hall in the industrial city of Manchester. Where one member of the audience delivered the most famous heckle in the history of pop music. Stopping Dylan in his tracks and reminding him of the fact that he'd always put to the back of his mind, though he'd always known there were some who would never let him forget it. There was no reason for him to be ashamed of it, it is a badge of honour. But standing onstage, in front of a mainly adoring crowd, but with hostile elements whose catcalls and jeers may have been just a foretaste of something much worse, is not really the best moment to be forced to dredge up one's insecurities.

Until that moment, the concert at the Manchester Free Trade Hall had been much like any other on the tour. Dylan played the first half alone, his regular acoustic set, accompanied just by his guitar and harmonica. He opened with 'She Belongs to Me', followed by 'Fourth Time Around', 'Visions of Johanna' and 'It's All Over Now, Baby Blue'. All gentle easy songs with compelling lyrics, as tuneful as Dylan could ever be, nothing to alert the audience (unless they'd read the reviews of his earlier concerts) that acoustics were not all that he would deliver. 'Desolation Row' ran for nine minutes, its beguiling lyrics sounding even weirder in the dark, vast auditorium. He closed the set with 'Just Like a Woman' and with a nursery rhyme, 'Mr Tambourine Man'.

The second half opened, as it had done all through the tour, with a bunch of musicians walking onto the stage. They and Dylan had been playing together for nine months but they still hadn't got round to giving themselves a collective identity. At this point they were billed as Levon Helm and The Hawks, despite Helm having left weeks earlier. They would briefly be repackaged as The Group until, shortly after the end of the tour, they incarnated themselves for the final time as The Band.

The audience weren't bothered about names. Some were growing restless, they hadn't paid to watch a rock band. Most were enjoying the evening, they were happy to be watching their idol; *Blonde on Blonde* wasn't out yet, but they had all heard the single version 'Rainy Day Women #12 & 35', and many of them would have bought a copy of *Highway 61 Revisited*. So they had a pretty good idea of what he might play. But the discomfort of their neighbours, those who had paid to see a folk singer, not an artist who might dare play something from his most recent albums, was unsettling. As The Hawks picked up their instruments the atmosphere in the hall grew tense.

Dylan and The Hawks launched into 'Tell Me, Momma', a rock number that sounded more like something from The Rolling Stones than pre-electric Dylan. C.P. Lee described it as a 'bone-crushing aural assault'.[7] It wasn't even an old favourite; nobody knew it; he had only played it for the first time a few weeks earlier. And it was loud, very loud, louder than anybody had ever heard from a bunch of musicians before. The noise, the unfamiliar song, and the growing discomfort of the folk purists in the auditorium all added to the tension. Something was bound to give.

'I Don't Believe You (She Acts Like We Never Have Met)' was next. The audience knew this one, it had been on his 1964 album, *Another Side of Bob Dylan*. On the album it was just Dylan and his guitar, now he was singing it to an electric backing. But that was just about OK, nobody seemed to mind too much, Dylan was back in folk mode. But as 'Baby, Let Me Follow You Down' started, so did the protests. They were mild at first, some slow handclapping, the sort of polite English objection heard at cricket matches when the action slows, and a few boos. But when some in the audience turned on those making the noise, telling them to shut up, things began to deteriorate.

Quite used to this sort of thing by now, Dylan and his musicians played on. Their volume more or less drowned out the catcalls, other than between numbers, but onstage they kept going. It was still the case that more people in the audience were enjoying the music than the vociferous few making their dissent known. The band got through 'Just Like Tom Thumb's Blues', 'Leopard-Skin Pill-Box Hat', 'One Too Many Mornings' and 'Ballad of a Thin Man'. The last number of the evening, 'Just Like a Rolling Stone', was about to begin.

And then it came. It seemed as if the hall had grown silent in anticipation of what was to happen next, but maybe the heckler was just waiting for the right moment. Either way, the cry came through loud and clear.

'Judas!'

Silence ticked by for the briefest of instants, a spattering of applause, and Bob Dylan standing on the stage looking a bit stunned, not sure what to make of the shout he'd just heard. Dutifully, the band launched into the opening of 'Like a Rolling Stone', but Dylan wasn't ready yet. He marched up to the microphone. 'I don't believe you,' he yelled. Then 'You're a liar.' Somebody, no one is quite sure who, yelled something that sounds like 'Play fucking loud!', but it might have been a different instruction and 'Like a Rolling Stone' crashed through the hall.

Did it matter? As a synonym for traitor the word 'Judas' has been used in English for a very long time. People generally use the word without thinking twice about its origins or what it means. The heckler almost certainly did. If, as he confessed 30 years later to Andy Kershaw, it was a young law student named John Cordwell:

> I was angry that Dylan . . . not that he'd played electric, but that he'd played electric with a really poor sound system . . . That, and it seemed like a cavalier performance, a throwaway performance compared with the intensity of the acoustic set earlier on. There were rumblings all around me and the people I was with were making noises and looking at each other. It was a build-up.[8]

But it wasn't 'a build-up' for Bob Dylan, nor for any of the other Jews in the audience (the Manchester Jewish community is England's second largest, so there were probably quite a few). Because, for Jews, the name Judas has connotations that extend far beyond the simple meaning of traitor. Judas Iscariot was, of course, the apostle who, according to the Gospels, betrayed Jesus, handing him over to the Romans and sending him to his crucifixion. The name Judas is

Greek for Judah, the Israelite tribe from which the word Jew comes. Since the Middle Ages, Judas has been depicted in European art as ugly, twisted, with a bent nose and an aggressive stare, the Jew who is to be despised. The name Judas is an antisemitic trope, it was used to represent all Jews in patristic literature, medieval catechisms, passion plays and into the modern age. Even when not explicitly fingered as Judas, Jews were tarnished with characteristics typically attributed to him, of treachery, corruption, greed and deceit.[9] In Christopher Marlowe's antisemitic play, *The Jew of Malta*, one of the characters says the hat that the Jewish anti-hero Barabbas wore was the one which Judas left under the tree where he hanged himself. Bob Dylan knew who Judas was, even if his heckler did not. It was Dylan, after all, who had told his listeners as far back as *The Times They Are A-Changin'* that they had to decide whether Judas also had God on his side.

Hearing the word 'Judas' hurled at him, at the end of a long, controversial and exhausting tour, would have stung Dylan. His gobsmacked retort of 'I don't believe you' was a reflex reaction, it made little sense, he just had to let fly. Years later, talking about those who complained that he plagiarised the work of other artists, he told *Rolling Stone*: 'These are the same people that tried to pin the name Judas on me. Judas, the most hated name in human history! If you think you've been called a bad name, try to work your way out from under that. Yeah, and for what? For playing an electric guitar?'[10]

Dylan didn't know it, and nor did his abuser, but the cry that became the most famous heckle in rock-music history helped bring the curtain down on the first part of his career. Not immediately, the tour carried on, with gigs in Glasgow, Edinburgh, Paris, Newcastle and the Albert Hall. But the crescendo, the climax, had been reached, he was descending from the peak, performatively and emotionally. His insecurities had been breached. He'd done so much work and after it all, after everything he had gone through, all he had done for the musical culture of the 1960s, for the generation for whom he had never been the spokesman, for the civil rights and peace movements, and for the careers of all the artists who had found fame, success and wealth on the back of his compositions, at the end of it all he was still abused as a Jew.

The tour ended, Dylan returned home, burnt out, frayed and exhausted. A few weeks after his return, on 29 July 1966, he was out on his motorbike. Details are sketchy, conspiracy theories abound, but the underlying facts are clear. He came off his bike and was injured. He brushed it off in his autobiography, saying simply, 'I had been in a motorcycle accident and I'd been hurt, but I recovered. Truth was that I wanted to get out of the rat race.'[11] Get out of the rat race he did. He retreated to his home and family. It would be August 1967 before he entered a recording studio again, and a further seven years before he went back on the road.

Dylan's early career was over. By the time he recorded his 1967 album, *John Wesley Harding*, rock had gone psychedelic and nobody was looking to him for any kind of leadership. Which probably suited him just fine. He could play the music he wanted, and change his style as often as it suited him. Without being bothered by folk purists, hecklers or cries that sounded like antisemitic abuse, even if they weren't intended to be.

ACKNOWLEDGEMENTS

I first heard about Bob Dylan when I was walking to school with my friend, the late and much missed Stuart Cohen. He said, 'We must go and see this guy from America, Bob Dylan. He's saying some really interesting things.' So we went to the Albert Hall to see him. It was 1965 and we soon found out that Dylan was about much more than just saying interesting things. This book is dedicated to Stuart Cohen's memory, one of the most intelligent and creative people I have ever known, and a great guitarist too, who left this world far too soon.

Thank you to all those who have helped and encouraged me in the making of this book. To David Stone, who knows more about Bob Dylan than I ever will, for reading the final draft and for his many helpful and useful remarks and pointers. To The Fabulous Micky C and Gillian Freedman for an astonishing number of Dylan quotes and references, and my brother Jeremy who sat, gobsmacked with me, while Dylan performed an entire concert at Wembley Arena with his back to the audience. To Adrian Litvinoff for sharing memories of Stuart. To Robin Baird-Smith who encouraged me to write the book, and made sure I did, and to his wonderful successors at Bloomsbury: my enthusiastic, erudite and ever-supportive editor, Octavia Stocker, to Continuum's energetic and innovative publisher Tomasz Hoskins, to the wonderful, knowledgeable and always helpful Sarah Jones without whom none of my books would end up in print, to my copy-editor, the sharp-eyed Richard Mason, whose knowledge of grammar and the correct way to write is staggering, to Rachel Nicholson, Katherine Macpherson and Xanthe Rendall in the UK publicity and marketing departments, and Rachel Ewen and Hubert Adjei-Kontoh in the USA.

And, as always, to those who ask me the questions that make me think more deeply about my writing and who have no hesitation in telling me when I am wrong. To Josh, Mollie, Melody and Louis, to Dan, Sam, Clare, Eli, Bonnie, Leo, Dylan(!) and Remi. And to everyone else who, sometimes unwittingly, has had a hand in making this book. And of course to Karen. Having spent a year or so sharing me with Leonard Cohen, she thought I had got rock stars out of what remains of my hair. Then along came Bob Dylan. Always encouraging, she makes sure I have a life outside of writing; I couldn't have written any of my books without her.

NOTES

INTRODUCTION

1 Alexandra Schwartz, 'The Rambling Glory of Bob Dylan's Nobel Speech', *New Yorker,* June 6, 2017.

I STARTIN' OUT

1 Anthony Scaduto, *Bob Dylan*. New York: Signet, 1971.

2 Tom Lehrer, 'National Brotherhood Week'. 1965, https://tomlehrersongs.com/. Unlike nearly every other major recording artist (including Dylan, whose lyrics we were not permitted to print), Tom Lehrer has renounced all rights to his songs.

3 Robert Shelton, Elizabeth M. Thomson and Patrick Humphries, *No Direction Home: The Life and Music of Bob Dylan*. Rev. and updated edn. London: Omnibus Press, 2011.

4 Bob Dylan, *Chronicles*, Volume 1. New York: Simon & Schuster, 2004, p. 34.

5 David P. Szatmary, *Rockin' in Time: A Social History of Rock and Roll*. Englewood Cliffs, N.J.: Prentice Hall, 2004, p. 21.

6 Elijah Wald, *Dylan Goes Electric!*. New York: HarperCollins, 2015, p. 13.

7 David K. Dunaway, 'Charles Seeger and Carl Sands: The Composers' Collective Years', *Ethnomusicology* 24, no. 2 (1980): 159–68.

8 Winston Churchill, 'Sinews of Peace' speech, Westminster College, Fulton, Missouri, 5 March 1946.

9 Bill Smith, 'Village Vanguard, New York', *Billboard*, 4 February 1950, p. 51.

10 Bob Dylan, *My Life in a Stolen Moment*. New York: Town Hall Inc., 1963.

11 Joan Baez, *And a Voice to Sing With: A Memoir*. New York: Summit Books, 1987, p. 40.

1 2   Steve Onderick, *Diamond Dave Whitaker Part 2: Bob Dylan, Woody Guthrie, and the Joint Heard Round the World*, https://www.youtube.com/watch?v=ioXQzPEmXXA&t=389s.

1 3   Stephen J. Whitfield, *The Culture of the Cold War*. Baltimore, MD: Johns Hopkins University Press, 1991.

2 MAKING AN IMPACT

1   Hillel Italie, 'Manny Roth, Colorful Owner of New York's Cafe Wha? Club, Dies at 94', *Washington Post*, 2 August 2014; Douglas Martin, 'Manny Roth, 94, Impresario of Cafe Wha?, Is Dead', *New York Times*, 1 August 2014; Dylan, *Chronicles*, p. 10.

2   Shelton et al., *No Direction Home*, p. 75.

3   Howard Sounes, *Down the Highway: The Life of Bob Dylan*. New York: Grove Press, 2001, p. 104.

4   Introductory words to the TV series *Star Trek* (1966–9).

5   John F. Kennedy, Inaugural Address, 20 January 1961.

6   David Van Ronk and Elijah Wald, *The Mayor of MacDougal Street: A Memoir*. Cambridge, MA: Da Capo, 2005.

7   Interview with Cameron Crowe for *Biograph*, original US stereo 5LP boxed set, Columbia C5X 38830, 7 November 1985. Quoted in Sean Wilentz, *Bob Dylan in America*. London: The Bodley Head, 2010.

8   Nick Murray, 'Wavy Gravy Recounts His Bizarre, Star-Crossed Hippie Journey', *Rolling Stone*, 17 October 2014.

9   Jack Kerouac, *On the Road*. New York: Viking Press, 1957, p. 54.

1 0   Clellon Holmes, 'This Is the Beat Generation', *New York Times Magazine*, 16 November 1952.

1 1   Dylan, *Chronicles*.

1 2   Ibid.

1 3   'Woody Guthrie', *Arena*, BBC, 1988; https://www.youtube.com/watch?v=9EnXnFgnkUc; Martin McQuade, 'Ramblin' Jack Elliott Reflects on His Friendship with Woody Guthrie and Why Bob Dylan's Act Made Him Stop Playing Harmonica Onstage', *Guitar Player*, 8 August 2022.

1 4   *The Ballad of Ramblin' Jack Elliott*, dir. Aiyana Elliott, 2000, Crawford Communications, United States.

15 McQuade, 'Ramblin' Jack Elliott . . .', *Guitar Player*.

16 *New York Times*, 29 September 1961, https://archive.nytimes.com/
    www.nytimes.com/books/97/05/04/reviews/dylan-gerde.
    html.

17 Shelton et al., *No Direction Home*, p. 132.

18 Interview with Nora Ephron and Susan Edmiston, 1965, quoted
    in Jonathan Eisen, *The Age of Rock, Sounds of the American Cultural
    Revolution: A Reader*. New York: Random House, 1969.

3 PROTESTIN'

1   *Broadside* #14, October 1962.

2   Amanda Petrusich, 'A Story About Fred Trump and Woody Guthrie
    for the Midterm Elections', *The New Yorker*, 6 November 2018.

3   There is some doubt about the date of the programme and whether
    it was ever broadcast. The interview transcript is at https://
    expectingrain.com/dok/int/gooding.html.

4   https://www.youtube.com/watch?v=gEvKe2WLumI.

5   Lisa W. Foderaro, 'City Cracking Down on Performers in
    Washington Square Park', *New York Times*, 4 December 2011.

6   Aaron J. Leonard, *Whole World in an Uproar: Music Rebellion and
    Repression 1955–1972*. London: Repeater, 2023.

7   *No Direction Home*, 2005, dir. Martin Scorsese, 4h 22 (in Trivia
    section, 1h 54).

8   Susan Green, 'Fifty-Two Years and Countless Cats: Good-Bye, My
    Friend', 3 March 2011; https://www.criticsatlarge.ca/2011/03/
    fifty-two-years-and-countless-cats-good.html.

9   Shelton et al., *No Direction Home*, p. 113.

10 FBI Report printed in Leonard, *Whole World in an Uproar*.

11 Sis Cunningham and Gordon Friesen, *Red Dust and Broadsides: A Joint
    Autobiography*, ed. Ronald D. Cohen. Amherst, MA: University of
    Massachusetts Press, 1999.

12 *Broadside* #1, February 1962.

13 *Broadside* #2, March 1962.

14 Bob Dylan, Broadside Show and Sessions 1962–63, https://www.
    youtube.com/watch?v=OYmsw-FFAkg&t=91s.

15 *Broadside* #3, April 1962.

16   *Broadside* #6, late May 1962.

17   *Broadside* #141, January–June 1979.

18   *Billboard*, 20 July 1963.

19   Studs Terkel Wax Museum in Chicago, 1963, https://www.youtube.com/watch?v=D-HAqPX8eGY.

20   Allen Ginsberg speaking in *No Direction Home*, dir. Martin Scorsese.

21   Alan Light, '"The Freewheelin' Bob Dylan": Inside His First Classic', *Rolling Stone*, 27 May 2016.

4 FREEWHEELIN'

1   https://newportjazz.org/storyville/how-a-boston-club-birthed-the-newport-jazz-festival-in-1954.

2   George Wein and Nate Chinen, *Myself Among Others*. Cambridge, MA: Da Capo, 2003.

3   Baez, *And a Voice to Sing With*, p. 61.

4   Ron Olesko, Remembering Theo Bikel, https://singout.org/remembering-theodore-bikel.

5   Quoted in Wald, *Dylan Goes Electric*, p. 126.

6   *Billboard*, 17 August 1963.

7   Barry Kittleson, 'New Folk Breed Spells Meat', ibid.

8   Barry Kittleson, 'A Legend Under Construction', *Billboard*, 27 April 1963.

9   *Cash Box*, 10 August 1963, p. 211.

10   Emancipation Proclamation, 1 January 1863, https://www.archives.gov/exhibits/featured-documents/emancipation-proclamation/transcript.html.

11   Martin Luther King, '"I Have a Dream" Speech', 28 August 1963.

12   Andy Greene, 'Flashback: Bob Dylan Performs at the 1963 March on Washington', *Rolling Stone*, 9 June 2020.

13   Quoted in Shelton et al., *No Direction Home*, p. 129.

14   Ralph J. Gleason, 'A Folk Singing, Social Critic', *San Francisco Chronicle*, 24 February 1964, reprinted in Ralph J. Gleason and Toby Gleason, *Music in the Air: The Selected Writings of Ralph J. Gleason*. New Haven, CT: Yale University Press, 2016, p. 151.

15   'Let Us Now Praise Little Men', *Time* magazine, 31 May 1963.

16 Andrea Svedberg, 'I Am My Words', *Newsweek*, 4 November 1963.

17 Scaduto, *Bob Dylan*.

18 Kerouac, *On the Road*, p. 17..

19 https://alldylan.com/december-13-the-bob-dylan-speech-at-the-bill-of-rights-dinner-1963.

20 Toru Umezaki, 'Breaking through the Cane-Curtain: The Cuban Revolution and the Emergence of New York's Radical Youth, 1961–1965', *The Japanese Journal of American Studies*, no. 18 (2007): 187–207.

21 Nat Hentoff, 'What Bob Dylan Wanted at Twenty-Three', *The New Yorker*, 16 October 1964.

22 'A Letter from Bob Dylan', *Broadside* #38, January 1964, available at https://singout.org/broadside/issues-p2.

5 A-CHANGIN'

1 Interview with Robin Pike, *ZigZag*, October 1974, quoted in Harry Freedman, *Leonard Cohen: The Mystical Roots of Genius*. London: Bloomsbury Continuum, 2021.

2 James Slack, 'Judge James Pickles, Who Once Asked "Who Are The Beatles?", Dies at 85', *Daily Mail*, 23 December 2010.

3 'Grammar School Bans Beatle Haircuts', *The Times*, 18 November 1963.

4 'Singers: The New Madness', *Time* magazine, 15 November 1963.

5 https://www.bjorner.com/DSN00340%201963.htm.

6 Hentoff, 'What Bob Dylan Wanted at Twenty-Three'.

7 Scaduto, *Bob Dylan*, p. 175.

8 Dave Van Ronk speaking in *No Direction Home*, dir. Martin Scorsese.

9 Kerouac, *On the Road*, pp. 10, 9.

10 Dylan, *Chronicles*, p. 57.

11 Allen Ginsberg, Lawrence Ferlinghetti, Mary-Ann Milford and Peter B. Howard, *Howl, and Other Poems*. San Francisco, CA: City Lights Pocket Bookshop, 1956.

12 *The Times*, 18 May 1964, p. 4.

13   David Hajdu, *Positively 4th Street: The Lives and Times of Joan Baez, Bob Dylan, Mimi Baez Farina and Richard Farina* (New York: Farrar, Straus and Giroux, 2001), pp. 201–2.

14   Hentoff, 'What Bob Dylan Wanted at Twenty-Three'.

6 MOVIN' ON

1   *Broadside* #14, October 1962.

2   Sherry Gershon Gottlieb, *Hell No We Won't Go! Resisting the Draft during the Vietnam War*. New York: Viking, 1991.

3   Thomas Hobbes, *Leviathan*, 1, 13.

4   Ian MacDonald, *Revolution in the Head: The Beatles Records and the Sixties*. New York: Henry Holt, 1994.

5   Hentoff, 'What Bob Dylan Wanted at Twenty-Three'.

6   Wein and Chinen, *Myself Among Others*, p. 326.

7   John Hughes, *Invisible Now: Bob Dylan in the 1960s*. Farnham: Ashgate Publishing, 2013, p. 86.

8   Irwin Silber, 'An Open Letter to Bob Dylan', *Sing Out!*, November 1964.

9   Ibid.

10   Paul Wolfe, 'The New Bob Dylan', *Broadside* #53, 20 December 1964.

11   'A Letter from Bob Dylan', *Broadside* #38, 20 January 1964.

12   Phil Ochs, 'An Open Letter from Phil Ochs', *Broadside* #54, 20 January 1965.

13   Speech by Mario Savio on the steps of Sproul Hall, Berkeley, 2 December 1964, https://www.americanrhetoric.com/speeches/mariosaviosproulhallsitin.htm.

14   Wendy Lesser, Greil Marcus and Mario Savio, 'Two Anniversary Speeches', *The Threepenny Review*, no. 62 (1995): 33–5.

15   Rob Fitzpatrick, *New Musical Express*, 12 September 2005.

16   Ibid.

17   Statement of the Government of the People's Republic of China, 16 October 1964, https://china.usc.edu/atomic-bomb-statement-government-peoples-republic-china-october-16-1964.

18   Barry Goldwater, Address 'Accepting the Presidential Nomination at the Republican National Convention in San Francisco', 16 July 1964, https://www.presidency.ucsb.edu/node/216657.

7 BACK HOME

1   Neil McCormick, 'The Classic Sixties Album Cover that Betrayed Bob Dylan's State of Mind', *Daily Telegraph*, 2 April 2020.

2   Scaduto, *Bob Dylan*, p. 242.

3   Clinton Heylin, *The Double Life of Bob Dylan,* Vol. 1, *1941–1966: A Restless Hungry Feeling*. London: The Bodley Head, 2021.

4   Jim Farber, 'Bob Dylan Unseen: Daniel Kramer Discusses Rare Images from the 1960s', *Guardian*, 25 May 2016; Kory Grow, 'See How Bob Dylan's Iconic "Bringing It All Back Home" Cover Was Made', *Rolling Stone*, 29 September 2015.

5   Max Jones, *Melody Maker*, 27 March 1965.

6   *New York Times*, 28 September 1997.

7   'The Folk Song Revival: A Symposium', *New York Folklore Quarterly* 19, no. 2 (June 1963).

8   Silber, 'An Open Letter to Bob Dylan'.

9   Interview with Jenny de Yong and Peter Roche, *Sheffield University Paper*, 30 April 1965, reproduced in *Interviews with Bob Dylan*, https://www.interferenza.com/bcs/interv.htm.

10 Shelton et al., *No Direction Home*, p. 204.

11 Ray Coleman, 'Beatles Say – Dylan Shows the Way', *Melody Maker*, 9 January 1965.

12 John Wilson, *Paul McCartney: Inside the Songs*, BBC Radio 4, 25 October 2021, https://www.bbc.co.uk/sounds/play/po9zf8hc?partner=uk.co.bbc &origin=share-mobile.

13 Bob Spitz, *Dylan: A Biography*. New York: McGraw-Hill, 1989.

8 ELECTRIC SHOCK

1   Russell Clarke, *The Times*, 23 August 2012.

2   *Billboard*, 12 June 1965.

3   Steven R. Strake, 'Eulogy to Malcolm X', *Broadside* #56, 10 March 1965.

4   Tom Paxton, 'Goodman, Schwerner and Chaney', *Broadside* #56, March 1965.

5   'Letter from Moses Asch of Folkways', ibid.

6   *New York Times*, 28 January 1965.

7   *Esquire* #382, September 1965.

8   Titled in *Broadside* as 'It's All Right Ma, It's Life and Life Only'.

9   Julius Lester, 'Talking Vietnam Blues', *Broadside* #56, March 1965.

10 'Civil Rights Workers Call Watts the "black ghetto"', *AP Press*, 14 August 1965, accessed at https://apnews.com/article/riots-race-and-ethnicity-los-angeles-ca-state-wire-lifestyle-99b96775 1b4a80 2103411 1ef63df488a.

11 Thomas Pynchon, 'A Journey into the Mind of Watts', *New York Times Magazine*, 12 June 1966.

12 Cited by Michael Hann, 'P.F. Sloan: The 1960s Enigma Admired by Bob Dylan and Jimmy Webb', *Guardian*, 17 November 2015, and elsewhere.

13 Nat Hentoff, 'Playboy Interview: Bob Dylan', *Playboy*, March 1966.

14 Phil Ochs, Letter to *Village Voice*, 12 August 1965.

15 Leonard, *Whole World in An Uproar*.

16 Seth Rogovoy, *Bob Dylan, Prophet, Mystic, Poet*. New York: Scribner, 2009.

17 For example, http://www.bobdylancommentaries.com/dylan-and-the-bible, or Colbert S. Cartwright, *The Bible in the Lyrics of Bob Dylan*. Bury, Lancashire: Wanted Man, 1985.

18 See my book *Leonard Cohen: The Mystical Roots of Genius*.

19 Interview with Martin Bronstein, CBC, Montreal, 20 February 1966, https://www.youtube.com/watch?v=JozbOTHdAUQ. (A misprint in the first book to quote this interview has the interviewer's name as Marvin Bronstein. The error has been copied by legions of Dylan biographers and Wikipedia ever since.)

20 Interview with Nat Hentoff, *Playboy*, February 1966.

21 *Billboard*, 12 June 1965.

22 Karl Dallas, 'Focus on MacColl', *Melody Maker*, 18 September 1965.

23 Dominic Lynskey, 'Beatlemania: "the Screamers" and Other Tales of Fandom', *Observer*, 29 September 2013.

24 Berkeley's Vietnam Day Committee, reprinted in Massimo Teodori, *The New Left: A Documentary History*. Indianapolis, IN: Bobbs-Merrill Co., 1969.

25 Reproduced in Robert N. Strassfeld, 'Lose in Vietnam, Bring Our Boys Home', *North Carolina Law Review* 82, no. 5 (2004).

26 Al Kooper, *Backstage Passes & Backstabbing Bastards: Memoirs of a Rock 'n' Roll Survivor*, updated edn. New York: Backbeat Books, 2008, p. 45.

27 Andy Gill, 'Back to the Land', *Mojo*, November 2000, p. 82, quoted in Glen O'Brien, *Antipodean Apocalyptic: Bob Dylan in Melbourne, 1966*, https://www.academia.edu/5947497/Antipodean_Apocalyptic_Bob_Dylan_in_Melbourne_1966.

28 Compare, for example, the account in Howard Sounes, *Down the Highway: The Life of Bob Dylan*. New York: Grove Press, 2001, with that in Wilentz, *Bob Dylan in America*.

29 Marion Meade, 'Does Rock Degrade Women?', *New York Times*, 14 March 1971.

30 David J. Garrow, *Bearing the Cross: Martin Luther King, Jr. and the Southern Christian Leadership Conference, 1955–1968*. New York: William Morrow, 1986, pp. 545–6.

31 Ronald Reagan on the unrest on college campuses, 1967, https://www.gilderlehrman.org/history-resources/spotlight-primary-source/ronald-reagan-unrest-college-campuses-1967.

9 JUDAS

1 Craig McGregor, 'Bob Dylan's Anti-Interview', *Sydney Morning Herald*, 13 April 1966, quoted in O'Brien, *Antipodean Apocalyptic*.

2 Uli Schmetzer, *Sydney Sun*, April 1966, quoted in O'Brien, ibid.

3 'Bob Dylan Destroys his Legend in Melbourne', *Variety*, April 1966.

4 Vincent Doyle, 'Dublin: Night of the Big Letdown', *Melody Maker*, 11 May 1966.

5 D.H.S., 'Pop Goes Bob Dylan – And Boo Go Fans', *Leicester Mercury*, 16 May 1966.

6 David Sandison, 'Dylan Booed – but Stays Ahead on (Electric) Points', *Leicester Chronicle*, 20 May 1966.

7 C.P. Lee and Paul Kelly, *Like the Night: Bob Dylan and the Road to the Manchester Free Trade Hall*. London: Helter Skelter, 1998.

8   Andy Kershaw, 'Bob Dylan: How I Found the Man who Shouted "Judas"', *Independent*, 23 September 2005. Others, however, dispute John Cordwell's account, favouring the claim by Keith Butler that he was the one who shouted 'Judas'. Cordwell and Butler are both dead, so who it really was will never be known.

9   Hyam Maccoby, *Judas Iscariot and the Myth of Jewish Evil*. London: Peter Halban, 1991.

10   Interview in *Rolling Stone*, 12 September 2012.

11   Dylan, *Chronicles*, p. 114.

INDEX